SMITH'S GUIDE™ TO EXECUTIVE CLEMENCY

FOR STATE AND FEDERAL PRISONERS

First Edition, April 2014

Petitions for Earl Washington, Jr., Joseph Payne, Sr., and William Saunders reprinted with permission from the National Death Penalty Archive, Special Collections & Archives, University at Albany, SUNY.

ISBN-10: 0989592413
ISBN-13: 978-0-9895924-1-3
Library of Congress Control Number: 2014937121

Published by
redbat books
2901 Gekeler Lane
La Grande, OR 97850
www.redbatbooks.com

Text set in Chaparral Pro.

Book design by Kristin Summers, redbat design | www.redbatdesign.com

SMITH'S GUIDE™ to Executive Clemency

for State and Federal Prisoners

By
Zachary A. Smith

redbat books
2014

TABLE OF CONTENTS

DISCLAIMER

This book is not an alternative to professional assistance by an attorney. This book does not provide licensed, professional legal advice. It's author is not a lawyer; its text is for informational purposes only. The material contained herein is not intended to substitute for professional assistance by an attorney. Never disregard professional legal advice, and never delay in seeking it or hiring an attorney to represent you, because of anything you read in this book. It is the responsibility of you, the reader, to seek out and secure legal advice on how to proceed with state or federal clemency proceedings.

The information in this book has been carefully researched, and all efforts have been made to ensure accuracy. The author and publisher assume no responsibility for any damages or losses incurred during, or as a result of, the application of the information presented here. All information should be carefully studied and clearly understood before taking any action based on the contents of this book. The reader assumes full responsibility for the consequences of his or her own actions, filings, and strategic decisions.

INTRODUCTION

For the last eighteen years, I have studied and practiced law in prison. After personally exhausting all the legal remedies available to me in state and federal courts, I started considering a clemency application and undertook the arduous task of studying every case I could find in which executive clemency had been granted: Jamie and Gladys Scott, Stacey Lannert, Nelson Hopkins, Sidney Cornwell, Darrel Mease, Lynda Branch, Betty Coleman, Michael Ford, Shirley Lute, Jonnie Lee Wilson, and Richard Clay. I also pored over the details of high-profile cases—those of Casey Anthony, Dale Helmig, Mark Woodworth, Jodi Arias, and the West Memphis Three: Damien Echols, Jason Baldwin, and Jessie Misskelly—for an idea of how they became so well known. Slowly, patterns of key psychological principles began to show themselves in every one of these cases.

I have in the following pages, laid out every aspect of the clemency process, step by step: the relief available, the statutory regulations (for all fifty state jurisdictions as well as federal), the grounds for executive clemency, the self-development, personal growth and transformation processes, social intelligence, communication skills, clemency campaign strategies, how to prepare a clemency application, examples of successful applications, and much more.

It is my intent for this book to evolve the mindset of the average prisoner, but it is my dream for it to eventually revolutionize the rehabilitative process, igniting a movement of personal growth and transformation throughout America's prison population...starting right now with *you*.

Whichever is the case, this book should prove to be an invaluable resource for you and any other prisoner fighting for his or her freedom. Armed with knowledge unknown by most other clemency applicants, you will gain a serious advantage in your future endeavors.

—Zachary A. Smith

<1> OVERVIEW OF EXECUTIVE CLEMENCY

Executive Clemency Process

> *Executive clemency had proved to be the "fail safe" in our criminal justice system... it is an unalterable fact that our judicial system like the human beings who administer it, is fallible.*
>
> —Justice William H. Rehnquist

As Supreme Court Chief Justice William H. Rehnquist wrote in *Herrera v. Collins, 506 U.S. 390, 415 (1993)*, the judicial system is fallible and clemency is a critical safeguard. The use of clemency in addressing miscarriages of justice has increased as a result of legislation restricting a prisoner's ability to appeal (i.e., the Anti-Terrorism and Effective Death Penalty Act of 1996) and Supreme Court decisions such as *Herrera*, which held that the federal courts can not entertain a prisoner's freestanding innocence claim.

Executive clemency is a broad power available to most state governors and the President of the United States. This authority is derived from state statutes and state constitutions for governors, and from the United States Constitution and United States Code for the President. A state governor, or the President (for federal convictions only), may grant pardons (invalidating both the guilt and punishment of the prisoner), reprieves (temporarily postponing punishment), and commutations (reducing the severity of the punishment) after conviction, for all offenses except treason and cases of impeachment. The elected official granting clemency may impose conditions, restrictions and limitations as he or she deems appropriate. A prisoner has no inherent constitutional right to being granted clemency.

Clemency Process by State

The governors of Alabama, Alaska, California, Colorado, Hawaii, Iowa, Kansas, Kentucky, Maine, Massachusetts, Michigan, New Jersey, New Mexico, New York, North Carolina, North Dakota, Oregon, Rhode Island, South Carolina, Vermont, Virginia, Washington, West Virginia, Wisconsin, and Wyoming, have sole authority to either grant or deny clemency applications.

The governors of Arizona, Delaware, Florida, Louisiana, Montana, Oklahoma, Pennsylvania, and Texas, must have the according recommendation from a board or advisory group to grant clemency.

In the states of Arkansas, Illinois, Indiana, Maryland, Mississippi, Missouri, New Hampshire, Ohio, South Dakota, and Tennessee, the governor may receive a non-binding recommendation of clemency from a board or advisory group.

In Connecticut, Georgia, Idaho, Minnesota, Nebraska, Nevada, and Utah, a board or advisory group holds executive authority to grant or deny clemency.

Types of Executive Clemency

The types of clemency are: pardons, commutations of sentence, reprieves, and remission of some court ordered fines.

Pardons are granted to prisoners who've proven or can prove their innocence.

Commutations are granted to prisoners who demonstrate rehabilitation, disparity of sentence, or dubious guilt.

A reprieve temporarily relieves a prisoner's punishment, mostly granted in death penalty cases to stay an execution for a period of time.

The remission of fines is a reduction or cancellation of court-ordered fines imposed against a prisoner.

However, not all states offer every type of clemency relief mentioned above. The types of relief available in each state are listed in the appendix of this book.

Eligibility

The eligibility requirements for prisoners filing for clemency varies from state to state. You can find the requirements for your state listed in the appendix of this book. If you are a federal prisoner, the eligibility requirements also appear in the appendix.

Grounds for Executive Clemency

Executive clemency may be granted on a number of grounds, such as: correcting an injustice which may have occurred during your trial, or there is newly discovered evidence that exonerates you; releasing you because you are afflicted with a life-threatening medical condition; reducing an excessive sentence; or acknowledging that your institutional adjustment has been exemplary, and that the ends of justice have been achieved because you have been rehabilitated.

Unlike any other kind of remedy, arguing for clemency is a unique legal strategy. It is begged for, not demanded. Again, you have no constitutional right to clemency. So due diligence must be exercised when preparing an application, and in mounting a campaign for your freedom.

Application Process

Your state may require you to send off for a clemency application. Some states do not require any standardized clemency application, only that the request for clemency be in writing. Those that do, and those that do not, are specified in the appendix. For convenience, the addresses for the board of pardons and parole and the governor's office, whichever is needed for a particular state, will also be provided there.

<2> CLEMENCY REVIEW, INVESTIGATION, AND RECOMMENDATION

Clemency Review

The initial clemency review process is similar in all states, as well as in federal jurisdictions, and consists of a board review of the application for compliance with informational requirements, the creation of a case file, and assignment to a field officer for investigation.

In most states, the case file is referred to a probation or parole officer to investigate. That officer then prepares a report (similar in form and content to a presentence investigation report) for the board whose responsibility it is to decide the application or make a recommendation to the governor.

In other states, the attorney general or the governor's office is responsible for reviewing the application and conducting an investigation, as is the procedure in federal cases. You can find the initial review process specific to your state, as well as the process applicable to federal prisoners, in the appendix of this book.

Investigation

The individual assigned to investigate your clemency application will do a thorough investigation, assessing all the issues raised, to determine the merits of your case. The information obtained, both positive and negative, will be summarized in the report.

The format used in these investigative reports are standard to most state and federal correctional agencies, varying only slightly in form, terminology, and content provided for interagency review. The following outline is the clemency report format used in Missouri.

- ***Introduction*** The investigator will outline the reason for the clemency request, including references to any specific collateral consequences being claimed as a result of the conviction, and the number of previous clemency applications that have been filed, if any.
- ***Present Offense*** The investigator will outline the present offense(s), a brief summary of the circumstances surrounding the present offense(s), and the date and type of release from incarceration, expiration of sentence date, and the prisoner's adjustment under supervision, if applicable.

- ***Victim Impact*** The investigator will contact the victim(s) or family members. If unable to contact either one, the investigator will use any information or documentation addressing this issue, and briefly summarize it.
- ***Arrest and Conviction Record*** The prisoner's arrest and conviction record will be listed in a similar format to that used for "Present Offense."
- ***Conduct Since Conviction*** The investigator will outline and assess the prisoner's conduct since being convicted. The investigator's assessment will cover issues such as social, employment, and financial stability, including thoroughly assessing any history of mental health or substance abuse issues, particularly related to criminality, in order to determine whether those issues have been successfully resolved. Any positive achievements of the prisoner are also outlined in this section.
- ***Official and Community Attitude*** The investigator will include any comments and recommendations from the law enforcement agency that arrested the prisoner, the prosecuting attorney, the sentencing judge, and any community member(s) with knowledge of the prisoner or the offense.
- ***Evaluation and Recommendation*** The last section of the report will outline the investigator's recommendation regarding clemency, with his or her objective reason(s) for supporting the recommendation to grant or deny the prisoner's request. When the report is completed, it is forwarded to the board responsible for making the final decision, or making a recommendation to the governor.

The investigators, board members, and any other individuals playing an active role in the clemency process are well-educated, armed with college degrees in criminal justice, psychology, and sociology. It is the duty of these people to meticulously review a prisoner's case to determine whether he or she can be released without posing a threat to society. They are required to weigh the mitigating and aggravating factors, relying on information provided by the prisoner and gleaned during the investigation. They are actually looking for information that demonstrates the prisoner has acquired the Holy Grail: self-esteem.

But why is self-esteem so important? Let's take an in-depth look into the psychology of the human mind.

Self-Esteem

The definition of *self-esteem* is: confidence in one's own worth; self-respect. Oftentimes self-esteem is understood to be the same thing as confidence, but the two are not identical. Indeed, they are quite different. The difference is that self-esteem is a barometer for how much someone *generally* likes and respects oneself and how worthy he or she feels to receive good things in life. It is an ongoing personal trait. Confidence, on the other hand, is a measure of how comfortable and effective someone feels in *a certain situation* with regard to one's own knowledge and skill set, and one's ability to accomplish a specific outcome or complete a certain task. Confidence is a physiological response to an external stimulus, and, as such, is a temporary state that depends on the circumstances of a specific situation.

In practice, someone with high self-esteem will treat others with kindness and respect, invest in his or her own long-term well-being by engaging in things that will benefit his or her future, and sacrifice things that would be immediately pleasurable but of no benefit to long-term goals, therefore choosing to do what's right. A person with high self-esteem has self-love.

People gain self-esteem by doing what is right, which makes them feel good about themselves for the choices they make. and that is because doing the right thing is not often easy; it frequently involves making sacrifices. Challenges build one's self-esteem once they have been met and overcome.

When people do what's wrong (e.g., lying, cheating, robbing, stealing, abusing drugs or alcohol, having unprotected sex, hurting others, etc.), they feel guilt, shame, and embarrassment. These negative emotions affect how they feel about themselves and how they believe they are thought of by others, which eats away at their self-esteem. The reason for this is that they choose to do or have what *feels* good or makes them *look* good, instead of choosing to do what *is* good or right.

Choosing to do something just because it feels good—when we know it is wrong—takes away our sense of self-control. When we feel independent and in control of ourselves through the exercise of our freedom of choice, it is because we are exercising free will, overcoming base impulses and urges to do what is easy or merely feels good at the time. We need to respect ourselves and our choices in order to feel good about who we are, gaining self-respect and self-esteem in the process.

When someone lacks control, giving in to immediate gratification (such as by getting high, having unprotected sex with strangers, overeating, spending money compulsively, etc.), craving for attention (such as by buying things purely to impress others, acting arrogant, being loud, acting rudely, or disrespecting or deliberately offending others), or protecting or projecting a cultivated self-image (a delusional or skewed sense of one's abilities, appearance, and personality), they end up a slave to their impulses, dependent upon others to feed their emotional needs for approval and respect. And when they don't receive these things in abundant amounts, they become angry, lashing out at whoever they feel is the source of their emotional discomfort, or they act out in self-destructive ways.

Fear is the root cause of anger. It is triggered by the loss of control over some circumstance, self-image, or other aspect of the person's life. Those who get angry and act out violently are actually displaying low self-esteem.

The ego is the part of our personality that mediates between environmental demands of the external world (reality), our conscience/superego (social standards or beliefs that we have internalized; our idea of who we'd like to be), and our instinctual needs/id, (the correction of unconscious urges and desires that continually seek expression). The ego is partly unconscious and partly conscious. It obtains knowledge of the external world through our senses. The ego's purpose is to control the demands of the id in a reasonable, moral manner approved by the superego.

The ego holds everything together—our self-concept, our beliefs, values, and behaviors—keeping out whatever it thinks will hurt us, telling us how to see ourselves and how to demand others to see and act towards us.

Our level of self-esteem determines how much our ego becomes engaged. The ego's default defense mechanism is anger. But why? Because anger boosts the ego, giving us the sense of power and control that restores our illusion of freedom and independence. The more inflated our ego, the lower our self-esteem will be.

A humble person is someone with a under-inflated ego and high self-esteem. An arrogant person is one with an inflated ego and low self-esteem. And someone with a "Type B" personality—a doormat disposition—has low self-esteem and a deflated ego.

Someone who has a deflated ego and low self-worth will direct negativity inward, blaming and punishing themself for feelings of inadequacy and unworthiness.

In society, the most dangerous individual is someone who has an inflated ego and little or no sense of self-worth, because an arrogant individual will always direct his or her anger outward—whether it's by destroying things or hurting others.

As you can see, acquiring self-esteem and displaying it in your application can make the difference between receiving a favorable or unfavorable recommendation for clemency.

<3> ADAPTATION, INTENTIONAL SELF-DEVELOPMENT, AND SELF-ACTUALIZATION

Adaptation

Over two million years ago, our ancestors, naked and afraid, struggled to survive and propagate, clinging to life in a dire day-by-day existence in the dangerous savannas of Africa. They worked within the limitations of their environment, developing effective strategies for hunting wild animals and finding edible insects, nuts, and plants. They learned to make tools out of sharp-edged stones, which they then used for butchering animals, scraping hides, and chopping and carving wood. They discovered combustion, creating fire for staying warm and cooking meat, making the digestion of food easier.

These primitive people quickly learned the benefits of hunting in groups, and found safety in numbers from predators. They formed tribes. Chiefs of these tribes were selected based upon their dominance, survival skills, and prowess, and their status afforded them their choice in women. The other men were forced to compete and fight for the privilege to copulate with women, risking their lives at the hands of jealous rivals. Some men stealthily took women from other tribes. The men who didn't compete or fight for women were celibate, eventually dying off without spreading their genes.

Women selected mates based upon the men's survival skills and prowess instead of appearance, which took time to observe and confirm. As a result, women developed an evolutionary stable strategy of selecting mates based upon men's desirability to other women. If a woman showed an interest in copulating with a man, other women could use that preselection as a time-saving indicator of that man's survival skills and prowess. They could confidently choose him as a mate, thereby enhancing the chances of survival for themselves and their offspring. The only real choice a woman had in her tribe was in choosing a man for protection and copulation, but once the choice was made and submitted to, the man was then in a position of power and control over her. This explains why women were selective and cautious about choosing a man.

Our ancestors' tribes were nomadic and did not form settled communities. As tribes grew in population, more food was needed, forcing them to constantly be on the move. They were hunter-gatherers, owning few material possessions because carrying them around would have been a burden. Since possessions were few, the concepts of "rich" and "poor" did not exist. Tribe members were instead distinguished from one another solely by sex, age, and survival skills.

Our ancestors had the mental, emotional, and physical endurance to survive under extraordinary circumstances. They adapted to the movements and appetites of predators—becoming the hunters instead of being the prey—as well as to the unpredictable weather, and to the continuous threat of jealous rivals driven by their own instincts to survive and procreate.

It is an innate human ability to adapt mentally, emotionally, and physically to an environment, to use all available resources for immediate survival as well as future benefit. The skill of adaptability enables one to be flexible in an unpredictable environment, and responsive to the demands of the moment even if they temporarily divert from realizing future plans.

In order to master the skill of adaptation, you must consciously train your mind to focus on your immediate environment, dropping all psychological defense mechanisms (psychology texts specify these as repression, regression, reaction formation, projection, rationalization, and displacement), and shift your perspective to evaluate what are needs versus mere wants.

Take a realistic inventory of the resources currently available to you. Are they being used in the most beneficial way?

For example, if you receive money from friends, family, or working a prison job—then spend it all on food from the canteen, instead of saving that money by eating out of the dining hall—are you using the resources of your environment for future benefit? Of course not. But why? Because the flow of money could dry up at any time, leaving nothing to be used for future needs. Someone adapting to his or her environment would eat meals provided by the prison, spending only what was absolutely necessary, saving the rest for when it was needed. The food served by the prison, however unpalatable, has to be better than insects and roots, right?

Always remember that you are on a mission to secure your freedom. Once you are free, you can eat whatever you want. For now, your ability to adapt to your environment, exploiting all available resources for future benefit, is an essential part of your intentional self-development process.

Intentional Self-Development Process

What psychologists call intentional self-development is a dynamic process of personal growth in which a person makes plans designed to shape his or her self-concept (that is, sense of identity and self-worth) and personality (which is one's characteristic pattern of thinking, feeling, and behaving).

The process of intentional self-development is controlled by changing old thought patterns, limiting beliefs, negative emotions, and patterns of behavior, all within the aim of molding oneself into a person of value. Its focus is on understanding the self (who one is and who one was), setting goals for personal growth, and making action plans designed to direct the course of one's life, shaping and strengthening self-concept and personality throughout the process.

Of course, while engaging in the process of intentional self-development, you will find that not everyone will support your effort. There will be those who will not appreciate the new path you are taking. Some may even be hostile to it. Let that be their problem, not yours. Accepting this is a part of the adaptation process, letting go of people and things that only weigh you down and stunt your progress.

Intentional self-development will be challenging, and at times you will want to abandon your efforts. But if you stay persistent and work through the period of initial discomfort, you will come out of this process with a wisdom that will help accomplish whatever personal goals you set.

Identity/Self-Concept

We are a one-time phenomenon in this world. Our precise pattern of genes cannot be duplicated. We are the sum totals of good genes and bad genes, mixed together with good habits and bad habits, with good ideas and bad ideas. We can't change our genetic makeup. Our eye color, height, skin tone, and many other genetically determined traits are fixed, but we can change our bad habits into good habits, by way of instruction and persistent action.

Since habits are learned behavior, we can change them. The first obstacle to overcome when changing any bad habit is not to learn but to unlearn the pattern of thought and behavior that created it. Self-concept is shaped by unconscious thoughts and beliefs about oneself and how it is believed that one is seen, thought, and felt about by others. Our true self is buried underneath insecurities, bad habits, and limiting beliefs, all of which inhibit us. As long as we contend with these inhibitions, we can't live up to our true potential. We have to focus intently on discovering ourselves and bringing our best self to the surface.

From birth, our brains developed hundreds of neural connections, collecting ideas about who we are, whether good or bad, smart or stupid, attractive or ugly, confident or afraid, etc. As a result of repetition, these identities hardened into a mental sculpture—a self-image. But this image isn't who we are, it's who we *think* we are. The conditioning circumstances that formed our self-image could be completely wrong. Nevertheless, how we see ourselves—true or false—creates our thoughts, beliefs, emotions, and behavior, which then contributes to our environment and determines our achievements.

When we attach self-worth to accomplishments or behavior, we are setting ourselves up for disappointment. We are giving away our control, letting our self-worth be determined by external factors or the approval of others. Self-worth can only come from within. Otherwise, no one would ever be capable of unconditional self-love and self-acceptance.

There will always be someone who doesn't love or accept you. Despite knowing that, once you can look at yourself in the mirror and say you love and accept who you are, unconditionally, regardless of approval from others or of your achievements, you'll be ready to take the next step.

Personal Growth and Transformation

The skill of programming one's mind is essential for personal growth and transformation. We have learned to believe things that may or may not be true. The unconscious mind doesn't care one way or the other whether something actually happened or we imagined it; the unconscious mind is simply programmed by the thoughts we hold in the forefront of our mind. In fact, our beliefs are untrue more often than not, and they create behaviors that we do not necessarily understand or want to continue. The unconscious mind is susceptible to almost any repeated suggestion.

For example, if you are uncomfortable with public speaking and often think about it, mentally rehearsing how bad things play out, feeling all the negative emotions associated with that negativity, a very real fear will be programmed into your unconscious. Then, whenever a situation arises that calls for you to speak in a public setting, your unconscious mind will replay the fearful thoughts, causing you to experience the negative emotions all over again, even though the original experience was a creation of your imagination.

Your unconscious mind can bring about most anything you believe, intellectually, to be true. But if your beliefs are not serving your best interests, or if they are limiting your success, you must take control by consciously reprogramming your unconscious mind. This can be done by using affirmations and visualizations of outcomes you want. But if the reprogramming is left unfinished, your unconscious mind will revert to old beliefs and patterns of behavior, and you will have to start the process anew.

You have to keep suggesting or affirming something until your unconscious mind is completely convinced that what you are suggesting or affirming is true. This is not as difficult as it may seem. The key is to be consistent in saying the same affirmations and doing the same visual exercises regularly. Once the unconscious mind has been reached, a positive feeling will result, and the belief or behavior you are striving to change or implement will become habitual.

Are you skeptical? Is your conscious mind having difficulty believing that intentional self-development is a learned skill nearly anyone can attain? Let's demystify this conundrum and ta~e an in-depth look at how we learn.

Processes for Learning, Unlearning, and Relearning

In the womb, our bodies develop nerve cells that make up what is known as our nervous system. By the day of our birth, each of us is equipped with one of the most amazing and complex organs known to biology—a human brain. As we begin to experience life, our brain's neural connections (networks of nerve cells) start refining the cerebral cortex (the outermost portion of the brain, playing an important role in consciousness). The various areas of the cerebral cortex, which are associated with thinking, memory, and language, are the last areas of the brain to develop, during childhood. As they do, our cognitive ability improves by way of assimilation, classical conditioning (also known as Pavlovian conditioning), operant conditioning (a type of learning in which behavior is strengthened if followed by reinforcement, or diminished if followed by punishment), observational learning (learning by watching and imitating the behavior of others), and modeling (the process of imitating an observed behavior).

Memory also plays a significant part in the learning process, as an information processing system. We process information in three key ways—by encoding its meaning, by visualizing it, and by mentally organizing it. Imagery is at the heart of mnemonic devices (such as the "peg" and "memory palace" systems), which can make people appear to have superhuman memories when it is actually a skill learned with practice.

However, the conscious mind is limited and can only store small chunks of information at a time. These chunks of information do not have to be a certain size; they can be anything, from the rules of a game, playing a musical instrument, driving a car, etc. The most effective way to learn is by consciously assimilating many small chunks of behavior, then combining them all so that they become habitual and unconscious. Forming habits frees up the conscious mind to learn even more skills.

A system of behavior modification techniques known as Neuro-Linguistic Programming TM (NLP) uses the following model for how the mind learns. It will help you understand the process better.

- ***Unconscious incompetence:*** You are doing something incorrect, but you don't know that you are doing it incorrectly.
- ***Conscious incompetence:*** You are doing something incorrect, and know it, but don't know how to do it correctly.
- ***Conscious competence:*** You are learning the correct way to do something, and are doing it correctly with focused attention.
- ***Unconscious competence:*** You no longer have to think about something or practice it, because you have mastered it, making it habitual.

You now know it is possible to consciously program your unconscious mind using the tools outlined in this chapter. The rest is up to you, and you alone.

People don't fail, they just stop trying. Don't be one of those people. Put in the time and effort, and you will attain your goals as a matter of course, leading you to self-actualization.

Self-Actualization

Self-Actualization is an innate growth drive that resides within all of us. But it is not activated until lower-level needs for safety, a sense of social belonging, and esteem are met.

Psychologist Abraham Maslow proposed that we are motivated by a hierarchy of needs. This hierarchy proceeds as follows. When our physiological needs are met, we become concerned with personal safety. If we acquire a sense of security, we then seek to love, to be loved, and to love ourselves. Having acquired self-esteem, we seek *self-actualization*, the fulfillment of our potential.

You can use Maslow's hierarchy of needs as a guide on your journey to realizing your full potential.

Self-Actualization
Need to live up to one's fullest and unique potential

Esteem
Need for self-esteem, achievement, competence, and independence; need for recognition and respect from others

Belongingness and Love
Need to love and be loved, to belong and be accepted; need to avoid loneliness and alienation

Safety
Need to feel that the world is organized and predictable; need to feel safe, secure, and stable

Physiological
Need to satisfy hunger and thirst

Limiting Beliefs

Harvey Stewart, at eighty-three years of age, was granted parole in April 2011, but was forced to stay in prison until he could be placed in a halfway house or nursing home. Harvey had nowhere else to go; he had outlived most of his relatives.

"So what do you want to do when you get out?" Harvey was asked.

"You think I want to get involved in some sex and get drunk? No. I want a good easy-going meal and a root beer. I said root beer," he exclaimed.

Harvey first entered the Texas prison system in 1951, sentenced to serve ten years for robbing a junk yard. And for six years, Harvey did time and little else until he was paroled.

Back on the street and not missing a beat, Harvey robbed brothels in Southwest Texas. He was also shot, and murdered a man in what he claimed was self-defense in 1958. Harvey escaped in 1965, but was caught a few days later. Be was paroled in 1984, then imprisoned again, for a new robbery case, in 1986.

At the time of his 2011 release, Harvey held the distinction of serving the most time of any Texas prisoner—nearly sixty years.

"Imagine that: sixty years down in this damn hole. I wouldn't recommend it. Man's got to be a damn fool to even stick his foot in here," Harvey said.

The nation's longest-serving female prisoner at the time, Betty Smithey, age sixty-nine, served forty-nine years in the Arizona Department of Corrections, until Governor Jan Brewer granted her clemency and reduced her sentence of life without parole.

"It's wonderful driving down the road and not seeing any barbed wire," Betty said, following her release on August 14, 2012. "I am lucky, so very lucky."

Many other prisoners are not so lucky, leaving prison not on parole but in body bags.

Our beliefs can be chains that bind us—to the past and the present, predetermining our future and keeping us from discovering our potential, restraining us from the experience of a rich and fulfilling life.

We adopt our beliefs from a variety of influential sources: upbringing, peers, environment, mentors, role models, books, movies, music lyrics, positive and negative experiences, authority figures, and through our unconscious rehearsal of behaviors. Most of the beliefs we adopt are untrue, but since we had no way of filtering them out, we merely adopted them.

For example, if a young boy is told that he will be run over by a car if he crosses the street, is that true? It could be. But it isn't likely if he looks both ways before crossing the street. The belief anchored with fear that he will be run over may save the boy's life. It serves the purpose of keeping him out of the street. But once he is grown and adopts the habit of looking both ways before crossing the street, the belief he had as a boy is obsolete and no longer serves him.

As a grown man, having the belief that he will be run over if he crosses the street would serve no purpose. The belief could become a phobia that keeps him from learning how to drive a car, going to work, shopping for food and clothes, or from going to see a movie with a woman who lives two blocks away.

This scenario sounds ridiculous, but we still hold outdated beliefs that no longer serve a positive purpose. Some of these beliefs still affect our behavior every day, without our awareness.

Here is a more realistic example of how beliefs can direct the course of a person's life. Suppose a boy named Johnny is in grade school. His teacher gives the class a spelling test and picks Johnny to spell the first word. But Johnny doesn't know how to spell it, because he did not study the list of words the teacher gave the class at the beginning of the week. Johnny was too busy playing in the street with his friends every day after school, so he tries to sound out the word. He gets it wrong.

The class bully yells, "You're stupid!" And the girl next to Johnny chimes in, "Yeah, you're stupid."

Everyone in the class laughs, including Joanne—the girl Johnny has a crush on.

On his walk home, Johnny mentally replays what happened that day in class—the embarrassment, the humiliation, the word "stupid" echoing in his head, and the ringing of Joanne's laughter in his ears.

When Johnny gets home, his father asks, "Are you deaf? Didn't I tell you to set the trash out this morning before you left for school? Go to your room and stay there for the rest of the night."

In his room, Johnny again plays through the events of the day in his mind, getting angry. He resents the teacher for calling on him, the class bully for embarrassing him, and his father for not simply taking the trash out himself.

The next morning, frustrated and certain that everyone thinks he is stupid, Johnny decides he does not want to attend school anymore. Instead, he starts hanging out with the thugs down the street. One day they ask him to steal some alcohol from a local store. Not wanting to disappoint them, Johnny goes into the store and comes back out with the goods: two bottles of grape Mad Dog 20/20.

Johnny is praised and respected by his boys. And as time goes by, the more daring his escapades become, earning him a reputation for being a ruthless criminal with no self-control, who eventually ends up in prison.

Now suppose that Johnny had gone home and told his father what happened in class, and his father, rather than yelling about the trash, said, "You're not stupid, Johnny. You just used the wrong strategy for spelling words. You have to picture the word in your mind instead of trying to sound it out. First take the word and write it down, then look up and to the left and imagine a big blank chalkboard. Write out the letters of the word, one by one on the chalkboard, until you have a clear picture of the entire word in your mind. Do that three to five times. See the word, spell it forward and backward while tracing over each letter in your mind."

With an effective spelling strategy, Johnny would have gone back to school ready for the next test. He would get the week's list of words and learn how to spell each one, forward and backward. He would also make a habit of spelling every new word he encountered in books and magazines, becoming the best speller in his class, even eventually winning the school's spelling bee.

As these stories demonstrate, we will be held back by our limiting beliefs unless we are consciously aware of them and take action to change them. Anything that we believe about ourselves, someone else, or our environment will become a kind of self-fulfilling prophecy. Anytime we tell ourselves that we can not do something that is humanly possible, that is a limiting belief. Understand that most limits are the limits we set for ourselves. Make a habit of recognizing these limiting beliefs and changing them.

Whenever you fail to get the outcome you want, analyze yourself and the situation until you find an error, then determine what you realistically could have done differently to turn things around. In doing this, you will develop the habit of correcting mistakes in your mind instead of having them play out in real time. If there was nothing you could have realistically done differently, accept that and move on.

When you become aware of a limiting belief, do not automatically place blame on anyone else, just forgive, forget, and move on. And when something happens to go wrong in the future, acknowledge that it is your fault and your fault alone. Accepting responsibility is a good thing, because it means you are in control.

You can affirm "I learn things quick and easy" until learning things "quick and easy" becomes a habitual reality. And the reality is this—by changing your beliefs, your behavior will change to match them, improving the quality of your life.

Self-Assessment

On the next pages you will find self-assessment exercises that will help you determine what you need to work on. It is important that you be honest with yourself while doing these exercises. The answers you write down will be invaluable as you proceed through the clemency process, particularly in the part of the process addressed in the chapter that follows. Not completing these exercises will only result in additional complications later. The effort now will yield significant reward.

Identity

How do you believe other people perceive you?

____

____

____

____

How would you like others to perceive you?

____

____

____

____

Name three of your traits that you would like to change (this may include: antagonism, aggression, argumentative, codependency, laziness, bad posture, smoking, gambling, lying, cheating, substance abuse, stealing, questionable hygiene, gossiping, overeating, neediness, fidgeting, talking fast, frequent vulgarity, impulsivity, lack of self-control, risk-taking, supplicating, compulsive masturbation, promiscuity, self-mutilation, depression, low ambition, unreliability, insecurity, envy, jealousy, selfishness, insensitivity, low integrity, bad manners, poor listening skills, low work ethic, humorlessness, frequent negativity, reactivity, reaction-seeking, or any others you see fit).

____

____

____

____

Name three new behaviors or characteristics that you would like to adopt.

____

____

____

____

Values

List ten of the most important values (e.g. family, love, wealth, good health, trust, faithfulness, friendship, etc.) to you. Elicit your core values by asking yourself: *What is really important to me in life? What motivates me or inspires me? What needs to be true for me?* When you are finished, go back and rewrite your values (e.g., family, love, friendship, health, stability, independence, etc.) in the order of importance, 1 being the most important, 10 being the least.

1. ____
2. ____
3. ____
4. ____
5. ____
6. ____
7. ____
8. ____
9. ____
10. ____

Beliefs

List ten beliefs about yourself that you consider to be true at this time in your life ("I look for the good in everything," or "I don't deal well with criticism," for example.)

1. ____
2. ____
3. ____
4. ____

5. ______________________________

6. ______________________________

7. ______________________________

8. ______________________________

9. ______________________________

10. ______________________________

Skills and Skill Sets

List ten skills and skill sets that you possess (e.g., verbal communication, playing music, writing, storytelling, visual art, hairstyling, giving manicures and pedicures, computer programming, auto repair, building and fixing things, playing sports, etc.). List everything you're good at.

____

____

____

____

Goals

Name three goals that you want to achieve to make your life more fulfilling (e.g., learning a specific skill, getting into shape, buying a house, writing a book, starting a business, etc.).

____

____

____

____

Why would the achievement of these goals improve your life?

____

____

____

____

What is preventing you from achieving them?

____

____

____

____

What is your personal mission in life? Write it below, along with the timeline you set for its accomplishment.

I am on a mission to ____

____

within ____________________ days/weeks/years.

Suggestions for Improvement

To take a giant leap in the self-development process, focus on developing self-control and discipline. Train yourself to think before you act. This is an issue many have; and it lies at the base of a host of other personal limitations. If this is an issue for you, make it a habit to affirm, "I think before I act, weighing all the pros and cons." In time you will discover yourself to be more in control, making better decisions, day to day.

Start analyzing your past and present behavior—as well as that of other people—until you understand the physical, social, and psychological reasons behind it. With time and practice, you will no longer take things personally, because you will understand that everyone else is merely running the program they were given. You will begin to see all of the beliefs that have limited you and are limiting others. But do not attempt to reprogram someone else, let others be. Work on improving only yourself. Keeping a journal will help.

You will also improve your life by working on your communication skills and developing higher social intelligence. This will be discussed in Chapter 6.

In this chapter, you learned who you are, what you value most, and what you want to achieve in life. You now have the tools to identify limiting beliefs and change them effectively.

It is important to take the intentional self-development process seriously and to give a detailed account, in your clemency application, of the journey you are on toward self-actualization.

If you attempt to shortcut the process and present a false or inflated personal profile in your application, those investigating your case will Perceive that dishonesty and render their recommendation accordingly.

You are an artist; the sculpture you are shaping is you. Your art is self-actualization, it is a way of life. Don't get discouraged.

<4> APPLICATION FOR EXECUTIVE CLEMENCY

Preparation of Clemency Application

This chapter addresses the preparation of your clemency application for submission. As a trademark of all *SMITH'S GUIDE*™ titles, you can find, at the end of this chapter, examples to look to while preparing your documents—in this instance, clemency applications filed and granted in actual cases.

Although the format recommended by *SMITH'S GUIDE*™ is similar to that used in the examples, this chapter provides additional subject matter, such as writing a personal letter, that will help you stand out as a person of value to society.

Note that the words *application* and *petition* are used interchangeably throughout the examples. These words refer to the same thing, but you should use whichever one your state uses to describe its clemency instrument.

State Forms, Cover Page, and Table of Contents

Some states require prisoners to use specific forms. In such instances, fill in all information for which space on the form is provided and write "see attached application" where there is not enough space to fully answer any question. Place the completed state form(s) on top your clemency application.

The cover page should be titled *Application for Executive Clemency for [your name, DOC number, and address]* at the top.

The table of contents should not be prepared until after the entire application is completed. Doing so will enable you to list the page numbers where certain information can easily be located.

Introduction

The introduction should encapsulate your reason(s) for asking for clemency. It needs to be concise while also including succinct details so the investigator assigned to your case can determine whether you are asking for a pardon, commutation, or some other relief. It should not be more than three pages.

Summary of the Offense

If you are presenting an actual innocence claim, you should give a brief account of the facts underlying the conviction(s), a procedural history, the results of prior legal proceedings (direct appeal, postconviction proceedings, or other collateral attacks), and a thorough presentation of all the evidence supporting your innocence. Copies of all documentation supporting the claim should be listed in the Table of Appendices (addressed later in this chapter) and attached to your application. (See example petition for Earl Washington).

If you are requesting a commutation, or some other clemency relief, you should give a brief account of the facts underlying the conviction(s), your social history, and a narrative of your self-development. (See example application for Sidney Cornwell).

Social History

Your social history should give a narrative of your upbringing, information about your parents and your relationship with them, and information about your other family members—siblings, children, etc. Your social history should be a detailed account of your childhood and other life events leading up to your incarceration. (See example of application for Sidney Cornwell).

If you had a good childhood and upbringing until something changed it, give a detailed narrative of what happened and its lasting or profound effect on you.

Do not put on a show, just be unguarded and truthful about your life and current situation.

Yes, some of the events you describe will be embarrassing, and relating them may make you feel uncomfortable, however this is a good thing. Embarrassment means you are being honest and open about yourself.

Self-Development and Personal Transformation

Unless you are making an actual innocence claim, it is important that you provide information about your self-development and personal transformation. As discussed in Chapter 2, the investigation will seek out information indicating that you have acquired self-esteem, corrected your thinking errors, developed self-control and discipline through the practice of setting and accomplishing goals, and are now on your way to self-actualization.

Give a detailed narrative of the process you have taken. Explain how you identified errors in your thinking and how you corrected them, as well as any other issues you had to resolve within yourself (e.g., substance abuse, abusive relationship, lack of self-control, self-hatred, anger, difficulty taking rejection, insecurity, etc.). Use what you learned in the last chapter. If you had a belief that limited you, describe what it was and how you overcame it.

If you still have issues, admit them and describe the actions you are now taking to address them. If you believe you need professional help with something, be forthright about it. This will show that you are being introspective and are serious about making positive changes in your life and becoming a productive member of society.

You should provide information of your achievements, such as completing educational courses, vocational training, and institutional programs. Attach copies of these records and certificates to your application, as appendices. If you do not have any such certificates, then you should take and complete as many programs as you can. If you do not have the equivalent of a high school diploma, take whatever steps are necessary to get one. Doing so will show that you have taken advantage of, or are currently availing yourself of, every opportunity available to you.

You should provide information of your employment history prior to incarceration. If you have not been formally employed, list any jobs you have worked during confinement. If you have not had any prison jobs, find one and maintain it. Displaying a good work ethic will help greatly in your clemency effort. If you have a medical condition which prevents you from working, explain it, and why it keeps you unemployed, in detail.

Future Employment Plan, Goals, and Accomplishments

It is important to show the determination and ability to find gainful employment upon your release from prison. Otherwise, you will be a financial burden on your family, friends, and society at large. To overcome whatever doubts those investigating or deciding your clemency request may have, let your skills, education, vocational training, and employment history speak on your behalf.

Take what you have learned in Chapter 3 and give a detailed plan of your goals. Provide a realistic timeline for accomplishing these goals upon your release. If you have already started putting your plan into action, describe what you have been doing. You must have a sensible plan for your life, one that makes it clear that you will not take a second chance for granted.

Basis for Clemency Request

You can use the statement below to introduce your personal letter and attachments. If you are asking for a pardon or relief other than a commutation, you will need to modify the statement accordingly.

> *For the foregoing, [Your Name] would request that the [Governor/Clemency Board] take notice of [his/her] statement and attachments in support of [his/her] request for a commutation of sentence.*

Conclusion

To conclude your application, you can use the example below, modifying it where appropriate, or draft one of your own.

Based upon the foregoing, [Your Name] respectfully requests the [Honorable Governor/Clemency Board], consider this Application for Executive Clemency, and prays for the relief requested herein. [He/She] further prays for any other and further relief which may be deemed just and proper under the circumstances.

Respectfully submitted,

[Sign Your Name]

[Date]

Personal Letter

The personal letter is usually the most difficult aspect of the clemency application process, because prisoners try to write what they think the governor or parole board wants to hear. But that is not the purpose of the letter. Its purpose is as an instrument to convey your personality and demonstrate your development of positive identity characteristics. It is your story of how certain situations and circumstances affected your life and set you on the road that led to where you are today. It is the story of how you come to understand yourself and what actions you took to change yourself into the person of value you are now.

The beginning of your story should be strong, setting a tone that makes it possible for the governor or clemency board to empathize with you. You might do this by starting your letter with an opening like the following.

> *I have come to the end of a very long road. There is nowhere else I can go, nor anything I can do to change the past. My current reality is unchangeable, and I take full responsibility for the reckless decisions I have made in my life. As I sit here, sentenced to spend thirty years in prison, I'd like to tell you my story.*

Word your story so that each event in your life is described in terms of sensations and emotions, not just facts. Delve into your childhood and describe the experiences that impacted you the most, how they made you feel, and what you think about them. Describe in detail the challenges you faced during your incarceration and self-development.

It may help you to imagine how a movie about your life would unfold, then write that story. Describe your self-development and personal transformation, all the ups and downs. Describe how you think and feel about decisions that affected people who love and care about you. If you do not have anyone, describe how that solitude feels, and how you learned to love and care about yourself.

Toward the letter's end, write about your goals and what you want to do with your life. Contrast this with an account of how you spend your time—reading books, drawing, writing, playing sports, or other positive, creative, or productive activities.

To end your letter, make an honest request for what you want and thank the governor or clemency board for taking the time to consider your request.

Table of Appendices

The table of appendices should list, in alphabetical or numerical order, all documents and attachments accompanying your clemency application, such as court records, statements, letters, copies of certificates, etc.

If possible, you should include pictures of yourself with your family, friends, both inside and outside of prison. If you paint, draw, write, etc., you should include anything that shows the creative skills you possess.

You may chose to include letters of support from family and friends, or to have those sent separately. Some states require you to submit letters of support and recommendation at the time of your application's submission. Whether or not this is a requirement of your state can be found in the appendix of this book. If it is, you must submit these letters with your application; however, if it is not, you may wait to send them until beginning your clemency campaign, which is the subject of the next chapter.

Reviewing Your Clemency Application Before Submission

When you are finished with your application and have compiled all the necessary documentation and attachments, carefully reread your application in its entirety, looking over all documentation and attachments one more time, to ensure that everything is in its proper order.

Make full and complete copies of your application and all its attachments. Some states have a set number of copies you must file, other states do not. Check your state's filing requirements and then send the exact number of copies of your application to the appropriate destination.

You should retain a full and complete copy for yourself, and one each for the sentencing judge and prosecutor. Even if your state does not require letters of recommendation from the judge and prosecutor to accompany your application, you should still make an effort to secure them, by sending a copy of your application with a letter asking them to provide the governor or clemency board with a recommendation on your behalf. Softening the opposition will be discussed in the next chapter.

Example Clemency Application for Sidney Cornwell

APPLICATION FOR EXECUTIVE CLEMENCY
FOR
SIDNEY CORNWELL
Ohio State Penitentiary
#340-473

THE OFFICE OF THE
OHIO PUBLIC DEFENDER

ROBERT K. LOWE
Assistant State Public Defender
[redacted]
Columbus, Ohio 43215-0708
[redacted]

and

LINDA E. PRUCHA
Supervisor, Death Penalty Division
[redacted]
Columbus, Ohio 43215-0708
[redacted]

and

ANDREW KING
Assistant State Public Defender
[redacted]
Columbus, Ohio 43215-0708
[redacted]

October 6, 2010

Example Clemency Application for Sidney Cornwell (cont.)

Table of Contents

i

Example Clemency Application for Sidney Cornwell (cont.)

Introduction

Sidney Cornwell faces execution on November 16, 2010, for the murder of Jessica Ballew. In 1996, Sidney committed a horrible crime; he fired a weapon at a house and killed Ms. Ballew. He is genuinely and deeply sorry for this.[1] He is also profoundly remorseful for wounding Samuel Lagese, Donald Meadows, and Marilyn Conrad.[2] As Sidney states in his letter to Gov. Strickland: "I take full responsibility for my actions, and causing the death of Jessica Ballew. I was reckless, and my actions of that night have cause *(sic)* a great deal of pain for everyone this act may have involved."[3]

Today, Sidney is a changed man who has a positive impact on those around him—both the inmates on death row and the people outside the prison with whom he has contact. Sidney is a role model for other prisoners. Over the past nine years, Sidney has been a model inmate.

Sidney's transformation did not occur overnight nor is it to avoid execution. Sidney began to accept responsibility for Ms. Ballew's death in 2005. Until then, he was in denial that he shot and killed a three-year-old girl. When Sidney came to grips with his actions and began to accept responsibility—first with himself and then with counsel—he was at the age of maturity and able to admit his actions.

Sidney now asks the Parole Board to consider the following reasons to grant clemency in his case.

- Sidney was abused as a child and repeatedly exposed to domestic violence.
- Sidney suffers from untreated testosterone deficiency and Klinefelter's Syndrome.
- Risk factors throughout Sidney's childhood led him to participate in gang activities.

[1] Ex. 1, Sidney Cornwell's letter to Gov. Ted Strickland (Sept. 18, 2010).
[2] Id.
[3] Id.

Example Clemency Application for Sidney Cornwell (cont.)

- Sidney suffers from neurocognitive deficits.
- Sidney's age at the time of the crime favors mercy in this case.
- The jury at Sidney's capital trial never heard crucial mitigating evidence of Sidney's life.
- Sidney has adapted to confinement and conformed to the strictures of incarceration.
- Sidney's death sentence is disproportionate to other Mahoning County homicides, thus, Sidney's case is not the worst of the worst.
- A black capital defendant in Mahoning County is 71.4% more likely to receive a death sentence than is a white defendant.

Summary Of The Offense

In June of 1996, Sidney Cornwell had been living in a dope house for approximately three months, rarely leaving that location. On June 10, Sidney, along with other members of the Crips gang, decided to walk the streets looking for girls. Bloods members Richard "Boom" Miles and Michael Williams located Sidney, Edward McGaha, Phillip Fuzell and, because of something said earlier in the day to Boom's sister, began firing a shotgun at Sidney and his fellow gang members. Edward was grazed in the head and treated at a hospital. Sidney and his group returned to the home of Edward's mother. Later in the day the Bloods drove by the house and gunfire was again exchanged. No one was injured.

Sidney went to the house of another Crips member, Heavy, where plans were made to find Boom. After drinking and smoking marijuana, Sidney and the other Crips got into stolen vehicles. At approximately 2 a.m. on the morning of June 11, three Crips vehicles approached an apartment where Boom was known to sell crack. The first two cars passed the building. The third vehicle stopped. On the front porch of the apartment were Donald Meadows, Susan Hamlett, and unseen by Sidney, Hamlett's niece, three-year-old Jessica Ballew. According to

2

Example Clemency Application for Sidney Cornwell (cont.)

reports, there was no porch light and the inside lights could not be seen from outside. All three cars had turned their headlights off. Sidney, who was in the third car, asked if Boom was there. Meadows and Hamlett said that he was not. Sidney replied, "tell Boom this," and started shooting. Jessica Ballew was shot twice and killed; Donald Meadows was wounded, as were two people inside the apartment, Marilyn Conrad and Samuel Lagese.

Susan Hamlett called the police. After abandoning the car and his weapon, Sidney was arrested and taken into custody.

I. Sidney was abused as a child and repeatedly exposed to domestic violence.

Sidney's mother, Beverly Cornwell Terry, was a young mother and wife. She married Sidney Cornwell, Sr. when she was just seventeen. And prior to that marriage, Beverly was a single mother living on public assistance. Although she became financially secure through marriage, it was a tempestuous relationship. The couple fought throughout her pregnancy with Sidney, and her husband physically abused her while she was pregnant. At some point Beverly moved out and lived with her mother. In her 1999 affidavit, she recalled this period as the worst time in her life. She nearly suffered a nervous breakdown.[4] It was so bad that she considered aborting her pregnancy, a decision that her family convinced her not to make.

Drugs, like violence, became a part of Sidney's life even before he was born. His mother smoked marijuana almost every day of her pregnancy. And Sidney's exposure to drug use only increased once he was born. His mother and father smoked marijuana in front of the kids. Plus, Sidney's father abused alcohol, cocaine, and LSD so much so that he spent most of his money on his addictions. In 1999, he acknowledged his addictions, but blamed his drug abuse on his

---

[4] Ex. 2, Affidavit of Dr. Kristen Haskins.

3

Example Clemency Application for Sidney Cornwell (cont.)

wife's infidelities.[5] Also, he admitted that both his parents and all his siblings abused drugs and/or alcohol.[6]

Violence, too, became a regular part of Sidney's life. When Sidney was a young boy, his father beat up a man that came to the house to shut off the power because of nonpayment. Sidney's father physically abused Sidney, the other children, and Sidney's mother. The abuse got so bad that Beverly moved out and took the kids to a battered woman's shelter run by the YWCA. Finally, she decided to permanently escape the violence by divorcing Sidney Cornwell, Sr. In the divorce, she got the house and custody of the children. Although the physical violence subsided with their father's absence, it did not end his abuse. Initially, he was content to "spy" on Beverly and the children, by standing outside watching them and yelling at them, but it soon escalated into much more.

Sidney's father put sugar in his ex-wife's gas tank and threw a brick, with "bitch" written on it, through their window hitting two of the children. And he frightened the children; they recalled him hiding in the bushes and yelling at them. The violence toward their mother escalated even further when he pulled a gun on his ex-wife. Her brother decided to protect her and shot Sidney Cornwell, Sr. in the chest. While things got better for Beverly with Sidney, Sr. out of the home, they got worse for the kids.

Several months after Sidney was born, his mother Beverly obtained a job at GM working 10-12 hour shifts. Beverly obtained this job because she was planning on leaving Sidney Sr. and needed a job out of necessity. One day while Beverly was away at work, Sidney Cornwell, Sr. showed up at the house and kidnapped the children. Beverly's oldest child and Sidney's half sister, Shanel Phillips was babysitting the children, but she was in eighth grade at the time and

[5] Ex. 3, Affidavits of Sidney Cornwell, Sr.
[6] Id.

4

Example Clemency Application for Sidney Cornwell (cont.)

unable to do anything to stop her former step-father. Beverly filed a report and asked for police assistance, but it would be years before Sidney returned home. She did not immediately seek out the children, in part, because Sidney Cornwell, Sr. threatened her if she came after the children.[7] So, the children spent the next several years living with their abusive father in Pennsylvania.

Sidney and his siblings were kidnapped and taken to Pennsylvania.

Sidney was in the third grade when he was kidnapped and moved to Pennsylvania. And things went from bad to worse for him and his siblings. Initially, the children moved into a two bedroom house, with hardly enough room for them all.[8] And until they moved out of that house, they had little contact with their mother or their half-sister.[9] During the entire time in Pennsylvania, their father would beat them savagely, sometimes for 10 or 20 minutes.[10] When he beat the children, he used switches, belts, or his bare fists. Every few days, the children would receive these beatings that left bruises on their arms and chests. LaShonda recalled being beaten so bad that her blood was spattered on the wall. According to his siblings, Sidney received the worst of the beatings because his father thought Sidney was fat and lazy. His father acknowledged beating Sidney more and leaving marks on his body.[11]

Sidney Cornwell, Sr.'s drug habit continued while in Pennsylvania. In fact, some of the beatings he inflicted were due to his frustration of being without money and in need of a fix.[12] Marcus recalls seeing his father on his hands and knees scrounging around on the floor looking for crumbs of crack. The children had very little to eat and had to wear raggedy clothes because

[7] Transcript of the Mitigation Hearing, p.70.
[8] Transcript of the Mitigation Hearing, p.71.
[9] Transcript of the Mitigation Hearing, p.138.
[10] Ex. 4, Affidavits of Marcus Cornwell.
[11] Ex. 3, Affidavits of Sidney Cornwell, Sr.
[12] Ex. 4, Affidavits of Marcus Cornwell.

Example Clemency Application for Sidney Cornwell (cont.)

their father used his money for drugs instead of food and clothing for the children. Sidney Cornwell, Sr. even used the child support money he got from his ex-wife to buy drugs.

Sidney's father was not only a physically abusive drug addict, but he was also a terrible role model for his children. Because their father wouldn't spend money on them, LaShonda would steal drugs from her father and sell them to get money for herself and her brothers.[13] It went further than that with Sidney—his father taught Sidney how to weigh and sell drugs. At the young age of 12, when Sidney should have still been playing games, his father had him out on the street selling drugs. In addition to mentoring Sidney in the ways of being a drug dealer, his father coached Sidney to be violent.

Sidney was beaten up at school by another boy. Once Sidney Cornwell, Sr. learned about the fight, he told his son that he better beat up the boy the next day or he would be beaten by his father.[14] Sidney knew that his father was serious, so he went to school the next day and beat up the boy. Sidney Cornwell, Sr. acknowledged teaching Sidney that "he needed to be willing to fight to protect himself and his family."[15] Because of the Klinefelter's Syndrome, Sidney likely suffered prolonged periods of frustration, which could explain why he began acting out violently when he was uprooted and returned to Youngstown and immediately faced gang violence.[16] And the coaching he received from his father to be violent likely helped overcome his natural tendencies.

Even though their mother knew about the abuse and neglect, she did nothing of consequence to intervene.[17] Once they moved to Sharon, Pennsylvania, she would visit, but she made no efforts to either get them help or get them back. Living with their father was so bad,

---

[13] Ex. 5, Affidavits of LaShonda Cornwell.
[14] Ex. 6, Affidavits of Beverly Terry.
[15] Ex. 3, Affidavits of Sidney Cornwell, Sr.
[16] Ex. 8, Report of William Zipf, M.D.
[17] Transcript of the Mitigation Hearing, p.151.

6

Example Clemency Application for Sidney Cornwell (cont.)

that LaShonda ran away, hitchhiking back to Youngstown.[18] Although Beverly temporarily took LaShonda in, she did nothing to help her two sons still under the thumb of their abusive father.

Sidney's testosterone deficiency and Klinefelter's Syndrome were not adequately treated.

Sidney suffers from Klinefelter's Syndrome mosaic, which was undiagnosed and untreated during his adolescence. Klinefelter's Syndrome is an abnormal chromosomal pattern in which cells carry an extra female sex chromosome having an XXY pattern as opposed to the normal male pattern of XY. The extra X chromosome is associated with problems causing late motor development, late speech development, learning problems, socialization problems, and problems associated with muscle tone/strength, visual perception, and coordination. Reading skills in particular may be poor, resulting in poor school performance. The muscle and coordination problems make it difficult to achieve success in sports. Additional problems can include psychological distress and frustration due to the lack of academic, athletic, and social success. The Klinefelter's Syndrome mosaic pattern can have a variable pattern of symptoms but can include the full clinical spectrum. Sidney's surgery for male gynecomastia suggests a more marked degree of the condition.[19]

Klinefelters can have a profound impact on the mental and social development of the children that have it. Dr. Daniel Davis reports that "[p]ersonality features associated with Klinefelter's includes low self-esteem, poor impulse control, anxiety, and social immaturity in groups, excessive shyness, excessive aggression, depression, difficulties in social skills development."[20] And it impairs language skills and executive functioning.[21] Further, in one

[18] Transcript of the Mitigation Hearing, p.75.
[19] Ex. 8, Report of William B. Zipf, M.D., p. 2-3.
[20] Ex. 9, Report of Daniel Davis, Ph.D., p. 14.
[21] Id.

Example Clemency Application for Sidney Cornwell (cont.)

study, 69% of participants with Klinefelter's had problems with controlling aggression.[22] Due to these issues, Klinefelter's requires "prospectively planned and timed support for young men with Klinefelter syndrome to ameliorate current poor psychosocial outcomes."[23] But Sidney never received any such support.

Sidney was admitted to a hospital when he was thirteen years old for surgery to reduce the size of his breasts. He was diagnosed with Testosterone Resistant Syndrome; Hypotestosteronemia (low levels of testosterone); and Macromastia (enlarged breasts). He had cup size DD breasts. He also had hypoplastic genitalia (underdeveloped genitals/incomplete or arrested development of genitals). Doctors removed 1,227.8 grams and 1,308.0 grams of breast tissue. The final diagnosis was Testosterone Deficiency Syndrome with manifestations of macromastia.[24]

Although these physical symptoms are signs of Klinefelter's Syndrome, he was never evaluated or tested for this genetic disorder. Nor does it appear that his testosterone deficiency received further treatment. He received no counseling, or additional attention from his family or school. Instead, his family continued to pressure and ridicule him about his weight and inability to be a successful athlete, and his school merely suspended him when he acted out and misbehaved.

Klinefelter's Syndrome went undiagnosed and untreated during Sidney's entire childhood, yet it likely played a key role in Sidney's social, academic, and mental development. Sidney required extra attention to succeed in school, but he did not get it.[25] Instead, he suffered from ridicule and a total lack of understanding by anyone in his family. His mother, his father,

---

[22] Id. p. 13.
[23] Id.
[24] Ex. 10, Greenville Regional Hospital Report.
[25] Ex. 8, Report of William Zipf, M.D.

8

Example Clemency Application for Sidney Cornwell (cont.)

and even his siblings thought Sidney was fat and lazy and referred to him as "fat ass."[26] Other kids called him Pop 'n Fresh, Doughboy, Porky, and fat hamburger.[27] He was teased about his weight to the point of tears.[28] Because Sidney was told his weight issues were his fault—rather than a typical symptom of his genetic disorder—it created a "negative self-fulfilling prophecy" where Sidney's world view and his beliefs about the future became increasingly negative.[29]

At thirteen years of age, Sidney was 5'6", weighed 225 lbs., and had DD cup breasts.[30] A young boy having breasts made him a target of harassment. Sidney recalls that he was the only kid with breasts and that "it was hell."[31] The only treatment he ever received for his disease was a breast reduction surgery. And that came about only because he spoke to another kid that told Sidney that he had surgery to remove them.[32] Although the surgery removed Sidney's large breasts, it left him with large scars that embarrassed him. He coped with it by telling people either that he had been stabbed in a knife fight or that he had been shot.[33]

In an effort to fit in and overcome his poor self-image, Sidney tried to play football like his older brother. No doubt he also hoped it would please his father.[34] Unfortunately, his attempt to play football was doomed from the start. Sidney would get winded walking to school.[35] And, despite the surgery, his weight never came under control. Further, it is not uncommon for patients with Klinefelter's Syndrome to have delayed development that would leave Sidney less coordinated than his peers.[36]

---

[26] Ex. 4, Affidavits of Marcus Cornwell.
[27] Ex. 11, Affidavit of Shanel Phillips.
[28] Ex. 11, Affidavit of Shanel Phillips.
[29] Ex. 9, Report Dr. Daniel Davis, Ph.D., p. 16.
[30] Ex. 10, Greenville Regional Hospital Report.
[31] Ex. 9, Report of Daniel Davis, Ph.D., p. 5.
[32] Id.
[33] Ex. 4, Affidavits of Marcus Cornwell.
[34] Id.
[35] Id.
[36] Ex. 8, Report of William Zipf, M.D.

9

Example Clemency Application for Sidney Cornwell (cont.)

Even if Sidney were able to overcome all the physical barriers that stood in his way, his delayed intellectual development affected his learning and his grades, ultimately frustrating any attempts to participate in extra-circular activities through school. When Sidney began school, he was noted as slow and had trouble learning to read.[37] Again, it is not uncommon for patients with Klinefelter's to suffer from learning disabilities. When Sidney was tested at 19, he had a lower than normal IQ; he had an eighth grade spelling level; he was in the fifth percentile for arithmetic. But there is no evidence that the schools ever stepped in to provide Sidney with the help he needed. Instead, he fell further and further behind.

Eventually, Sidney began acting out when he arrived at middle school. He began regularly receiving suspensions, on the average of two or three a month. Rather than try to address Sidney's underlying problem, the schools just kept suspending him, which served only to reinforce his behavior. And by the time he reached high school, he was absent often and had mostly failing grades. Sidney's failure in sports and school left him without any portion of his life where he had success.

Sidney's condition did not improve when he moved back home to Youngstown. His father sent him back to live with his mother, when Sidney Sr.'s second marriage fell apart and his drug addiction got worse. Although Sidney left an abusive drug addict, who urged Sidney to be violent and sell drugs, he returned to live with an absent mother. She worked long shifts and was not around to help Sidney—she basically worked and slept.[38] Moreover, LaShonda believed that her mother was not interested in the "care and safety of her children."[39] And when LaShonda

[37] Ex. 2, Affidavit of Dr. Haskins.
[38] Transcript of the Mitigation Hearing, p.132.
[39] Ex. 5, Affidavits of LaShonda Cornwell.

10

Example Clemency Application for Sidney Cornwell (cont.)

got pregnant her mother kicked her out, even though Beverly had been a unmarried teenage mother herself.[40]

Beverly did very little to remedy any of the problems Sidney was having. Sidney's school records show that she was informed about his behavior, but she never did anything to help. When Sidney returned home, he even asked to go to a different school. Despite making decent money, Beverly did nothing but leave Sidney to fail in a school system that could not or would not help him.[41] And this may have been all Sidney needed to put his life on the right track because despite the abuse he suffered, he did somewhat better when he lived in Sharon, Pennsylvania.[42] Overall, his mother had a minimal influence in making Sidney's life better.[43]

Sidney's Klinefelter's Syndrome still went untreated, making his weight a continuing issue for him. When he was 15 and 270 lbs., his step-father offered Sidney $2,000 dollars to lose 50 lbs.[44] This offer illustrates how little his family tried to understand his condition. Sidney was a teenager with an undiagnosed and untreated disease that impacted his appearance and his ability to learn. He failed at football and was failing at school. His mother was disinterested in his life, and when his father took an interest in his life, it was to be abusive and a terrible role model. And the school's suspensions did nothing but further isolate Sidney and deprive him of any positive role model.

Sidney's Klinefelter's and poor socialization left him without any healthy way to deal with his frustrations. Instead, his frequent exposure to violence as a child taught him to use aggressive behavior to solve his problems and allowed him to compensate for his lack of self-

---

[40] Transcript of the Mitigation Hearing, p.89.
[41] Transcript of the Mitigation Hearing, p.144.
[42] Transcript of the Mitigation Hearing, p.196.
[43] Transcript of the Mitigation Hearing, p.203.
[44] Ex. 12, Affidavit of Parker Terry.

11

Example Clemency Application for Sidney Cornwell (cont.)

esteem.[45] Until he was large enough to retaliate with violence, Sidney was the target of bullying. But once he grew larger than his bullies, he became like the "Incredible Hulk" and beat them up whenever they teased him.[46] As Dr. Davis put it, "his size and anger provided fertile ground for physical aggression to be developed and rewarded."[47]

Sidney found himself a troubled teenager alone in a violent and gang-infested city. In fact, the city was so bad, Sidney's brother, Marcus, fled it back to Pennsylvania to live with a family his football coach found for him.[48] Marcus was jumped and asked right away to go back to Sharon.[49] Although Marcus' escape allowed him to avoid the worst elements of Youngstown, the years of abuse and neglect left him nearly as scarred as his younger brother. Despite being successful in sports, having a positive family influence, and graduating high school, Marcus was driven to attempt suicide.[50] Even all the advantages Marcus had over Sidney were barely enough to convince him that life was worth living.

Sidney was not offered the same opportunity to escape and try to turn his life around. He was forced to stay behind. Even worse, now he was separated from his brother, perhaps the only positive male role model he had in his life. Everything in Sidney's life had led him to feel like an outsider, and he no doubt yearned to be accepted. That compulsion to fit in somewhere proved to be so powerful that Sidney turned to the Crips as a place to find that sense of belonging, protection, and family.

Sidney was a large kid, but even that did not stop him from getting jumped when he returned to Youngstown.[51] Now, instead of just one person abusing him, he was surrounded by

[45] Ex. 9, Report of Daniel Davis, Ph.D., p. 15.
[46] Id. p. 4.
[47] Id. p. 15.
[48] Ex. 4, Affidavits of Marcus Cornwell.
[49] Transcript of the Mitigation Hearing, p.79.
[50] Transcript of the Mitigation Hearing, p.200.
[51] Transcript of the Mitigation Hearing, p.198.

12

Example Clemency Application for Sidney Cornwell (cont.)

many young men who were aggressive and violent. Not only did Sidney lack the social support to deal with the violence, but he lacked the necessary skills to escape the violence and the budding gang culture around him.

II. The risk factors throughout Sidney's childhood led him to participation in gang activities.

As detailed above, Sidney was exposed to a number of risk factors in his childhood. These factors were not counterbalanced with any opportunities to find a more positive path for his behavior. He was the victim of severe neglect by his parents, physical and psychological abuse, and extensive ridicule and social rejection not only by his peers but also by his own family.

He had already witnessed violence within his own family. In school, which might offer an avenue for a young person to obtain an education and the possibility of a better future, he did poorly in classes, leading to failure and disciplinary problems. He was offered no counseling or alternative education opportunities. He received no additional treatment for testosterone deficiency and the genetic disorder of Klinefelter Syndrome, which Dr. Davis states would have made him less vulnerable to a gang lifestyle.[52] He had no help from an adult to deal with the learning and behavior problems that became increasingly apparent as he became an adolescent.

Not surprisingly, Sidney began living more and more in the streets, where he became involved in drug sales and gang activity. The violence he witnessed in the streets only added to the damage already done to his brain development and psychological health. To understand Sidney at nineteen years of age, it is important to understand the significance of gang participation in his young life.

---

[52] Ex. 9, Report of Daniel Davis, Ph.D., p. 16.

13

Example Clemency Application for Sidney Cornwell (cont.)

A gang is a surrogate family

When a gang becomes a surrogate family for an individual such as Sidney, the gang replaces the positive role models and goals of a "normal" teenager with activities and role models that are antisocial and pro-criminal. A youth whose needs are not being met by his own family and community initially finds acceptance, belonging, and protection in a gang. The gang then becomes a source of greater and greater influence on the decisions that young person will make. "Gangs often become a sort of 'surrogate family' and are often able to exert great influence on ...decision making at a time when even normal adolescents value the opinions of their peers more than they value the opinions of the adults in their lives."[53]

Participation in a gang increases the likelihood that a teenager, like Sidney, will become involved in criminal activity. Once in the gang they are subject to the will of the "OGs" (Original Gangsters). The OGs "'call the shots' behind the scenes and exploit younger members, who are eager to please them and gain approval, in part due to their unfulfilled need for such acceptance and 'success' in other areas of their lives..."[54] For Sidney, the gang offered him a chance at the "success" that he could not achieve either in school or in the eyes of his family.

Once in a gang, the behavior of boys begin to change. There is pressure to rise in the ranks. The younger gang members develop a need to appear strong. Instead of following healthy, pro-social role models and institutions, they follow the norms of the gang, with an increased risk for criminal and violent behavior, which accompanies an increased risk for personal victimization. Sidney, already damaged by his exposure to violence as a young child,

[53] Ex. 13, Report of C. Ronald Huff, Ph.D., Sept. 30, 2010, p. 2.
[54] Ex. 13, Report of C. Ronald Huff, Ph.D., Sept. 30, 2010, p. 3.

14

Example Clemency Application for Sidney Cornwell (cont.)

also witnessed and was victimized by, extensive violence in the streets.[55] As a gang member he was shot at several times and feared being killed.

Sidney's story is similar to other young people who have been drawn into gang activity. Young people in gangs progress from "hanging out," to joining the gang, to ever more serious activity that usually leads to arrest. Ironically the gang, seen initially as a "family" providing protection and belonging, puts youths at increased risk for incarceration and homicide.[56]

At this most vulnerable time in his life, when most in need of constructive guidance and protection, Sidney's parents "did not monitor his behavior or set limits effectively." He failed in school, misbehaved, and was suspended. Instead of receiving counseling or additional academic help, he was removed from school. This made him even more vulnerable to gang influence; gang members readily accept such young people who are already searching for belonging and acceptance, and the gang offers a different kind of protection. Sidney also grew up in an area "where gang activity, violence, drug sales, and high crime rates exist," which increased the risk that he too would end up in a gang.[57]

Once in a gang, Sidney was "far more likely to be involved in crime, including very serious violent crime, and to possess powerful, highly lethal weapons…" than youths not in a gang.[58]

> Youth involved in gangs who carry weapons for self-protection and status seeking and who also may be involved with drugs are at high risk for violence. These youth are often impulsive and frequently lack the cognitive problem-solving skills

---

[55] Ex. 13, Report of C. Ronald Huff, Ph.D., Sept. 30, 2010, p. 3.

[56] Ex. 14, Flannery, Daniel J., Huff, C. Ronald, Manos, Michael, "Youth Gangs: A Developmental Perspective", pp. 175-204 in T.P. Gullotta, G.R. Adams, & R. Montemayor (Eds.), Delinquent Violent Youth , Thousand Oaks, CA, Sage Publications, 1998, pp. 177, 189.

[57] Ex. 13, Report of C. Ronald Huff, Ph.D., Sept. 30, 2010, p. 4; Ex. 14, Flannery, Daniel J., Huff, C. Ronald, Manos, Michael, "Youth Gangs: A Developmental Perspective", pp. 175-204 in T.P. Gullotta, G.R. Adams, & R. Montemayor (Eds.), Delinquent Violent Youth , Thousand Oaks, CA, Sage Publications, 1998, p. 179.

[58] Ex. 13, Report of C. Ronald Huff, Ph.D., Sept. 30, 2010, p. 4

15

Example Clemency Application for Sidney Cornwell (cont.)

to settle disputes calmly. Fistfights turn into more lethal confrontations because guns are present.[59]

Disputes escalate when other participants provoke further confrontation, or when conflict is continued at a later time.[60]

Sidney's initial need for acceptance and protection became something dangerous and uncontrollable, which he could not have fully foreseen. Sidney's low IQ, physical, emotional, and behavioral problems and the dysfunctional environment of his developmental years "can help explain how dysfunctional behavior can be learned in a context where gangs, guns, drugs, and violent behavior are ubiquitous facts of everyday life for too many young people like [Sidney]."[61]

A drive by shooting changed several lives forever.

One critical day in the life of Sidney Cornwell began with events that are all too familiar to young men on the streets. An encounter with a rival gang led to retaliation, which escalated to further retaliation. In the end a child was dead, and three people were wounded. But the beginnings of this tragedy occurred much earlier.

Sidney's behavioral development and maturation were severely impaired. His "life chances were constrained by [Klinefelter's S]yndrome, which clearly can affect physiological, psychological, intellectual, and social functioning."[62] His medical problems exacerbated the abuse, neglect, and violence that marked his childhood years. He suffers from neurocognitive deficits, including deficits in executive functioning, which have been empirically linked to

[59] Ex. 14, Flannery, Daniel J., Huff, C. Ronald, Manos, Michael, "Youth Gangs: A Developmental Perspective", pp. 175-204 in T.P. Gullotta, G.R. Adams, & R. Montemayor (Eds.), Delinquent Violent Youth , Thousand Oaks, CA, Sage Publications, 1998. p, 183-4.

[60] Id., at 184-5.

[61] Ex. 13, Report of C. Ronald Huff, Ph.D., Sept. 30, 2010, p. 5; Ex. 14, Flannery, Daniel J., Huff, C. Ronald, Manos, Michael, "Youth Gangs: A Developmental Perspective", pp. 175-204 in T.P. Gullotta, G.R. Adams, & R. Montemayor (Eds.), Delinquent Violent Youth , Thousand Oaks, CA, Sage Publications, 1998. p. 178.

[62] Ex. 13, Report of C. Ronald Huff, Ph.D., Sept. 30, 2010, p. 6.

16

Example Clemency Application for Sidney Cornwell (cont.)

impulsive acts of aggression and violence.[63] His limitations in learning and school performance were compounded by his feelings of rejection due to his physical appearance and lack of athletic skills. "In such cases…compensatory, acting-out behavior that leads to subsequent expulsions (separation from the school, one of society's main socializing institutions) can help drive young people further into 'the streets' and into gangs….Once in a gang….young people become socialized into a normative system that values violence and 'toughness,' including criminal behavior."[64] Sidney's impulsive and aggressive actions, like the actions of many young gang members seeking to display gang loyalty and achieve acceptance, led to the unintended shooting of a young girl. The needs that propelled him toward this end had never been met earlier in his life by the adults who could have most helped him.

III. Sidney suffers from neurocognitive deficits.

On September 23-24, 2010, Sidney was evaluated by Dr. Nicholas Doninger, a psychologist. Dr. Doninger conducted a comprehensive interview and neuropsychological testing of Sidney. Dr. Doninger's findings support the conclusion that Sidney suffers from deficits in executive functioning.[65]

Sidney reported to Dr. Doninger several incidents of head trauma. He suffered two closed head injuries as a young child. In addition, he required stitches after splitting his head open in a fall on a driveway. In 1995 he received treatment in the emergency room for a closed head injury received in a car accident. In 1996 he received buckshot wounds to his face in a gang-related drive by shooting.

[63] Ex. 16, Report of Nicholas A. Doninger, Ph.D., Sept. 23-24, 2010, p. 13.
[64] Ex. 13, Report of C. Ronald Huff, Ph.D., Sept. 30, 2010, p. 6.
[65] Ex. 16, Report of Nicholas A. Doninger, PhD.

17

Example Clemency Application for Sidney Cornwell (cont.)

Sidney also reported some drug use, including the regular use of marijuana by eighth grade. He reported occasions of excessive drinking. Crack cocaine was discovered on his person in high school. He never received any drug counseling or substance abuse treatment.

Dr. Doninger's report indicates that Sidney's mother used marijuana during her pregnancy, and that she was slapped in the face by Sidney's father while pregnant. Sidney was exposed to considerable family violence while growing up, including physical violence directed at Sidney by his father. While living with their father in Pennsylvania, the children were poorly cared for.

The report also indicates that Sidney was slow in school, and he had difficulty learning to read. He had extensive behavioral problems, resulting in suspensions for fighting, insubordination, excessive tardiness, and crude language. Yet, he received no counseling or tutoring. By high school he was failing all his classes and regularly missing school.

On the WAIS-IV, Sidney obtained a current Full Scale IQ (FSIQ) of 86 placing him within the Low Average range of intelligence classifications and at the 18th percentile relative to age-matched peers.[66] Additional test scores are contained in Dr. Doninger's report attached as Ex. 16. All these tests and factors are relevant to Dr. Doninger's conclusions.

Dr. Doninger concluded that Sidney's performances generally fall within the average range with respect to basic academic skills. Learning and delayed recall indices for visual material were in the mildly to moderately impaired range, reflecting difficulties in organizing more abstract material. Fine motor dexterity, as well as motor strength, was mildly to moderately impaired bilaterally. Performance was impaired across most measures of executive functioning, "a broad class of cognitive abilities, which enable an individual to engage in appropriate, socially responsible, goal directed conduct and to modify behavior in response to

[66] Id. p. 8.

18

Example Clemency Application for Sidney Cornwell (cont.)

environmental changes." Dr. Doninger observed mild to moderately severe deficiencies in abstract reasoning/problem solving, conceptual flexibility, capacity to learn from experience, identification of rules, planning and organization.[67]

It is established that deficits in executive functioning may be indicative of a functional abnormality in the frontal lobes of the brain. Resulting behaviors may include difficulty suppressing or modulating ongoing behavior, withholding a wrong or unwanted response (impulsivity), appreciating errors in performance or the social impact of behavior, responding appropriately to changing environmental demands, and empathy.

> Several events documented in Mr. Cornwell's background underscore the ecological validity or "real-world" manifestations of executive dysfunction; including, involvement with drugs after directly witnessing the impact of substance dependence on his father, using marijuana during his incarceration for the instant offense, assaulting others resulting in injuries seemingly disproportionate to the threat posed by the victim's behavior, and failing to capitalize on a couple opportunities to earn legitimate sources of income opting instead for the fast money of selling drugs. The timing of these events suggests impairments in judgment, reasoning, and capacity to modify behavior particularly under conditions of heightened arousal, which were present before the murder of which he has been convicted.[68]

Impairments in executive functioning do not invariably lead to violence and aggression, but Sidney had several other risk factors in his environment and life at the time of this offense. He was the victim of parental absence, physical and emotional abuse, lack of affection, poverty, academic failure, behavior problems at school, school dropout, gang membership and delinquent friends, availability of drugs, and exposure to violence. All of these factors would have limited his choices, and denied him the support of a more positive environment. In addition, Sidney's Klinefelter's Syndrome, which may result in "significant cognitive psychiatric and behavioral

[67] Id. p. 11-12.
[68] Id. p. 12.

19

Example Clemency Application for Sidney Cornwell (cont.)

problems compared to non-disabled children," was not mediated by any family or community intervention or support. [69]

Dr. Davis, a psychologist with Klinefelter's experience, concurs in Dr. Doninger's evaluation. Dr. Davis is able to further explain the relationship of Klinefelter's to Sidney's executive functioning deficits. Dr. Davis explains that due to Sidney's "executive function disturbances associated with Klinefelter's, he was unable to fully think through his behaviors, plan and anticipate consequences or make appropriate judgments."[70] Dr. Davis explains that because Sidney "had been exposed to violence as a youth, [he] had aggressive behavior develop as a likely compensatory response to poor self-esteem and lacked the requisite problem solving and social skills to negotiate his environment non-violently."[71]

In sum, Sidney's history of prenatal substance exposure, head trauma, substance abuse, developmental vulnerabilities, and chromosomal abnormality contributed to his deficits in executive functioning, "which are critical to one's capacity to interact effectively with others." At the time of this offense, he lacked the supportive environment crucial to overcoming these disadvantages.[72]

IV. Sidney's age at the time of the crime favors mercy in this case.

> Retribution is not proportional if the law's most severe penalty is imposed on one whose culpability or blameworthiness is diminished, to a substantial degree, by reason of youth and immaturity. Roper v. Simmons, 543 U.S. 551, 571 (2005)

Sidney Cornwell was barely past his nineteenth birthday at the time of this offense. Although he was statutorily and constitutionally eligible for the death penalty, his youth and lack

---

[69] Id. p. 12-13
[70] Ex. 9; Report of Daniel Davis Ph.D., p. 15.
[71] Id.
[72] Ex. 16, Report of Nicholas A. Doninger, Ph.D., p. 13; Ex. 9, Report of Daniel Davis Ph.D., p. 16.

20

Example Clemency Application for Sidney Cornwell (cont.)

of maturity calls for mercy. Nineteen year-olds are immature and lack good judgment, even when raised in the best of circumstances. However, Sidney was not raised in the best of circumstances; he was raised in the worst of circumstances. From birth, he was abused, neglected, and never given the proper support.

Although we permit individuals to drive at age sixteen and vote at age eighteen, this does not mean they are mature at those ages. An international study by the National Institute of Mental Health and UCLA's Laboratory of Neuro Imaging shows that intellectual maturity comes at age twenty-five.[73] This study found that the cortical areas of the brain thicken during childhood and into adolescence.[74] And in the frontal cortex, gray matter peaks around age 11 and 12 years old.[75] There is a slight difference between girls and boys with the brain of girls developing slightly quicker than boys.[76] Then, the brain goes through pruning, which means connections within the brain that are not used are lost.[77] The connections that do survive the pruning process gain strength in transmitting information when myelin, a fatty cell material, develops and acts as insulation around the neural connections.[78] The research shows that this insulation process does not occur in the prefrontal cortex until the early 20s or later.[79]

"The prefrontal cortex coordinates higher-order cognitive processes and executive functioning."[80] The executive functions are the supervisory cognitive skills for goal-directed

[73] Ex. 17, Elizabeth Williamson, Brain Immaturity Could Explain Teen Crash Rate (Washington Post Feb. 1, 2005); Ex. 18, Robert Davis, Is 16 too young to drive a car? (USATODAY, March 2, 2005).
[74] Ex. 19, Johnson, Blum, Giedd, Adolescent Maturity and the Brain, p. 217 (Journal of Adolescent Health 45 (2009)).
[75] Id.
[76] Id.
[77] Id.
[78] Id.
[79] Id.
[80] Id.

21

Example Clemency Application for Sidney Cornwell (cont.)

behavior, planning, working memory, strategizing, attention, and impulse control.[81] All of these skills work together to allow an individual to pause, evaluate the situation, consider options, plan reactions, and then implement that plan.[82] If an individual has poor executive functioning, then that individual has difficulty properly accessing, planning, and carrying-out an appropriate judgment or decision.[83] This area of the brain is the last area of the brain to mature.[84] This is evident from the clemency interview. The Board asked Sidney why he shot at the individuals on the porch if he was trying only to scare them. Sidney answered that he was not thinking, and that he didn't think it through. In part, because he was only 19 at the time of the offense, Sidney's brain was not fully matured and his decisions lacked the benefit of adult mental processes.

Additionally, parenting has a big impact on the way the brain is wired.[85] "The aspects of brain development most closely tied to human behavior can be affected for better or worse by the care we give our children."[86] Although the brain is resilient, early exposure to violence, stress and other environmental pressures increase risk of impulsive actions and high blood pressure.[87] The American Academy of Pediatrics has indentified factors that show abusive childhood experiences trigger violent behavior.[88] These factors are as follows: witnessing domestic violence or substance abuse within the family, being poorly or inappropriately supervised, and being the victim of physical assault.[89] Sidney was abused and neglected as a child, exposed to many forms of violence including domestic violence, and teased about his weight. He suffered

[81] Id.; Ex. 20, ABA Juvenile Justice Center, Adolescence, Brain Development and Legal Culpability (January 2004); Ex. 21, Inside the teenage brain. An interview with Jay Giedd (Frontline – PBS).
[82] Id.
[83] Id.
[84] Ex. 19, Johnson, Blum, Giedd, Adolescent Maturity and the Brain, p. 217 (Journal of Adolescent Health 45 (2009)).
[85] Kotulak, Ronald, Inside the Brain: Revolutionary Discoveries of How the Mind Works p. 35 (1996).
[86] Id. at p. 11.
[87] Id. at p. 9.
[88] Ex. 20, ABA Juvenile Justice Center, Adolescence, Brain Development and Legal Culpability (January 2004).
[89] Id.

22

Example Clemency Application for Sidney Cornwell (cont.)

from the effects of Klinefelter's Syndrome, and was exposed to drug use and subsequently abused drugs. Sidney also suffers from neurological damage and has high blood pressure.[90] All of these factors placed Sidney's prefrontal cortex at a high risk for improper wiring, meaning he did not possess the usual ability to control risky behavior when he was nineteen.

Dr. Davis evaluated the interplay of Sidney's executive function deficits, Klinefelter's Syndrome, and childhood experiences. Dr. Davis concluded that:

> Because he has the executive function disturbances associated with Klinefelter's, he was unable to fully think through his behaviors, plan and anticipate consequences or make appropriate judgments. He lacked, more than the usual teenager who does not have executive functioning issues, the ability to reason through and control his behavior. As well, because he had been exposed to violence as a youth, [he] had aggressive behavior develop as a likely compensatory response to poor self esteem and lacked the requisite problem solving and social skills to negotiate his environment non-violently, he developed increasingly aggressive behavior. His executive functioning deficiencies prevented him from being able to see through the consequences of these behaviors and also to control and manage his considerable anger.[91]

Sidney's father sent him down the wrong path at an early age and his mother did little to stop it. As a result, Sidney's ability to properly evaluate situations and make good choices was severely impaired. Through neglect and abuse, Sidney was taught to protect himself by using violence. Sidney's actions were the wrong choice. The result was tragic and can never be made right. However, under these circumstances, Sidney's youth and the parental teachings must carry significant weight in determining what sentence is ultimately appropriate for him for this crime. Sidney should not be executed.

[90] Ex. 16.
[91] Ex. 9, Dr. Davis at p. 15.

23

Example Clemency Application for Sidney Cornwell (cont.)

V. The jury at Sidney's capital trial never heard crucial mitigating evidence of Sidney's life.

Trial counsel's performance was deficient.

Sidney was convicted of aggravated murder with a death penalty specification. It lay within the power of the jury to spare his life. Both the Sixth Circuit Court of Appeals and the United States Supreme Court have repeatedly acknowledged the importance of mitigating evidence at a capital trial, and the defendant's right to present such evidence. Indeed, "[t]he Constitution requires States to allow consideration of mitigating evidence in capital cases." Carter v. Bell, 218 F.3d 581, 594 (2000) (quoting McKoy v. North Carolina, 494 U.S. 433, 442 (1990)) Consistent with this requirement, Ohio Revised Code § 2929.04(B) provides that in a capital case, if one or more aggravating circumstances have been proved beyond a reasonable doubt, the jury must consider and weigh the "nature and circumstances of the offense, the history, character, and background of the offender," as well as several enumerated mitigating factors, including any other factors in mitigation of the imposition of the sentence of death. The defendant faces the prospect of being put to death unless counsel obtains and presents mitigating evidence. In spite of this imperative, Sidney's trial attorneys allowed their expert at trial to present inaccurate and incomplete information about Sidney's life. At the most crucial moments of his trial, Sidney's attorneys failed him. Defense counsel failed to examine medical records, failed to explore the possibility that Sidney had the genetic disorder Klinefelter's Syndrome, and failed to present adequate testimony about Sidney's involvement in a gang.

Only a small portion of trial testimony addressed Sidney's weight problem and surgery to reduce the size of his breasts. His sister, LaShonda, testified:

> Oh, he was like—nobody—he was like heavy—like real big, you know, and it was like my father want like him and my brother be playing sports; you know, all of us to play sports, whatever. Corky [Sidney] never really played sports. He was

24

Example Clemency Application for Sidney Cornwell (cont.)

> lazy, you know. So he used to be like, you know, whupping him cause he wouldn't be able to–you know—I mean, people used to just, you know, call him names and stuff like that, you know. He never really fit in, so—you know what I mean?[92]

Sidney's attorneys allowed LaShonda to further testify that Sidney didn't seem to care about his weight, and that even after breast surgery, "he was still like lazy."

On cross-examination, the prosecutor in his questions emphasized that LaShonda had tried to tell Sidney to lose weight, that their father had tried to tell him to lose weight, but that Sidney "never did what you told him to do?" and "when you and your father told him to do something, move around, lose some weight, he didn't do it?" LaShonda answered that Sidney "took his lazy time to do stuff."[93] Beverly Cornwell Terry, Sidney's mother, referred to Sidney's surgery as "cosmetic" surgery.[94]

As expert evidence, defense counsel presented the testimony of psychologist Dr. James Eisenberg. When asked about the effect of childhood experiences, Dr. Eisenberg referred to Sydney's surgery as "liposuction:"

> It affects them in a number of ways. A couple of things are going on here with Sidney. You know, he's overweight as a young child, very overweight from what the pictures indicate, so overweight—in fact, as a 13-year old, he is so embarrassed by his weight—he's being made fun of at school—they're calling him Porky, Porky—that he literally asks his mom to see if he can get a chest reduction. Not to be crude, but what he told me is that he didn't want to have these titties and this—that kids were making fun of him at school. And he does. He does, in fact, at 13-years old, has a reduction. I asked him, "Some kind of liposuction?" Which is a pretty profound statement. It says something about his identity, self-imagine [sic], self-worth, the way people are making fun of him. And he goes ahead and has this reduction.[95]

---

[92] LaShonda Cornwell at P.TR. 73-74
[93] Cross exam. of LaShonda Cornwell at P.TR. 86-87
[94] Beverly Cornwell Terry at P.TR. 150-51
[95] Dr. James Eisenberg at P.TR. 198-99

25

Example Clemency Application for Sidney Cornwell (cont.)

Dr. Eisenberg did not give the jurors any further information about Sidney's surgery or medical problems. Defense counsel allowed the jurors to believe that Sidney merely had liposuction because he was too lazy to work off the weight.

In closing argument the prosecutor argued to the jury:

> ...So did that give him the right to do this, a bad childhood?
>
> It was the school's fault. They didn't have enough programs for him, or his mother said the principal didn't like her, didn't like him. Twenty-four suspensions in five years. Sidney, as his sister said, as his friends said, Sidney is willful. Sidney is stubborn. He does what he damn well pleases. Sidney's fat. You know, if fat kids had a right to kill people, I'm way overdue... Did he work out with weights, run, watch what you eat, what all the rest of us have to try and do? No, he went for liposuction. He had a fat reduction. For God's sake, Sidney's lazy."[96]

Defense counsel's objection was overruled.

Defense counsel's witnesses' testimony indicates that no one could say for certain what kind of surgery Sidney had, what it was for, or what diagnosis, if any, was provided by doctors at the time of the surgery. Significantly, no one addressed the physical and emotional burdens Sidney was dealing with until Sidney himself asked for breast reduction surgery. Even then, no follow up treatment or counseling was provided, and his family continued to ridicule him.

The trial testimony paints Sidney in a negative light, as someone just too lazy to change, who had cosmetic surgery to fix how he looked because he wouldn't exercise the weight off. This impression was exploited by the prosecutor in closing argument.

Defense counsel, and Dr. Eisenberg, never told the jury that Sidney was admitted to Greenville Regional Hospital, Greenville, Pennsylvania with Testosterone Resistant Syndrome, Hypotestosteronemia (low levels of testosterone), and Macromastia (enlarged breasts). The jury was not told that Sidney was admitted for bilateral simple mastectomies due to his cup size DD

---

[96] Prosecutor at P.TR. 274

26

Example Clemency Application for Sidney Cornwell (cont.)

breasts. He also had hypoplastic genitalia (underdeveloped genitals/incomplete or arrested development of genitals).[97] Defense counsel never told the jurors this information or that Sidney's family did not obtain additional treatment for him. Nor was the jury told that Sidney suffers from Klinefelter's Syndrome. Defense counsel, therefore, could not tell the jurors the profound impact these medical conditions would have had on Sidney's life.

Sidney should not have received a death sentence at the time of trial. Sidney's case contains significant mitigating evidence that warrants a life sentence. Had trial counsel investigated Sidney's medical history, the incorrect image that Sidney was "merely" a fat, lazy person never would have been presented. Instead, a medical condition that Sidney could not control, and for which he never received treatment, would have made Sidney more sympathetic to jurors.

Trial counsel failed to conduct a complete and thorough investigation into Sidney's medical history. As Judge Moore concluded in her dissent in the Sixth Circuit Court of Appeals' review of Sidney's case, trial counsel knew that Sidney was hospitalized at age thirteen for a double mastectomy, but never located the medical records or provided them to Dr. Eisenberg. This constituted deficient performance.[98]

Had counsel obtained Sidney's medical records and given them to Dr. Eisenberg, the jury would have learned that Sidney was suffering from Testosterone Deficiency Syndrome—a medical condition. His medical records and symptoms would have led to a diagnosis of, and testimony about, Klinefelter's Syndrome—a genetic disorder that causes weight gain, enlarged breasts, underdeveloped genitals, and language, learning, behavioral, and psychological issues. As Judge Moore noted, "Dr. Eisenberg could have corrected the image of Cornwell being

---

[97] Ex. 10, Greenville Regional Hospital Report.
[98] Cornwell v. Bradshaw, 559 F. 3d 398, 417 (6th Cir. 2009)(Moore, J., dissenting).

Example Clemency Application for Sidney Cornwell (cont.)

portrayed by informing the jury that Klinefelter Syndrome was the likely cause of Cornwell's various problems, not laziness. This information would have allowed the jury to view Cornwell in a much more sympathetic light—not as a teenager who had been lazy and taken the easy road in his life, but as a teenager who suffered the burdens of a genetic disease that he could not control and for which he never received a diagnosis, let alone treatment. Furthermore, evidence of Klinefelter Syndrome would reduce Cornwell's blameworthiness in a way that the weight-related evidence alone did not."[99]

The jury was not told about the devastating impact of Klinefelter's Syndrome on Sidney's life.

Young men with Klinefelter's Syndrome have problems with self-esteem, anxiety, and depression. In Sidney's case, "his underlying genetic vulnerabilities likely lead to an increased risk of these problems in a psychosocial environment that was already primed for the development of such psychological problems." Other personality features associated with Klinefelter's Syndrome include poor impulse control, social immaturity in groups, excessive shyness, excessive aggressiveness, and difficulties in social skills development. Boys with Klinefelter's Syndrome have verbal and language deficits.[100]

Sidney was teased and ridiculed by his family and peers because of his size and weight, physical characteristics that were caused by his genetic abnormality. To compensate, he became a bully. Because he was alienated and isolated from his family and peers, he was particularly vulnerable to involvement in a gang, who "provide a pseudo family and community to alienated and disenfranchised youth." His detrimental family environment, coupled with the learning and executive functioning problems seen in Klinefelter's Syndrome, rendered school non-important. When he lost his eligibility to play sports due to his grades, he had no reason to stay in school.

[99] Id. at 419.
[100] Ex. 9, Report of Daniel Davis, Ph.D., Oct. 7, 2010, p. 13, 14.

28

Example Clemency Application for Sidney Cornwell (cont.)

Gang life became even more attractive to him.[101] Once in a gang, his behavior became increasingly more aggressive.

Sidney's executive function disturbances are typical of those associated with Klinefelter's Syndrome. "[H]e was unable to fully think through his behaviors, plan and anticipate consequences or make appropriate judgments. He lacked, more than the usual teenager who does not have executive functioning issues, the ability to reason through and control his behavior." In addition, his exposure to violence as a child and youth increased the risk of aggressive behavior in compensation for his low self esteem.[102]

Sidney's Klinefelter's Syndrome went unrecognized and undiagnosed in his childhood and teenage years. "[H]e was told (and believed) that his physical condition was the result of a personality failing rather than a disorder. Developing that sort of negative self-fulfilling prophesies about oneself easily leads into other negative beliefs about yourself, your world and your future." Behavior then follows those negative beliefs. No one ever interceded to change Sidney's negative and dysfunctional beliefs about himself.[103]

In cases of Klinefelter's Syndrome, "testosterone replacement therapy (which [Sidney] did not receive) has been shown to have considerable benefit upon the psychological functioning of the individual. If that had happened, it is clearly possible that his vulnerability to the gang life style and his problems with anger and aggression would have been significantly reduced." This information was never given to Sidney's jury.[104]

[101] Id. p. 15
[102] Id.
[103] Id. p. 16.
[104] Id.

29

Example Clemency Application for Sidney Cornwell (cont.)

Sidney's jury was not adequately informed of the risk factors and disadvantages acting upon his young life. Sidney was deprived of the fair consideration of his life history by the jury at his capital trial. His case calls for clemency.

VI. Sidney has adapted to confinement and conformed to the strictures of incarceration.

Sidney has been incarcerated on Ohio's death row since 1997, which was shortly after his 20th birthday. Sidney has a few Disciplinary Control incidents that occurred between 1999 and 2000 and has some minor conduct reports.

The United States Supreme Court has held that evidence of a defendant's ability to make a peaceful adjustment to prison life is relevant to mitigate a death sentence.[105] The Ohio Supreme Court also recognizes a defendant's adjustment to incarceration as a mitigating factor.[106]

Sidney has a very short list of disciplinary actions that resulted in disciplinary control (DC). Sidney has had three incidents that resulted in DC: Rioting or encouraging others to riot, Jan. 28, 1999; Threatening bodily harm to another (yelling under his door and threatening to break door down), May 2, 1999; Fighting with another inmate, Feb. 26, 2000.[107] These three incidents each happened within the first three years of being on death row, while he was at Mansfield Correctional Institution and before Sidney turned 25-years-old. Sidney has had approximately six conduct reports that did not result in DC: disrespect to staff (1999 and 2001); disrespecting staff and creating a disturbance (2001); disobedience of a direct order (1999); disobedience of a direct order and possession of contraband (2001); and possession of contraband, (2008).

---

[105] Skipper v. South Carolina, 476 U.S. 1 (1986).
[106] State v. Simko, 71 Ohio St. 3d 483, 497 (1994).
[107] Ex. 22, Institutional Summary Report (IRS).

30

Example Clemency Application for Sidney Cornwell (cont.)

All of these incidents, except the 2008 possession of contraband occurred within the first four years of Sidney's incarceration, while at Mansfield, and before Sidney turned 25-years-old. The majority of these incidents can be related to Sidney's transition to death row and the fact that the brain does not mature until a person is 22-25 years old. Overall, Sidney has been a compliant inmate and was placed in the extended privilege unit at the Ohio State Penitentiary [OSP] based upon his Rules Infraction Board record.

Sidney's prison records includes a Security Threat File. This file exists because Sidney was a member of the Crips gang. It was membership in this gang that led to the events for which he is incarcerated. Since accepting responsibility for the events that led to Jessica's death, Sidney has denounced his involvement and membership in the Crips. Sidney has not participated in any activity that would indicate that he is a security threat at this time. His institutional record speaks for itself—he is not a security threat.

Within the confines of prison, Sidney is bettering himself. Sidney has consistently held a job since July 1999.[108] Sidney has held positions of recreation worker, barber, porter, and laundry attendant.[109] Sidney also achieved his GED in Dec. 2007, completed the Stress Management program in Jan. 2009; completed the Film Group Project I in March 2010, and is currently enrolled in Film Group Project II.[110] He has accepted his circumstances and is prepared to spend the rest of his life in prison.

Sidney has volunteered twice to speak with Corrections Administration graduate students about life on death row.[111] Professor Nathan, University of Toledo, was granted permission to take his class to OSP, SOCF, and other prisons, where they heard from different prison staff,

[108] Ex. 23, DRC Job History File.
[109] Id.
[110] Ex. 22, Institutional Summary Report (IRS).
[111] Ex. 24, Professor Vincent Nathan's letter.

31

Example Clemency Application for Sidney Cornwell (cont.)

took tours, and heard from certain inmates.[112] His class was able to have an extended conversation with death row inmates. Sidney volunteered and was granted the opportunity to speak to Professor Nathan's class on two separate occasions: March 15, 2008 and December 11, 2009.[113] The topic discussed was the individual's own experience spending time on death row awaiting execution.[114] Professor Nathan is truly thankful to Sidney for his willingness to share his hopes, fears, and day-to-day experiences on death row with strangers.[115] Professor Nathan states that Sidney's participation is "unusual and courageous positive behavior on the part of a prisoner facing the reality of the ultimate punishment."[116] Sidney is not just sitting idly on death row; he is sharing and teaching when possible, which has a dramatic impact on others.[117]

While on death row, Sidney accepted Christ into his life. Sidney actively attends worship services and bible study.[118] Sidney's faith assists him in all of his decisions. This faith has also led Sidney to have a better understanding of the harm that he caused both Jessica's family and his own. Sidney's faith has also assisted him in accepting and being remorseful for his actions.[119] Sidney is taking the steps to confess his actions to Jessica's family and ask for their forgiveness. Sidney hopes to have the opportunity to speak directly with Jessica's family to personally express his remorse.

Sidney's religious conversion is not new found. Sidney started the hard and slow life conversion after he came to grips with his actions. Since accepting religion into his life, Sidney has actively participated in religious services and bible study.[120] Sidney also sends letters to

[112] Id.
[113] Id.
[114] Id.
[115] Id.
[116] Id.
[117] Id. ; Ex. 25, Chaplain Bob Gentile's letter.
[118] Ex. 25, Chaplain Bob Gentile's letter; Ex. 26, Chaplain Lyle Orr's letter.
[119] See State v. Landrum, 53 Ohio St. 3d 107, 125 (1990); State v. Carter, 64 Ohio St. 3d 218, 228 (1992).
[120] Ex. 25, Chaplain Bob Gentile's letter; Ex. 26, Chaplain Lyle Orr's letter.

32

Example Clemency Application for Sidney Cornwell (cont.)

loved ones sharing the word of God and encouraging them to accept the word of God into their lives.[121] Sidney not only speaks the word of God, but speaks to others and encourages them to live better.[122] As Chaplain Gentile explains: "Sidney is a gifted individual and his knowledge, experience and encounters can prove to be of assistance to children and adults facing difficult and similar choices such as Sidney's."[123]

It took time for Sidney to personally accept responsibility for his actions because he was in denial that he had killed Jessica.[124] As the car drove up to the apartment, his intent was to find Boom. Upon learning that Boom was not there, Sidney wanted to send a message to Boom that they were looking for him. Without thinking, he fired his weapon to scare the two adults on the porch. Killing Jessica or even wounding anyone was not the intended message. Sidney did not see Jessica on the porch and once he learned that his actions caused the death of a child, he went into a state of denial. Sidney carried this denial for years when he could no longer live in denial and accepted responsibility for his actions.

Sidney has done what society expects someone in his situation to do: accepted responsibility, expressed remorse, acknowledged the permanent loss of his freedom, and altered his behavior. Because he has made a positive adjustment to the correctional institution and poses no risk of future dangerousness, Sidney Cornwell should be permitted to live the rest of his life in prison.

---

[121] Ex. 25, Chaplain Bob Gentile's letter.
[122] Ex. 26, Chaplain Lyle Orr's letter.
[123] Id.
[124] Ex. 1, Sidney Cornwell's letter to Gov. Strickland.

33

Example Clemency Application for Sidney Cornwell (cont.)

VII. Sidney's death sentence is disproportionate to other Mahoning County homicides, thus, Sidney's case is not the worst of the worst.

In 1999 Anthony Anderson and Kevin Calwise planned to rob Wadell Casey, a known drug dealer.[125] They obtained weapons and proceeded to Casey's home.[126] Upon arriving at Casey's house, they came upon Lashawnda Aziz, Casey's girlfriend, and her two infant children, DeShun and Brea. Casey was not present.[127] Anderson knew Aziz was five months pregnant with Casey's child.[128] Anderson and Calwise entered the home and shot Brea, who sustained three massive gunshot injuries to her face and one to each her neck and hand.[129] Lashawnda was shot twice in the head while DeShun was shot three times to the head.[130] The unborn child died along with Lashawnda.[131] Anderson was 25 years old, and Calwise was 22 years old. Both were sentenced to life without the possibility of parole.[132]

In 2008 Michael Davis set fire to a house because he was angered over the theft of his cell phone.[133] This crime was acknowledged by authorities as the largest mass murder in the city's history as six individuals were killed in the blaze.[134] Two adults and four children (ages 2, 3, 5, and 8) were killed.[135] Davis was 18 years old at the time of the crime.[136] Davis is Caucasian and the victims were black.

Davis was indicted with aggravated murder with the O.R.C. § 2929.04(A)(5) and (A)(7) death specifications for each victim. Davis was also indicted with the O.R.C. § 2929.04(A)(9)

[125] Ex. 27, State v. Calwise, 2003 Ohio 3463, P1-P5 (Ohio 7th Dist. Ct. App. 2003).
[126] Id.
[127] Id.
[128] Id.
[129] Id.
[130] Id.
[131] Id.
[132] Id.
[133] Ex. 28, Survivors describe fatal fire in testimony at Davis trial, Vindy.com (Oct. 9, 2008).
[134] Ex. 29, Judge enters innocent pleas for Davis at arraignment, Vindy.com (Feb. 1, 2008).
[135] Ex. 28, Survivors describe fatal fire in testimony at Davis trial, Vindy.com (Oct. 9, 2008).
[136] Id.

34

Example Clemency Application for Sidney Cornwell (cont.)

specification for the four child victims. The jury acquitted Davis of the mass murder specifications and child killing specifications.[137] The jury convicted Davis of the felony murder specification. Davis presented his age (18 years old); IQ (75); the fact that he was abused and neglected as a child (mother unable to care for him because she worked and sibling cared for him by abusing him and not taking to school); that he was poorly educated (did not attend school regularly and in special needs class); employment at Burger King and McDonalds; and psychological make-up caused lack of in-sight (learning disability, unable to think clearly, made stupid decisions, did not understand consequences of actions).[138] The jury recommended life with the possibility of parole after thirty years, and subsequently that sentenced was imposed.[139]

In Sidney's case, there was one child victim who died, and three individuals were injured. Sidney was charged with one aggravating circumstance. Sidney's mitigation consisted of the following: Sidney was 19 years old at the time of the crime, he was abused and neglected as a child (mom worked and was never around for Sidney; born into the world as an unwanted child; lower range IQ; problems in school; despite this family past, Sidney has the love and support of mother and siblings.[140] The mitigating factors between Davis and Sidney are comparable, yet Davis received Life to 310 years while Sidney got the death penalty.

While the murder of Jessica Ballew is tragic, and Sidney is deserving of serious punishment for causing this tragedy, it is not the "worst of the worst."[141] A comparison of Sidney's crime to that of Anthony Anderson/Kevin Calwise and Michael Davis indicates that Sidney's crime is not the worst of the worst.

---

[137] Ex. 30, State v. Davis, Case No. 08 CR 128 (Judgment Entry of Sentence Oct. 28, 2008).
[138] Ex. 31, State v. Davis, Case No. 08 CR 128 (Judgment Entry O.R.C. 2929.03 Oct. 24, 2008).
[139] Ex. 30, State v. Davis, Case No. 08 CR 128 (Judgment Entry of Sentence Oct. 28, 2008).
[140] See State v. Cornwell, 86 Ohio St. 3d 560, 573-74 (Ohio 1999)
[141] See Roper v. Simmons, 543 U.S. 551, 568 (2005) (death penalty must be reserved for the "worst of the worst").

35

Example Clemency Application for Sidney Cornwell (cont.)

VIII. Sidney's jurors did not have the option of sentencing him to life without parole.

Life without parole was not a sentencing option when Sidney was sentenced to death in 1997. In 1996, the Ohio Legislature amended O.R.C. § 2929.03 to allow for a sentence of life without parole in capital cases. Until this change was adopted, jurors had only the sentencing options of death or life with the possibility of parole after twenty or thirty years. This law took effect July 1, 1996. The triggering date as to when this law took effect, is the date of the crime. Sidney crime took place June 11, 1996—a mere nineteen (19) days before life without the possibility of parole was a sentencing option.

The option of life without parole has afforded jurors the means to punish an offender without the risk that he will be one day released, thus avoiding death as the only alternative. When given a life without parole alternative, jurors' (and society's) support for the death penalty diminishes. A 1992 poll indicates that only 41 percent—less than half—of the jurors polled said that the death penalty was the appropriate sentence in capital cases; 37 percent favored life without parole.[142] Studies also show that support for the death penalty decreases when alternatives are available.[143] Not only does juror support decrease, but American support for the death penalty decreases to forty-eight percent when life without parole is an option.[144] Overall, American support for the death penalty has dropped to a new low since the early eighties.[145]

While changes in laws over time are inevitable, for Sidney, the absence of life without parole in 1994 operated like a reverse, arbitrary lottery—go to trial today, get death; go to trial tomorrow, get life without parole. The Legislative Branch changes laws. The Judicial Branch cannot correct the inequity born by this kind of change in the sentencing law, but the Executive

---

[142] View from the Jury Box, *The National Law Journal*, Feb. 22, 1993.
[143] See Sentencing for Life: Americans Embrace Alternatives to the Death Penalty, Death Penalty Information Center, April 1993.
[144] 2008 Gallup Poll, http://www.gallup.com/poll/111931/americans-hold-firm-support-death-penalty. aspx.
[145] Id.

36

Example Clemency Application for Sidney Cornwell (cont.)

Branch can. In comparison to the above described Michael Davis case[146] and the Anthony Anderson/Kevin Calwise cases, life without the possibility of parole is a compelling and frequently used sentencing choice for jurors when that option is available. Furthermore, since Sidney was nineteen at the time of this crime, life without the possibility of parole is a severe penalty.[147] This Board should recommend clemency to correct the arbitrary absence of the option of life without parole at the time of Sidney's trial.

IX. A black capital defendant in Mahoning County is 71.4% more than likely to get death than a white defendant.

A black individual is 71.4% more than likely to receive the death penalty in Mahoning County than a white individual. Since 1981, when Ohio's current death penalty statutes were enacted, Mahoning County has sentenced fourteen individuals to death.[148] Of those fourteen death sentences, ten were imposed upon black individuals and four upon white individuals.[149] Thus, 71.4% of Mahoning County's death sentences have been imposed upon black individuals. Of the ten black individuals sentenced to death, only three were with victims who were black.[150] The other seven were interracial crimes.[151] Only one of the four white defendants were for an interracial crime.[152]

A case in point where a white defendant did not get the death penalty for an interracial crime is Michael Davis. Davis is a white individual.[153] His six victims were black. Davis killed two adults and four children by setting a house on fire.[154] This crime was labeled the cities

[146] Michael Davis received six life with parole eligibility after 30 years to be served consecutively—essentially life without possibility of parole.
[147] See Roper v. Simmons, 543 U.S. 551, 572.
[148] See Ex. 32.
[149] Id.
[150] Id.
[151] Id.
[152] Id.
[153] Id.
[154] Ex. 28, Survivors describe fatal fire in testimony at Davis trial, Vindy.com (Oct. 9, 2008).

37

Example Clemency Application for Sidney Cornwell (cont.)

largest mass murder in history.[155] Davis got life with the possibility of parole.[156] Meanwhile, Sidney is black, victim is white, and he received the death penalty.

"[I]t is of vital importance to the defendant and to the community that any decision to impose the death sentence be, and appear to be, based on reason rather than caprice or emotion."[157] Perhaps race may not be the reason for this disparate treatment. But there is an unacceptable risk that considerations of race, however subtle, infected the prosecutor's decision to death indict Cornwell because this was an inter-racial crime. This spectra of racial bias alone is reason enough to grant clemency and impose a sentence of life without parole. Mahoning County did impose a death sentence upon a black individual who killed a black child in similar fashion as Sidney.[158] Drummond's death sentence is the result of a gang related crime. If Mahoning County is targeting inner-city-gang-related crimes; this would result in disparate treatment as it effectively targets inner-city black individuals for harsher punishment.

Disparate treatment of individuals underscores the arbitrary application of the death penalty on factors such as race.[159] It appears that race does play a part as to who gets the death penalty in Mahoning County. Sidney Cornwell deserves clemency.

Conclusion

Sidney accepts that he must pay for what he did to Ms. Ballew. Since that fateful event, Sidney has had the opportunity to mature not only biologically but as a person. Sadly, Sidney did not have the support and direction he needed as a young child. He was unwanted as a child, and his mother and father did not provide the love and guidance every child needs. Sidney now lives with structure and the love and support of family, friends, mentors, and religious leaders.

[155] Ex. 29, Judge enters innocent pleas for Davis at arraignment, Vindy.com (Feb. 1, 2008).
[156] Ex. 30, State v. Davis, Case No. 08 CR 128 (Judgment Entry of Sentence Oct. 28, 2008).
[157] Gardner v. Florida, 430 U.S. 349, 358 (1977).
[158] See State v. Drummond, 111 Ohio St. 3d 14 (Ohio 2006).
[159] See Furman v. Georgia, 408 U.S. 238, 249 (1972).

38

Example Clemency Application for Sidney Cornwell (cont.)

He has found a way to live life as best as he can under the circumstances he faces. Sidney is not the same person he was when he committed this crime. He is remorseful. Sidney started changing years ago when he could not live in denial for his actions. Change was not easy, yet he did change with the proper support people – the support he didn't have as a child. Sidney does not deserve to be executed. This board should recommend clemency.

For the reason contained in this application, Sidney's statement to the Board on September 27, 2010, and the evidence he will present at the Oct. 13, 2010 Clemency Hearing, Sidney respectfully requests this Board recommend to Governor Strickland that he commute Sidney Cornwell's death sentence to life imprisonment.

Respectfully submitted,

THE OFFICE OF THE
OHIO PUBLIC DEFENDER

ROBERT K. LOWE
Assistant State Public Defender
[redacted]
Columbus, Ohio 43215-0708
[redacted]

and

LINDA E. PRUCHA
Supervisor, Death Penalty Division
[redacted]
Columbus, Ohio 43215-0708
[redacted]

and

39

Example Clemency Application for Sidney Cornwell (cont.)

ANDREW KING
Assistant State Public Defender
[redacted]
Columbus, Ohio 43215-0708
[redacted]

Certificate of Service

I hereby certify that a true copy of the foregoing Application for Executive Clemency was electronically served upon Thomas Madden, Assistant Attorney General, [redacted] Columbus, Ohio 43215 and Ralph Rivera, Assistant Prosecuting Attorney, Mahoning County, [redacted] Fl., Youngstown, Ohio 44503 on this the 6th day of October, 2010.

Robert K. Lowe
Counsel for Applicant

40

Example Petition for Executive Pardon for Earl Washington, Jr.

EARL WASHINGTON, JR.:

AN INNOCENT MAN

PETITION FOR EXECUTIVE PARDON

Example Petition for Executive Pardon for Earl Washington, Jr. (cont.)

TABLE OF CONTENTS

i

Example Petition for Executive Pardon for Earl Washington, Jr. (cont.)

INDEX OF EXHIBITS

ii

Example Petition for Executive Pardon for Earl Washington, Jr. (cont.)

I. INTRODUCTION

This petition for a pardon seeks gubernatorial relief for an innocent man facing execution.

Earl Washington, Jr. is a 33-year-old, black man with mental retardation. His IQ score of 69 ranks him in the bottom 2% of the population. He functions at about the level of a ten-year-old child. He is cooperative, indeed gentle, deferential to those in authority, and eager to please any interlocutor. In a prosecution that relied exclusively on his own statements to the police -- and in which the jury was not informed of then-existing forensic evidence, known to the prosecution, that was facially inconsistent with his guilt -- Mr. Washington was convicted and sentenced to death for the rape and murder of a white woman. Unrepresented by counsel, he came within days of execution.

The justice of that conviction has been in doubt for years: the "confession" upon which it was based was the product of days of police rehearsal and re-shaping, and it emerged from the same series of interrogations that produced four other confessions that the Commonwealth has explicitly or implicitly acknowledged to be false.[1]

Recently, however, Virginia's state crime laboratory has put Mr. Washington's innocence beyond question. The crime laboratory

---

[1] Professor Ruth Luckasson of the University of New Mexico, a nationally-known expert on mental retardation and the death penalty whose report is included herewith, has reviewed all five of these confessions, and describes them as "archetypes of what can happen to people with mental retardation during intense questioning." Report of Professor Ruth Luckasson at 7 (Tab 1).

1

Example Petition for Executive Pardon for Earl Washington, Jr. (cont.)

performed DNA testing on semen left inside the body of Rebecca Williams and had its work subjected to verification by the same outside expert whose report was relied upon to pardon Walter Snyder, Jr. The test results, read in light of the prosecution's own undisputed testimony describing Rebecca Williams dying declaration, show that Mr. Washington did not commit the crime.

Yet the judicial system now offers to Mr. Washington only one remaining step, presentation of a certiorari petition to the United States Supreme Court -- and that Court will not consider the new evidence. Mr. Washington must seek relief from the Governor.

In addition to the absolute pardon on the capital conviction that simple justice demands, Mr. Washington seeks return of the good-time credit he has lost during the ten and a half years he has been wrongly incarcerated on Death Row. This action is necessary to restore the <u>status quo ante</u> with respect to unrelated non-capital convictions that followed from the same interrogation session by the police that led to the capital conviction. The non-capital charges, of burglary and wounding, resulted in a total sentence of 30 years. Mr. Washington should be eligible for parole on those charges, but, because the present situation is one not contemplated by Virginia's statutory structure, the Governor's intervention is needed to assure this result.

2

Example Petition for Executive Pardon for Earl Washington, Jr. (cont.)

II. <u>THE FACTS UNDERLYING MR. WASHINGTON'S CONVICTIONS</u>

The facts set forth in this section are not disputed, and are for the most part drawn from the opinions of the United States Court of Appeals for the Fourth Circuit in <u>Washington v. Murray</u>, 952 F.2d 1472 (4th Cir. 1991) ("Washington I") (Tab 3) and <u>Washington v. Murray</u>, 4 F.3d 1285 (4th Cir. 1993) ("Washington II") (Tab 4), as well as documents from the Joint Appendix ("J.A.") (Tab 5), submitted in connection with the latest appeal.

On June 4, 1982, Rebecca Lynn Williams, returning home at noontime with her two young children to her apartment in the town of Culpeper, was raped and stabbed. She could do no more than identify her assailant as a black man acting alone, and died a few hours later. <u>Washington I</u>, 952 F.2d at 1475. (Tab 3).

At trial, the officer who responded to the call testified, "I asked her if she knew who her attacker was. She replied, no. I asked her then if the attacker was black or white and she replied, black. I then asked her if there was more than one and she replied, no." (J.A., Vol. V, 1462). (Tab 5).

Similarly, Rebecca Williams' husband testified, "I asked her, you know, who did it, and the only thing she replied to me was, a black man, and that was about it." (J.A., Vol. V, 1464). (Tab 5).

Suspicion initially focused on one James Pendleton -- and forensic tests showed that seminal fluid stains on the bedding where the rape took place and hairs found in the pocket of a

3

Example Petition for Executive Pardon for Earl Washington, Jr. (cont.)

shirt found at the scene were consistent in some particulars with his, see Forensic Reports (Tab 6) -- but he was never charged, and the crime lay unsolved in the files of the Culpeper County Police Department. Washington I, 952 F.2d at 1475, 1478 & n.6. (Tab 3).

Almost a year later, on May 21, 1983, petitioner Earl Washington, Jr. -- "a black man, aged 22 at the time, with a general I.Q. in the range of 69, that of a child in the 10.3 year age group," Washington I, 952 F.2d at 1472 (Tab 3) -- was arrested on unrelated charges by the police in Warrenton, in Fauquier County.

These charges arose as follows. After Mr. Washington had spent a number of hours drinking heavily with family members, a dispute arose. Mr. Washington broke into a nearby house for the purpose of stealing a pistol which he knew to be there, and was surprised by the householder, Mrs. Helen Weeks. He hit her over the head with a chair, and returned to the gathering. As he entered the house with the gun at his side, it accidentally discharged, hitting his brother, Robert, in the foot. Mr. Washington fled into the woods, where the police found him a few hours later.

While in police custody, Mr. Washington "confessed" to five different crimes. In four of the cases, the "confession" proved to be so inconsistent with the crime it purported to describe that it was simply rejected by the Commonwealth as the unreliable product of Mr. Washington's acquiescence to the officers. In the

4

Example Petition for Executive Pardon for Earl Washington, Jr. (cont.)

fifth case -- which resulted in the present capital murder conviction and sentence -- the statement had to be re-shaped through four rehearsal sessions before reaching a form the authorities considered usable. See Police Reports and Statement of Earl Washington, Jr. (May 22, 1983). (Tabs 11 and 12).

Confession #1. The questioning began on the morning of May 21, 1993 when law enforcement officers of Fauquier County secured from Mr. Washington a waiver of his Miranda rights. They began by discussing the Weeks case, and obtained a "confession." According to a vivid account contained in this document, Mr. Washington had attempted to rape Mrs. Weeks. (J.A., Vol. I, 125). (Tab 5). But Mrs. Weeks testified to the contrary at the preliminary hearing (Tr., June 23, 1983, at 6-7) (Tab 7) and the Commonwealth dropped the charge of attempted rape. (Tr., June 23, 1983, at 25). (Tab 7). Thereafter, Mr. Washington pleaded guilty to statutory burglary (Va. Code, § 18.2-89) and malicious wounding (Va. Code, § 18.2-51), and was sentenced to consecutive 15-year prison terms. See Order dated May 1, 1984. (Tab 8). (These events are described in greater detail in the affidavit of former defense attorney (now Fauquier Commonwealth's Attorney) Jonathan S. Lynn. See Affidavit of Jonathan S. Lynn. (Tab 9). But on the morning of May 21, 1983, all of this lay in the future.

Confession #2. Having obtained Mr. Washington's "confession" to the Weeks crime, the police turned the conversation to an attempted rape that had occurred on Waterloo

5

Example Petition for Executive Pardon for Earl Washington, Jr. (cont.)

Road. Mr. Washington confessed to this too, but the charge was dismissed. Mr. Washington's "confession" was inconsistent with important facts in that case. See Order dated May 3, 1984. (Tab 20).

Confession #3. Next, the police obtained Mr. Washington's "confession" to a breaking and entering on Winchester Street. He was never charged with this crime. The victim saw him in a line-up and stated that he was not the assailant.

Confession #4. Mr. Washington then "confessed" to the rape of a woman named Rawlings. (1 J.A. 118-20). (Tab 5). He was charged with this crime, but the charge was dismissed by the Commonwealth. See Order dated May, 1, 1984. (Tab 10). The victim's description of the attacker was inconsistent with Mr. Washington and she had previously identified someone else as the assailant. See Affidavit of Commonwealth's Attorney Jonathan S. Lynn. (Tab 9).

Confession #5. At this point in the interrogation, according to handwritten police notes given to -- but never used by -- counsel who represented Mr. Washington in his capital case, "Because I felt that he was still hiding something, being nervous, and due to the nature of his crimes that he was already charged with and would be charged with, we decided to ask him about the murder which occurred in Culpeper in 1982. ... Earl didn't look at us, but was still very nervous. Asked Earl if he knew anything about it. Earl sat there and didn't reply just as he did in the other cases prior to admitting them. At this time

6

Example Petition for Executive Pardon for Earl Washington, Jr. (cont.)

I asked Earl - "EARL DID YOU KILL THAT GIRL IN CULPEPER?" Earl sat there silent for about five seconds and then shook his head yes and started crying." (1 J.A. 120). (Tab 5). See also Police Reports. (Tab 11).

The officers then asked Mr. Washington a series of leading questions about the crime and obtained affirmative responses.[2] This process eventually ceased, as the police notes frankly acknowledge, because the police had exhausted their store of information about the crime. (J.A., Vol. I, 121). (Tab 5). See also Police Reports. (Tab 11). Thus, for example, the Fauquier County officers did not know that Rebecca Williams had been raped (J.A., Vol. V, 1536) (Tab 5), and Mr. Washington did not supply any such information.

At this point, the Fauquier police called the Culpeper police and invited them to participate in the questioning. (J.A., Vol. V, 1537). (Tab 5). The following morning, May 22, 1983, Mr. Washington first had a further session with the Fauquier authorities at which, according to the officers' notes, "He went through the story (as on 05/21/83) again." (J.A., Vol. I, 127). (Tab 5). Then two officers from Culpeper, following oral Miranda warnings, began to interrogate Mr. Washington. (J.A., Vol. V, 1558). (Tab 5). No contemporaneous records of this session have

---

[2] For example, the interrogating officer testified that, as soon as petitioner stopped crying, "I told him, to clarify things, I told him I'm talking about the girl that was found stabbed lying naked outside the apartment in Culpeper. I asked him if that's the one and he said, yes." (J.A., Vol. V, 1535). (Tab 5).

7

Example Petition for Executive Pardon for Earl Washington, Jr. (cont.)

been produced, and it was apparently not recorded.

However, the interrogating officer later described the session in court. (J.A., Vol. V, 1560-61). (Tab 5). He testified that Mr. Washington initially wrongly identified Rebecca Williams as having been black, and only corrected the statement on being re-asked the question. (J.A., Vol. V, 1560). (Tab 5). This pattern was common throughout the interrogation: "I asked him to describe this woman. He had problems with describing." (Id.) See Washington I, 952 F.2d at 1478 n. 5. (Tab 3).

Thus, in addition to not knowing the race of Rebecca Williams when asked non-leading questions:

-- He described the victim as "short". (J.A., Vol. I, 121). (Tab 5). She was 5'8" tall. (J.A., Vol. V, 1479). (Tab 5).

-- He said that he stabbed the victim two to three times. (J.A., Vol. IV, 1064). (Tab 5). She had been stabbed 38 times. (J.A., Vol. V, 1474). (Tab 5).

-- He said he saw no one else in the apartment. (J.A., Vol. V, 1581). (Tab 5). The victim's two young children were present. (J.A., Vol. V, 1455-56). (Tab 5).

After approximately an hour of review of the facts, according to the police testimony, the officers informed Mr. Washington that they would ask him the same questions once more, this time reducing the conversation to writing. They did so, and the resulting document was admitted at trial as his "confession." (J.A., Vol. IV, 1026; J.A., Vol. V, 1585). (Tab 5). See also Statement of Earl Washington, Jr. (May 22, 1983). (Tab 12).

8

Example Petition for Executive Pardon for Earl Washington, Jr. (cont.)

During the afternoon of May 22, 1983, while Mr. Washington's statement of that day was being typed up for his signature, officers drove him to numerous apartment buildings in Culpeper in an effort to get him to identify the scene of the crime. Three times they drove into the apartment complex where the crime had actually occurred. On the third occasion, when asked to point out the scene of the crime, Mr. Washington "pointed to an apartment on the exact opposite end from where the Williams girl was killed. At the time, I pointed to the Williams apartment and asked him directly, is that the one?" This question obtained an affirmative response. (J.A., Vol. V, 1588). (Tab 5).

Similarly, the police officers had Mr. Washington identify as his own the shirt of unknown provenance that was found at the apartment and given to them by family members six weeks after the crime. <u>See</u> <u>Washington</u> <u>I</u>, 952 F.2d at 1478. (Tab 3).

During the guilt phase of the trial, the only evidence offered by the prosecution to link Mr. Washington to the crime consisted of his statements (including his identification of the shirt). <u>See</u> <u>Washington</u> <u>I</u>, 952 F.2d at 1477-78. (Tab 3).

Defense counsel failed to obtain or offer available evidence that:

-- The Commonwealth's own serologic analysis of the seminal fluid found on the blanket where the crime took place showed that it could not have come from Mr. Washington. <u>See</u> <u>Washington</u> <u>I</u>, 952 F.2d at 1476. (Tab 3).

-- The semen type was that of the Commonwealth's first

Example Petition for Executive Pardon for Earl Washington, Jr. (cont.)

suspect, James Pendleton. <u>See</u> <u>Washington</u> <u>I</u>, 952 F.2d at 1478 n.6. (Tabs 3 and 6).

-- The hairs found in the pocket of the shirt found at the crime scene were consistent in part with James Pendleton's facial hair, but did not compare to Mr. Washington's hairs. <u>See</u> Forensic Reports. (Tab 6). When the state crime laboratory pointed out this inconsistency to the Culpeper police and requested additional Washington hairs for comparison, the police refused. <u>See</u> <u>Washington</u> <u>I</u>, 952 F.2d at 1478. (Tabs 3 and 6).

Defense counsel also failed to show the process of suggestion by which the police officers had obtained the statement that was ultimately admitted into evidence, that Mr. Washington was wholly incapable of understanding <u>Miranda</u> warnings, and that his entire adaptive strategy for living in the normal world consisted of attempting to please his interlocutors by telling them what they wanted to hear.[3] In short, although "All the circumstances surrounding the 'confession' indicate that its contents came (intentionally or not) from the police and were

---

[3] Had defense counsel hired a competent mental health expert, the jury would have received the full context of the "confession" as now presented by Professor Luckasson: during the interrogations in all five cases, Mr. Washington "attempted to save face by using his coping strategy of seeming to understand, and he was taking as many cues as he could from [the officers'] behavior and words to try to 'get it right' ... [He] believed they 'knew' the facts so he was trying to guess until his guesses matched what they 'knew.'" Like Professor Luckasson's report, this expert's opinion would have relied upon the officers' own notes of the questioning, together with the extensive professional literature on the effects of police interrogation techniques in obtaining false confessions from people with mental retardation. Report of Professor Luckasson at 7 (Tab 1).

10

Example Petition for Executive Pardon for Earl Washington, Jr. (cont.)

simply parroted back by Earl piece by piece as he learned it," Report of Professor Ruth Luckasson at 7 (Tab 1), defense counsel failed to present any evidence whatsoever to this effect.

Defense counsel then made a closing argument which simply asked the jury to give Mr. Washington his day in court, without, however, discussing one iota of the evidence the jury had heard. (J.A., Vol. VI, 1977-79). (Tab 5). See Washington I, 952 F.2d at 1481. (Tab 3).

Not surprisingly, Mr. Washington was convicted.

At the punishment phase, defense counsel's jury argument took up in its entirety 27 lines in the record. After the prosecutor had graphically and repeatedly described the 38 stab wounds to 14 vital organs and the "pool of blood" in which the victim lay, defense counsel advised the jury that "this is Earl Washington's day in court and you must do him justice." (J.A., Vol. V, 1679-80). (Tab 5). He gave no reason why the jury should not impose the death penalty. As to the factors the jury should consider, he submitted that:

> there is really, not really, in that the course of human experience, any particular standard that governs in all with respect to punishment, so each of you, each of you must search within yourself to consider the crime and consider the gentleman whom you have found to be its perpetrator and look at him and look at the crime and determine what punishment is just for him. His life is in your hands. (Id.)

Not surprisingly, the jury sentenced Mr. Washington to death.

11

Example Petition for Executive Pardon for Earl Washington, Jr. (cont.)

III. THE PRIOR LEGAL PROCEEDINGS

Mr. Washington's conviction and death sentence were affirmed on direct appeal, Washington v. Commonwealth, 228 Va. 535, 323 S.E.2d 577 (1984), (Tab 13) cert. denied 471 U.S. 1111 (1985), with trial counsel serving as appellate counsel. See Washington I, 952 F.2d at 1475 n.2. (Tab 3).

That counsel ceased serving once certiorari was denied. Thus, in August of 1985, Mr. Washington was facing an execution date of September 5 utterly alone. The Commonwealth's view was that Mr. Washington, mentally retarded or not, should investigate, write and file his own petition for state habeas corpus relief, and then -- perhaps, if the petition seemed meritorious -- counsel might be appointed. The alternative was later starkly described under oath by Senior Assistant Attorney General James Kulp:

> Q. If you didn't hear from Mr. Washington, you were going to execute him whether he had a lawyer or not, isn't that correct?
>
> A. The order would have been carried out I am sure.
>
> Q. The order of execution?
>
> A. That is correct.[4]

Another inmate, Joseph M. Giarratano, made urgent efforts to call this situation to the attention of anyone who would listen, resulting in a frantic nationwide search for counsel -- during which 30 to 40 law firms declined the case, in almost all

---

[4] Transcript of Proceedings, July 11, 1986, Giarratano v. Murray, at 443.

12

Example Petition for Executive Pardon for Earl Washington, Jr. (cont.)

instances precisely because of the imminence of the execution date.

Finally, a New York City law firm was prevailed upon to volunteer. With Mr. Washington already having been transferred to the Penitentiary to await execution, a state habeas corpus petition was filed on his behalf in the Culpeper Circuit Court on August 26, 1985 (J.A., Vol. I, 69-275). That court stayed the impending execution, and no subsequent warrant was signed.

The state petition was dismissed without an evidentiary hearing on December 23, 1986 (J.A., Vol. III, 721-22). The Virginia Supreme Court denied a petition for appeal in a brief summary order dated February 26, 1988. (J.A., Vol. VII, 2224). Mr. Washington then sought federal habeas corpus relief from the United States District Court for the Eastern District of Virginia (J.A., Vol. III, 751-868), which dismissed the petition without a hearing (J.A., Vol. VII, 2182). Washington I, 957 F. 2d at 1475. (Tab 3).

In Washington I, the Fourth Circuit rejected on various grounds most of the claims of error, including an attack on the failure of counsel to elucidate for the jury the process by which the "confession" had been obtained. The Court of Appeals did, however, reverse the District Court's summary dismissal of Mr. Washington's habeas corpus petition and order an evidentiary hearing on his claim that trial counsel had been ineffective in that they "had received but failed to appreciate the significance of, and hence to introduce at trial, the results of exculpatory

13

Example Petition for Executive Pardon for Earl Washington, Jr. (cont.)

laboratory tests on semen stains found on a blanket recovered from the bed where the rape of Mrs. Williams occurred." Washington I, 952 F.2d at 1476. (Tab 3).

At the hearing on remand, all the experts agreed that the semen stains on the bedclothes could not have come from Mr. Washington -- and the Commonwealth's scientist revealed for the first time that she had so advised the prosecutor prior to trial (J.A., Vol. VII, 2291-92, 2226). (Tab 5). Mr. Washington's experts testified that this fact, in conjunction with the other forensic evidence in the case -- none of which counsel had ever been aware of or presented to the jury -- made James Pendleton the most likely suspect (J.A., Vol. VIII, 2340-41). (Tab 5). The Commonwealth's experts testified that if the stains had been contaminated by fluids from the victim -- a fact that no one could know, since there is no scientific test for making this determination (J.A., Vol. VIII, 2313, Vol. VII, 2227) -- then the test results could be explained (J.A., Vol VIII, 2227). (Tab 5).

The District Court ruled that the performance of counsel had been professionally reasonable, and, in any event, had not prejudiced Mr. Washington. Accordingly, it dismissed the petition. (J.A., Vol. VII, 2225). (Tab 5).

In Washington II, the Fourth Circuit affirmed by a vote of 2-1. All three panel members agreed that the failure of counsel to pursue and present the forensic evidence represented ineffective assistance. The majority ruled, however, that the error was harmless; the detailed nature of the "confession" made

14

Example Petition for Executive Pardon for Earl Washington, Jr. (cont.)

the prosecution's case so strong that even a jury which knew that the semen stains on the bedding could not have come from Mr. Washington would have convicted him and sentenced him to death. By the same 2-1 vote as before, the panel denied rehearing on October 8, 1993.

IV. <u>THE DNA EVIDENCE</u>

While the case was pending on appeal to the Fourth Circuit for the second time, the parties began discussions for the purpose of arranging for DNA testing of biological samples that had been taken from the body of the victim.[5] They eventually agreed that testing would be carried out both by the central laboratory of the Virginia Division of Forensic Science and by an expert chosen by Mr. Washington's attorney. (The latter was Dr. David Bing of Boston, whose results the Governor relied upon earlier this year in pardoning Mr. Snyder on rape charges.)

The Commonwealth reported its results first.[6] <u>See</u> Report of Jeffery Ban. (Tab 14). These were as follows: Mr. Washington

[5] Unlike the semen stains found on the bedding, which were at issue in the appellate proceedings, this material could not be blood-typed. Hence, until the invention of DNA testing several years after trial, there was no useful forensic examination of it that could be done. Thus, evidence concerning it has not at any time been the subject of judicial proceedings, nor, as noted in Part V below, could it be.

[6] Dr. Bing eventually determined that the amount of biological material left to him for testing was insufficient to enable him to obtain independent results on the critical sample, <u>viz.</u> the one taken from the victim. He did however confirm the Commonwealth's DNA typing of the other relevant individuals. <u>See</u> Report of David H. Bing, Ph.D. (Tab 15).

15

Example Petition for Executive Pardon for Earl Washington, Jr. (cont.)

has DNA type 1.2, 4; Rebecca and Clifford Williams both are of DNA type 4,4; the DNA type of the sperm found in Rebecca Williams body was 1.1, 1.2, 4. Thus, as the crime laboratory reported, the sperm contains a genetic characteristic (a 1.1 allele) that could not belong to any of these individuals.[7] Put another way, sperm with a 1.1 allele is inconsistent with both Mr. Washington and Mr. Williams.[8] Thus, the sperm must have been contributed by another person. Doubtless, this person was the real perpetrator of the crime. But in any event, it was not Mr. Washington.

To be sure, as the crime laboratory states, if some hitherto-unmentioned person (one with a 1.1 allele) had joined with Mr. Washington in raping Rebecca Williams, then this might provide an explanation for the test results.[9] That hypothesis, however, is entirely inconsistent with the known facts. Not only did the Commonwealth's case at trial rest on Mr. Washington's

---

[7] In the words of the Commonwealth's report, "Neither Earl Washington (HLA DQa Type 1.2, 4), Rebecca Williams (HLA DQa Type 4,4), nor Clifford Williams (HLA DQa Type 4,4), individually or in combination, can be the contributor(s) of the 1.1 allele previously detected on the vaginal swab." (Tab 14).

[8] In any event, Mr. Williams testified for the prosecution that he had not had intercourse with his wife for several days before the crime (J.A., Vol. V, 1465), as a predicate for the medical examiner's testimony that the sperm cells recovered from the victim's must have come from recent sexual activity, presumably the rape. (J.A., Vol. V, 1478-79). (Tab 5).

[9] In the words of the crime laboratory, "However, none of these individuals [Earl Washington, Clifford Williams, Rebecca Williams] can be eliminated as contributing to the mixture if another individual possessing a 1.1 allele is also present." (Tab 14).

16

Example Petition for Executive Pardon for Earl Washington, Jr. (cont.)

"confession," which made no mention of any such third person, but, as recounted above, Rebecca Williams stated specifically to two people (her husband, and a police officer) that she had been raped by only one man.

To give weight to a theory that would ignore those facts so as to evade the exculpatory force of the DNA evidence would be to undercut the validity of DNA testing in almost all cases, whether the results were favorable to the prosecution or the defense, since it could always be suggested that the adverse results were due to the activities of some mysterious stranger.[10]

The Governor has already demonstrated his appreciation of the force of this consideration. The situation here is precisely that which existed in Mr. Snyder's case. See Executive Clemency for Walter T. Snyder, Jr. (Tab 16). There, as reported by the Commonwealth Attorney for Alexandria, "It is clear that the only source for the relevant [sperm evidence] would be the assailant in the case, or someone else with whom the victim had recent sexual contact. All experts agree that a possible explanation of the results could arise from evidence of a third party donor of the tested material. However, they also all agree that this is very unlikely given that the victim stated at trial that she had

[10] Scientific considerations, as well as the known facts of the crime, make the suggestion particularly unconvincing in this case. The experts agree that the 4 allele noted in the laboratory report most probably is an artifact of the testing procedure, which was not sensitive enough to fully isolate the relatively small amount of sperm from the victim's bodily fluids. If so, then the actual genotype of the sperm sample is 1.1, 1.2 -- a result that is inconsistent with Mr. Washington's involvement even under the fanciful two-rapist scenario.

17

Example Petition for Executive Pardon for Earl Washington, Jr. (cont.)

not had sexual contact with anyone else for ten days prior to the rape." Thus, notwithstanding that the victim in that case had identified Mr. Snyder and that he "was found to be among possible contributors [of the sperm] based on blood type and secretion analysis" -- both inculpatory factors that are absent here -- the Commonwealth Attorney affirmatively supported the pardon request, and the Governor granted it. In this case, too, the Governor should grant a pardon, lest an innocent man be fantasized into the electric chair.

V. <u>THE CURRENT LEGAL STATUS: THE CAPITAL CHARGES</u>

The deadline for seeking Supreme Court review of the rulings of the Fourth Circuit is January 7, 1994. But the DNA test results could not under the rules be included in any petition for certiorari, because (due to their emergence after the Circuit Court's denial of rehearing) no lower court has ever considered them.

Thus, any certiorari petition would have to focus on a series of rulings (relating, for example, to semen on the bedclothes) that have become entirely outdated by events -- and to ignore the reality that new DNA testing on semen samples recovered from inside the victim shows that Mr. Washington could not have been the contributor. It would hardly evidence respect for the Supreme Court to ask it to grant review of matters that are now largely of historical interest, nor do we believe that the Governor should wish us to do so.

18

Example Petition for Executive Pardon for Earl Washington, Jr. (cont.)

In short, the petition that remains to be filed is not one that will enable Mr. Washington to present to the judicial system the new and compelling evidence that calls for relief.

VI. <u>THE CURRENT LEGAL STATUS: THE NON-CAPITAL CHARGES</u>

Mr. Washington's institutional records reveal that, with credit for jail time, his sentence on the non-capital charges began to run on March 20, 1984. Because of the capital sentence, he has not been receiving statutory good-time on these charges (Va. Code, § 53.1-116). In ordinary course, he would have received such credit, been eligible for parole, and -- in light of his good institutional record -- been released on parole.

Mr. Washington should be restored to the position he would have occupied if he had not been wrongfully convicted on the capital charges. But, as detailed in "Calculation of Good Time Credit," (Tab 17), the unusual nature of this case makes that relief difficult to obtain within the existing statutory structure. Thus, our first and principal reason for requesting that the Governor order that Mr. Washington be credited with all good-time accrued is simply to insure the erasure of a collateral consequence of the wrongful conviction.

That reason would apply in any such case. But in this instance there is a second reason as well. Mr. Washington's case is just the sort for which parole was designed, and the Virginia Parole Board should be given the opportunity to evaluate it. Thus it is especially important here that the Governor act to

19

Example Petition for Executive Pardon for Earl Washington, Jr. (cont.)

clear away lingering technical consequences of the capital conviction that might stand in the way of Board consideration.

A. <u>Mr. Washington's Productive Prior Life History</u>

As Professor Luckasson describes, for approximately eight years, between the time his schooling ended at the age of 15 and the time he was arrested, Mr. Washington maintained a clean criminal record and supported himself through a series of unskilled jobs. Interviews with four different employers reflect the same series of observations; Mr. Washington was slow, but kindly and hard-working. If one explained a task to him until he understood it, he would perform it diligently. As one put it, "Other guys would bad mouth you and be rude. Earl would just say, 'Yes, boss,' and do his job without further comment." Indeed, various employers felt well enough disposed towards him that they assisted him in such matters as opening a bank account and obtaining a driver's license. <u>See</u> Report of Professor Ruth Luckasson. (Tab 1).

B. <u>The Isolated Nature of Mr. Washington's Criminal Conduct</u>

Professor Luckasson's report also explains the reasons for believing that the single criminal episode in which Mr. Washington was involved, the assault on Mrs. Weeks, was an uncharacteristic response to a stressful situation. It was a single incident out of character with his entire history.

As discussed above, on the day of the incident, Mr. Washington had spent a very long day with his family prior to the episode drinking heavily. This in itself was uncharacteristic

20

Example Petition for Executive Pardon for Earl Washington, Jr. (cont.)

since Mr. Washington is normally no more than a moderate drinker, and it may have had a distinct influence on what followed. At the gathering, Mr. Washington got into a dispute with another man -- another uncharacteristic event since he is ordinarily not at all aggressive. He broke into a house across the street where he knew that a gun was kept on top of the refrigerator. Attempting to make off with it, he was surprised by the appearance of Mrs. Weeks. Lacking the verbal or social skills to try to explain or excuse his presence, he hit her over the head with a chair and retreated.

This is the only instance in which Mr. Washington has responded violently to a stressful situation. There is no reason to think it will be repeated, since:

1. His reaction was inconsistent with a lifetime of previous behavior -- as well as with his behavior during the ten years since then.
2. The episode itself taught Mr. Washington important lessons. "He is ashamed for having hurt someone and he understands that by behaving irresponsibly he caused her pain." Report of Professor Ruth Luckasson at 5. (Tab 1).
3. Despite his disabilities, Mr. Washington's adjustment to Death Row has been everything that could be asked. This is borne out by an institutional record that is free of all but the most minor sorts of infractions. As a responsible prison official stated to defense counsel, Mr. Washington has been "a model prisoner."

21

Example Petition for Executive Pardon for Earl Washington, Jr. (cont.)

VII. <u>CONCLUSION</u>

Earl Washington, Jr. is innocent of the crime for which he was almost executed, and for which he still faces the electric chair. Mr. Washington lacks judicial recourse. The pardon power was given to the Governor for just such cases. Justice requires that he exercise it here.

EARL WASHINGTON, JR.

By: ____________________
Of Counsel

Robert T. Hall
Hall, Markle, Sickels & Fudala, P.C.
[redacted]
Fairfax, Virginia 22030
[redacted]

Barry A. Weinstein
Virginia Capital Representation Resource Center
[redacted]
Richmond, Virginia 23219
[redacted]

Professor Eric M. Freedman
Hofstra Law School
Hempstead, New York 11550
[redacted]

Marie Deans
[redacted]
Richmond, Virginia 23230
[redacted]

Dated: December 20, 1993

22

Example Petition for Executive Clemency for Joseph Payne, Sr.

PETITION FOR EXECUTIVE CLEMENCY

of

JOSEPH PATRICK PAYNE, SR.

Paul F. Khoury
Michael A. Rotker
WILEY, REIN & FIELDING
[redacted]
Washington, D.C. 20006

Counsel for
Joseph Patrick Payne, Sr.

October 22, 1996

Example Petition for Executive Clemency for Joseph Payne, Sr. (cont.)

TABLE OF CONTENTS

Page

- i -

Example Petition for Executive Clemency for Joseph Payne, Sr. (cont.)

Page

- ii -

Example Petition for Executive Clemency for Joseph Payne, Sr. (cont.)

I.
THE COMMONWEALTH SHOULD NOT EXECUTE A MAN WHO MOST LIKELY IS INNOCENT

Joseph Patrick Payne is scheduled to be executed on November 7, 1996 for the 1985 burning murder of inmate David Dunford at Powhatan Correctional Center. A review of the evidence in Joe's case as well as the decisions of the state and federal habeas courts raises the real concern that the Commonwealth may be executing an innocent man, while it has put back on the streets of Virginia the convict who, by all accounts other than his own, actually committed the murder. This case is one of the rare few where clemency is appropriate.

A. Joe's Conviction is Based on The Word of "An Appalling and Known Prevaricator"

There likely has never been a capital murder conviction in Virginia based on weaker evidence of guilt than this one. The Fourth Circuit's recent decision denying Joe's appeal Exhibit 1 acknowledges that Joe's conviction "hinge[s]" upon the "eyewitness" testimony of one inmate, Robert Smith, a.k.a. "Dirty Smitty," who "a wealth of evidence demonstrat[es] . . . was an appalling and known prevaricator," and who received 15 years worth of sentence reductions in return for his testimony. No physical evidence linked Joe to the crime. The prosecutor, John Latane Lewis, III, concedes that "without question had [Smith] not been willing to testify, the Commonwealth would not have been successful in getting [a] conviction."

Although the jury did not hear this, the Department of Corrections ("DOC") investigators and the Commonwealth's Attorney

Example Petition for Executive Clemency for Joseph Payne, Sr. (cont.)

agree that, even among inmates, Smith stands out for his lack of credibility. They have testified that Smith is a "manipulative con man" who will lie whenever it is in his self interest; that Smith lied to them on a regular basis in attempts to receive more favorable treatment; and that Smith lied under oath in a number of other situations.

While the Commonwealth's Attorney represented to the jury that Smith had received 10 years worth of sentence reductions for his testimony, Smith ultimately received 15 years worth of sentence reductions and had a criminal sodomy charge, to which he had signed a sworn confession, dropped in exchange for his testimony. As a result of these reductions, Smith currently is walking the streets of Virginia rather than serving his 40 year sentence for a series of four armed robberies.

The Commonwealth admits that the prosecutor believed that Smith's credibility was so shaky, and the possibility of conviction so uncertain, that at the beginning of trial he offered Joe a plea bargain of life imprisonment and then dropped it to a 30-year sentence while the jury was deliberating. This would have had little effect on a man already serving a life sentence, but Joe turned down the deal, adamantly asserting his innocence.

B. Six Witnesses Say the Commonwealth's <u>Star Witness Committed the Murder</u>

Four inmate eyewitnesses (three of whom the jury never saw) have testified that they saw Smith commit the murder after Joe entered the shower room. Joe, Smith, Dunford and the inmates

- 2 -

Example Petition for Executive Clemency for Joseph Payne, Sr. (cont.)

allegedly involved in the conspiracy are white. All four of these eyewitnesses are black. Several of them explained that the murder was a "white thing" with which they did not initially want to be involved. They testified that they were coming forward because an innocent man is on death row for a crime they know he did not commit.

Two more inmate witnesses the jury never heard testified that directly after the murder, Smith boasted to them in the prison cafeteria line that he had just burned Dunford, gleefully sharing gruesome details of the murder. Another inmate witness has testified that on the eve of Joe's trial, Smith admitted that he was going to perjure himself and that he would "testify against his grandmother" to get the deal he was being offered.

C. **The Star Witness Recanted**

Over a year after Joe's trial, Smith gave us a 16-page, signed, sworn affidavit recanting his testimony against Joe and describing the life-threatening pressure corrections officials applied to coerce his testimony. Virtually all of the details of the recantation are corroborated by DOC records or the Commonwealth Attorney's files. (For example, the records confirm that Smith did indeed receive the additional inducements disclosed in the affidavit.) True to form, Smith subsequently recanted his sworn recantation, claiming that he had been coerced.

- 3 -

Example Petition for Executive Clemency for Joseph Payne, Sr. (cont.)

D. <u>The Courts Have Avoided Dealing With the Troubling Evidence Demonstrating Joe's Innocence</u>

Joe was given an evidentiary hearing in front of the state trial judge who had sentenced him to death. The judge refused even to admit into evidence Smith's sworn recantation and summarily found that all of the witnesses testifying on Joe's behalf were inmates not worthy of belief. Of course, the only evidence against Joe was the uncorroborated account of one inmate -- a suspect who had the greatest incentive to deflect the blame away from himself and whose testimony the Commonwealth procured in exchange for his freedom. In his conclusory seven-page order denying Joe's claims, the state habeas judge avoided making any findings about the abundant evidence of Smith's lack of credibility, instead emphasizing repeatedly that the jury believed Smith. The jury, however, never heard the evidence presented at the state habeas hearing. The state judge's refusal to address this abundant evidence undermining the credibility of Smith's trial testimony constituted a misapprehension of his fact-finding responsibilities in a state habeas proceeding. The federal courts that have reviewed Joe's case have denied relief, simply deferring to the state trial judge's flawed, perfunctory "findings."

E. <u>Clemency Is Appropriate In Joe's Case</u>

Based on the overwhelming evidence in the record of Joe's innocence, even as described by the Fourth Circuit, it is inconceivable that Joe would now be convicted of Dunford's murder. This is precisely the type of case where clemency is appropriate.

- 4 -

Example Petition for Executive Clemency for Joseph Payne, Sr. (cont.)

The Fourth Circuit in this case asserted that habeas corpus is not the "traditional forum" for Payne's claims of "actual innocence"; executive clemency is. *See* Exhibit 1, *Payne v. Netherland*, No. 95-4106, 1996 WL 467642 at *3 n.2 (4th Cir. Aug. 19, 1996), *citing Herrera v. Collins*, 506 U.S. 390, 400-02 (1993) (Clemency serves as the "fail safe" in our fallible legal system to ensure against the execution of an innocent man).

The fact that Joe is serving a life sentence for the 1981 murder of a convenience store clerk in Prince William County does not diminish his entitlement to clemency in the Dunford case. There was no justification for Joe's senseless actions that night in 1981, and he is serving a life sentence for that crime. Joe committed the 1981 murder in an alcohol and drug-induced stupor, immediately confessed, expressed remorse and attempted suicide several times after his arrest. The Director of the Forensic Unit of Central State Hospital, who normally testifies for the Commonwealth against defendants, examined Joe in connection with that prior crime and was convinced that he could be rehabilitated and did not have a propensity for violence. Joe has accepted his responsibility for that crime and has been punished. He is seeking clemency for a prison murder he did not commit.

If the death penalty is to remain legitimate and vital in the Commonwealth, it must be applied in a principled manner. This means that the death penalty should not be imposed where substantial evidence and the decisions of the habeas courts suggest that the man about to be executed probably is innocent of the crime

- 5 -

Example Petition for Executive Clemency for Joseph Payne, Sr. (cont.)

for which he was convicted. Granting relief in this case will, if anything, strengthen the Commonwealth's use of the death penalty. It will reaffirm that the Commonwealth administers this ultimate sanction in a fair manner and that executive clemency serves as a meaningful check on the system for those rare cases where substantial "lingering doubt" remains as to the guilt of the condemned man.

As you review the facts in this submission and the decisions of the habeas courts, we request that you keep in mind the following question: "Am I certain that the Commonwealth is executing the man who actually killed David Dunford?" If you cannot answer "Yes" to that question, then Joe should be granted clemency.

II.
THE EVIDENCE IN THE RECORD SUPPORTS JOE'S INNOCENCE

A. Murder and Department of Corrections Determination to Obtain a Capital Murder Conviction

On March 3, 1985, David Wayne Dunford, an inmate at Powhatan Correctional Center ("PCC"), was burned in his cell when an assailant padlocked his cell door, threw a flammable liquid into the cell and ignited the liquid with matches. Dunford died nine days later of burns suffered in the explosion.

One of the initial suspects in the case was inmate Robert Smith. Institutional officers claimed that Smith was seen around Dunford's cell at the time of the murder, and institutional reports indicate that Smith was in fact being investigated for his

- 6 -

Example Petition for Executive Clemency for Joseph Payne, Sr. (cont.)

involvement in the burning. *See* Exhibit 2, State Habeas Hearing Tr. 144; Mar. 12, 1985 Institutional Classification Committee Report.

Early in the investigation, Virginia DOC officials made it clear that it was "critical" to obtain a capital murder conviction in the Dunford murder. A similar burning murder had occurred at the Virginia State Penitentiary in 1982, and the Commonwealth had not obtained a conviction in that incident. On April 16, 1985, before anyone had been charged in the case, PCC Warden William Rogers wrote DOC Regional Administrator Fred E. Jordan seeking authorization to offer potential witnesses sentence reductions and emphasizing the need to obtain a capital murder conviction:

> [a]n inmate was burned in his cell . . . . **It is very critical to send a signal to others that this type of action will not be tolerated** and an extensive effort will be made to prosecute. **I can not think of a better signal to send than someone being convicted of capital murder.**

Exhibit 3 (emphasis added).

B. <u>**Joe's Trial**</u>

At Joe's trial in April 1986, the prosecution's case-in-chief consisted of the testimony of four inmate witnesses: Robert Smith, William Miller, Terry Stiltoner and Edgar Asher. Smith was the only Commonwealth witness who identified Joe as the murderer.

All four witnesses were inmates at PCC and had previously testified at an earlier trial against inmate Stephen Howard, who was convicted of conspiracy to murder Dunford. Each of these four witnesses had already received a ten-year sentence reduction in

- 7 -

Example Petition for Executive Clemency for Joseph Payne, Sr. (cont.)

exchange for their testimony in both trials. Exhibit 4. At Joe's trial, the Commonwealth's Attorney elicited from Smith testimony that he received a ten-year sentence reduction in return for his testimony in both cases. Exhibit 5. No information was elicited or disclosed about any other inducements given to Smith in return for his testimony against Joe.

None of the Commonwealth's inmate witnesses, other than Smith, claimed to have seen the murder. Rather, the three other witnesses admitted to their involvement in a conspiracy to kill Dunford, identified Howard as its organizer and leader, and asserted that Smith was also involved in the conspiracy. Although their accounts of the motive for the killing differed, they suggested to one degree or another that Dunford had run afoul of a white prison gang, the Pagans, of which Howard was a leader. *See* Exhibits 6 and 7, May 2, 1985 Statement of Robert Smith to Investigators. While they also alleged that the initial plan called for Joe to commit the murder, Exhibit 8, all three of these witnesses either testified or made statements to DOC Internal Affairs investigators prior to trial that Joe withdrew from the alleged conspiracy and backed out of the plan prior to the murder. Attached at Exhibit 9 is a summary of their testimony to that effect at Joe's trial and in pre-trial statements to investigators, along with the underlying transcripts.

Smith was the only witness to testify that he saw Joe commit the murder. Smith testified that on the day of the murder, he was

- 8 -

Example Petition for Executive Clemency for Joseph Payne, Sr. (cont.)

at the shower door on the top tier of PCC building C1 when he saw Joe commit the murder. Exhibit 10.

Smith also testified, and made statements acknowledging, that he was involved in a conspiracy directed by Howard to kill Dunford. Smith admitted he was involved in numerous discussions to plan Dunford's murder, participated in testing flammable liquid in Howard's cell several days prior to the murder, and kept the can of flammable liquid used to kill Dunford in his cell prior to the murder. Exhibits 11 and 7. He testified that, according to Howard's plan, he was supposed to put the padlock on Dunford's cell door. Exhibit 12. Smith further testified that he was scared of Howard and that Howard threatened to kill him if he did not follow through with the plan to kill Dunford. Exhibit 11 at Payne Trial Tr. 177.

No physical evidence connected Joe with the murder. The Commonwealth's capital murder charge thus rested squarely upon the uncorroborated eyewitness testimony of Smith. The Commonwealth's Attorney himself has repeatedly asserted that "[w]ithout question, had [Smith] not been willing to testify, the Commonwealth would not have been successful" in convicting Howard and Joe. Exhibit 13.

Defense counsel had subpoenaed sixteen potential witnesses to testify on Joe's behalf, but called only two witnesses at trial, and only one of any significance -- inmate Frank Clements. Exhibit 14. Clements testified that from his vantage point at the shower room door, he saw Smith commit the murder while Joe was in the shower. Exhibit 15. This account was consistent with, but more

- 9 -

Example Petition for Executive Clemency for Joseph Payne, Sr. (cont.)

detailed than, the testimony he had provided at Howard's trial, where he testified that he and Joe were in the shower room on the day of the murder when they heard a "woosh" and Smith came running into the shower.

Between the Howard trial and Joe's, one of defense counsel's associates had interviewed Clements, who explained that he did not go into more detail in his testimony at the Howard trial because he did not want to incriminate himself as a "watchperson." Exhibit 16. Clements indicated that he was prepared to provide all of the details at Joe's trial because Joe was facing a capital murder conviction. *Id.* The associate's notes of her pre-trial interview made it clear that Clements' testimony at Joe's trial would go beyond his testimony at Howard's trial, and suggested the need to allow Clements to explain the reasons for the difference. *Id.*

At Joe's trial, Clements testified exactly as he told the associate he would. But because co-counsel who called Clements to testify had not read the transcript of Clements' testimony at the Howard trial and was not aware Clements was going to testify he saw Smith commit the crime, Clements did not have an adequate opportunity to explain the reasons for the additional details in his testimony. Exhibit 17. The prosecutor was thus able to impeach him effectively on cross-examination.

The defense then rested on that low note, as it had already dismissed all of its remaining subpoenaed witnesses, some of whom would have been able to corroborate Clements' account. Exhibit 18. Counsel's decision to rest was made over Joe's vehement objection.

- 10 -

Example Petition for Executive Clemency for Joseph Payne, Sr. (cont.)

He insisted that he wanted to testify and to have the corroborating witnesses testify on his behalf. Exhibit 19.

Despite the missteps of defense counsel, the Commonwealth's Attorney felt that Smith's credibility was sufficiently shaky and the possibility of conviction so uncertain that he twice offered Joe plea bargains during the trial, first a life sentence and later a 30 year sentence. *See* Exhibit 20. The Attorney General's office characterizes it as follows:

> Not only did the defense team feel that it had done a good job in impeaching Smith, so did the Commonwealth. The Commonwealth's plea offer came down from life to thirty years while the jury was deliberating.

Exhibit 21, Brief For Respondent-Appellee in the Fourth Circuit, p.23 n.23.

Such a plea would have had a negligible effect on Joe, as he was already serving a life sentence, but Joe turned it down, adamantly asserting his innocence. The jury convicted Joe and, after a sentencing phase, sentenced him to death on the grounds that the crime was vile. The jury did not find the other statutory aggravating circumstances, *i.e.*, that Joe represented a "future danger" to society.

C. __State Habeas Hearing__

1. __Eyewitness Testimony Implicating Smith__

At the state habeas hearing, Joe produced significant evidence that he was innocent and that his conviction was unconstitutionally based on the perjured testimony of Robert Smith. In addition to Frank Clements, two other eyewitnesses, Eddie Phillips and Zeb

- 11 -

Example Petition for Executive Clemency for Joseph Payne, Sr. (cont.)

Artis, came forward after Joe's trial to support Joe's claim of innocence. These witnesses testified that they saw Smith burn Dunford after Joe had entered the shower on the morning of March 3, 1985. Neither of these witnesses had anything to gain by testifying on Joe's behalf. Both Phillips and Artis are black, and they testified that they are not friendly with Joe or with other white prisoners in general. Exhibit 22. Both men stated they were coming forward because "there's an innocent man . . . on death row for a crime that he did not commit." *Id.* at 78; *see also id.* at 72. A fourth inmate, Jeffrey Austin, also black, corroborated the eyewitness testimony of Phillips, Artis and Clements. He was subpoenaed and ready to testify at Joe's trial, but was never called to the stand.

Below are excerpts of the testimony of each of these witnesses at Joe's state habeas hearing.

a. Eddie Phillips

On the morning of the murder, Phillips was in a cell across and one tier down from that of Smith and the victim Dunford. *See* Exhibit 23.

> [T]his particular morning, I seen Joseph Payne and Frank Clements go in the shower together -- not really together, coming out of the tier, went in the same shower . . . .
>
> Q. Did you hear anybody yell to them or not while they were entering the shower?
>
> A. A guy from cell -- one cell from me, was out on the tier calling, . . . Jeffrey Austin . . . He asked Payne for some cigarettes. . . . [T]hat's when Payne stopped and told him that . . . he didn't have any

- 12 -

Example Petition for Executive Clemency for Joseph Payne, Sr. (cont.)

> cigarettes. Payne proceeded on to the showers. . . . And right across from me is -- this is where inmate Smitty's cell is. But he's one tier up, but right across from me. . . . [H]e come out the cell, and . . . he was standing on the tier. . . . And Smitty was observing the police [corrections officer] making his rounds. So after the police made his rounds, Smitty went back in his cell, come back out, had a can -- paint can like . . . and some matches. . . . And he had a pair of state jeans on with no shirt on. He went on down to [Dunford's] cell and had . . . a pad lock, you know, to put on Dunford's door -- put a lock on his door and threw . . . whatever he had in the can, I don't know what it really was . . . threw it in there -- threw a pack of matches and . . . .
>
> Q. All right. And what happened?. . . .
>
> A. It was a big ball of confusion -- a lot of smoke, fire and stuff jumping out of Dunford's cell. . . . Smitty jumps, goes in the shower, beside of Frank Clements -- [Clements] was standing at the shower had the door open, looking out the shower, and Smitty goes back and goes in the shower.

Exhibit 23, State Habeas Hearing Tr. 54-58 (the following day, Smith boasted about "burning the dude up"). Phillips described the murder as "a white thing," with which he initially wanted no involvement, especially since another life sentence would not have significantly affected Joe. *Id.* at 59-60. He explained that the reason he came forward only after Payne's trial is that he knows "they condemned the wrong man."

> [I]t was a white guy's problem, you know, and . . . I stay out of white folk's problems . . . [B]ut later on, to me, it won't no white or black problem [anymore], because they condemned the wrong man. So to me, it [became] a human problem.

Id. at 72.

- 13 -

Example Petition for Executive Clemency for Joseph Payne, Sr. (cont.)

b. Zeb Artis

On March 3, 1985, Zeb Artis was housed directly across from Dunford's cell on the same tier.

> As I was going back to my cell, I seen Frank Clements and Joe Payne heading to the shower. So I'm sitting at the side of the door by my cell and I'm looking out from the door, and I sees . . . Robert Smith leaning over the tier.
>
> Q. All right. And what do you remember that Robert Smith did?
>
> A. I seen Robert Smith duck into his cell and come back out of it as fast as he came in the cell. So I stepped out on the tier, and Robert Smith told me to get back in my cell. . . . He waved me off and told me to get back in my cell, so, you know, I went back in the cell.
>
> Q. And what does that mean to you, when somebody waves you off?
>
> A. Something going to go down. . . .
>
> Q. What did you see Robert Smith do at that time?
>
> A. At the time, I seen Robert Smith coming down the tier with a paint can in his hand, right, and he stopped around about one cell from the laundry room. And -- step to the side, and put the paint can down and put a padlock on the door. . . . After he did that, he took some stuff he had in a can and threw it in [Dunford's] cell. . . . And then . . . he had some matches in his mouth. He took the match and strike them and stepped to the side, and threw it inside the cell. . . . A cloud of smoke and flames finally come out of the cell, and it damn near went through mine -- hit my cell, because I'm straight across from the cell, and I seen him, and the coffee I had [in] my hands spilled all over the floor in my cell, right. Smitty stepped to his right and disappeared in the shower.

Exhibit 24.

- 14 -

Example Petition for Executive Clemency for Joseph Payne, Sr. (cont.)

When asked why he was coming forward for the first time only after Joe's trial, Artis responded "[b]ecause there's an innocent man there on death row for a crime that he did not commit." *Id.* at State Habeas Hearing Tr. 78.

c. Frank Clements

> [E]very morning, they ring this bell and it's time for them to open the doors. So I come out of my cell. Mr. Payne slept a cell before me. He came out his cell. He was ahead of me going to the shower. . . . And when we got to about the middle-ways of the tier, . . . Dirty Smitty was leaning on the rails, just leaning there. . . . When we got to the showers, and this guy named Superfly -- another nickname -- called up to Joe and asked him did he have a pack of cigarettes.
>
> Q. Is that Mr. Austin?
>
> A. Yeah. . . . And . . . Joe says no, he didn't have any, so we proceeded to the shower. . . . When we got in the shower, [Payne] got in the shower . . . I came to the door and opened it up to see who else was coming in the shower. I seen Dirty Smitty coming down the hall with a paint can in his hand. And he went to about two or three doors down from the shower. And it looked like he put something on this door, it was a lock or whatever. I assume it was a lock. And then he took the stuff in the can and he threw it in the cell. And I guess he threw a match in, because I heard -- that's when I heard the whoosh sound. . . . And then . . . [Dirty Smitty] comes in the shower.

Exhibit 25.

d. Jeffrey Austin

> On this particular morning, I seen Joe Payne and Frank Clements going in the shower on the top tier, which was C tier. . . . And at the time, I was getting ready to go to work in the kitchen, so I stepped out and asked him and Frank . . . Clements whether I could borrow some cigarettes from them, right. So both of

- 15 -

Example Petition for Executive Clemency for Joseph Payne, Sr. (cont.)

them replied they didn't know. They proceeded on into the shower on the C tier there.

Q. Did you see Robert Smith that morning?

A. Yes, sir. . . . He was about five cells down from the shower. He had on a pair of blue jeans. He was putting on some plastic kitchen gloves. . . . I observed him standing on the tier and I went on back into my cell to proceed to get ready to work in the kitchen. . . . Then . . . I heard an explosion. That's when I stepped out onto the tier, I seen Smitty, Robert Smith, running down to the shower . . . from the man's cell.

Exhibit 26.

The Commonwealth attempted to discredit the testimony of Joe's witnesses -- Phillips, Artis, Clements and Austin -- by cross-examining them (more than six years after the crime) concerning the minutiae of what each individual was wearing and who said what to whom. Although there were, understandably, some minor memory differences,[1] their accounts were consistent in all material respects.

None of the testimony of these eyewitnesses is inconsistent with the trial testimony of any Commonwealth witness, except, of course, Smith, or with any physical evidence presented at Joe's trial. In addition, unlike all of the Commonwealth's inmate witnesses at Joe's trial, the witnesses who came forward on Payne's behalf had nothing to gain as a result of their testimony.

---

[1] For example, on cross-examination, the Commonwealth tried to create differences as to whether Payne was wearing a towel or a robe, Exhibit 27, or whether Austin asked Payne for cigarettes or vice versa, *id.* at State Habeas Hearing Tr. 83, 286.

- 16 -

Example Petition for Executive Clemency for Joseph Payne, Sr. (cont.)

Other witnesses at the habeas hearing also implicated Smith. Two inmate witnesses, Jesse Pritchard and Van Parker, testified that directly after the burning, in the cafeteria line, Smith bragged about having killed Dunford, offering gory details about how the skin on Dunford's hands was seared to the bars of his cell door. Exhibit 28. Both witnesses were subpoenaed to testify at Joe's trial, but were dismissed by defense counsel and taken back to prison without being called to testify. *Id.* at State Habeas Hearing Tr. 219-220, 230-231; Exhibit 29, Federal Petition for Writ of Habeas Corpus, ¶¶ 81-82.

John Berlin, a former inmate in the Virginia correctional system and a friend of Smith's, also testified to a conversation with Smith on the eve of Joe's trial where Smith admitted that he was going to lie against Joe because "I'd testify against my grandmother today . . . to get the hell out of jail." Exhibit 30, State Habeas Hearing Tr. 256. When Berlin heard the news that Joe had been convicted of capital murder, he immediately contacted Joe's counsel to report his conversation with Smith. Exhibit 31, State Habeas Hearing Tr. 258-60; Federal Petition For a Writ of Habeas Corpus ¶ 84.

2. Recantation of Commonwealth's Only Eyewitness

At the hearing, Joe offered a 16-page, sworn, notarized, handwritten affidavit, signed by Smith on every page, taken at the Augusta Correctional Center on December 17, 1987 by Joe's habeas counsel in the presence of a witness, Marie Deans of the Virginia

- 17 -

Example Petition for Executive Clemency for Joseph Payne, Sr. (cont.)

Coalition of Jails and Prisons. Exhibit 32, Handwritten and Typewritten versions of Dec. 17, 1987 Affidavit of Robert Francis Smith. In the affidavit, Smith admitted that he perjured himself at Howard's trial and Joe's; that Joe was in the shower when the murder occurred; that Internal Affairs Investigators Thomas Fairburn and Garland Stokes told him what to say; and that he was allowed to coach other witnesses. The affidavit detailed threats made against Smith by the DOC investigators in an effort to coerce his testimony against Howard and Joe. *Id.* It also described inducements offered to him beyond the disclosed ten-year sentence reduction, including a promise that he would receive an additional sentence reduction and that a sodomy charge pending against him would be "taken care of" in return for his testimony. *Id.*

Virtually all of the details in the affidavit are corroborated by DOC records.[2] *See* Exhibit 33, Federal Petition For a Writ of Habeas Corpus ¶¶ 86-111 (summarizing the corroborated details). For example:

- DOC and court records confirm the additional five-year time cut and the dropping of a criminal sodomy charge Smith received in exchange for his testimony. *See* Smith's Affidavit, Exhibit 32, ¶¶ 20, 55; Exhibit 35, Smith's confession, sodomy charge, and subsequent dismissal of charge; 10-year sentence reduction dated Jan. 27, 1986, 5-year sentence reduction dated Sept. 5, 1986.
- Smith's recantation indicates that he suggested he be allowed to coach reluctant Commonwealth inmates on what

[2] Interestingly, Smith's version of the incident in his recantation corresponds with a pre-trial statement he made to defense counsel's associate Mark Tyndall, in which he claimed that Payne was in the shower when the murder happened. Exhibit 34.

- 18 -

Example Petition for Executive Clemency for Joseph Payne, Sr. (cont.)

to say and was given such an opportunity. Smith's Affidavit, Exhibit 32, ¶¶ 27, 30. The prosecutor's files corroborate that Smith wrote the prosecutor a letter asking to "help" Commonwealth witness William Miller with his testimony. Exhibit 36. Smith was given contact with both Miller and Commonwealth witness Terry Stiltoner prior to their testimony. Exhibit 37.

- Smith admitted in his affidavit that he continually vacillated in his willingness to testify against Joe and that at one point he threatened the prosecutor that he would call Joe's trial counsel to admit he perjured himself. *See* Smith's Affidavit, Exhibit 27, ¶ 52. According to Smith's affidavit, DOC investigators, in turn, threatened Smith with perjury charges if he changed his story and convinced him to write a letter to the prosecutor recanting this intention. *Id.* at ¶¶ 53, 54. In fact the prosecutor's file contains just such a letter from Smith, Exhibit 38, as well as other letters evidencing Smith's continual vacillation and attempts to receive additional favorable treatment. *See, e.g.*, Exhibit 39.

At the hearing, Smith disclaimed almost every assertion in the affidavit. He testified that although he had signed every page of the affidavit and initialed all crossouts, the words in the affidavit were not his; he did not know the content of what he was signing; and he was coerced into signing the statement, which was invented by Joe's habeas counsel. Exhibit 40. The court refused to allow Deans, who was present when Smith made the statements in his affidavit, to testify in order to refute Smith's testimony at the hearing. Exhibit 41. Asserting "I have an opportunity to demonstrate that Mr. Smith flat out lied to you just minutes ago," Joe's habeas counsel proffered that Deans would testify that the affidavit accurately represented Smith's statements during the meeting and that Smith had read the affidavit as it was prepared prior to signing it. *Id.* at State Habeas Hearing Tr. 209-10.

- 19 -

Example Petition for Executive Clemency for Joseph Payne, Sr. (cont.)

Joe moved to have Smith's affidavit introduced into evidence under the "declaration against interest" exception to the hearsay rule. Exhibit 42. He further argued that, in any event, in a habeas case involving the potential innocence of a condemned man, the Constitution prohibits the rigid application of evidentiary rules to bar introduction of such clearly relevant evidence. *Id.* The circuit court deferred decision on that issue and ultimately, in its February 6, 1992 order, summarily refused to admit the affidavit into evidence. Exhibit 43.

3. Testimony Concerning Well Known Lack of <u>Credibility of Commonwealth's Only Eyewitness</u>

Every witness at the habeas hearing who was asked about Smith -- including the Commonwealth's Attorney, the DOC Internal Affairs investigators who handled the case, and even Smith himself -- testified that Smith was a "manipulative con man" who would say whatever was necessary to benefit his needs. Exhibit 44 summarizes the testimony of Commonwealth Officials. Lead Investigator Fairburn agreed that even before Joe's trial, Smith lied regularly to Commonwealth officials in order to receive additional favorable treatment. Exhibit 45. Investigator Stokes testified that Smith lied under oath in a proceeding in Wise County Circuit Court concerning promises allegedly made to him in connection with Howard's case and Joe's case. Exhibit 46. Investigator Elwood Barrick testified that he believed Smith's sworn confession to sodomizing an inmate at knifepoint was a ruse Smith invented in order to obtain a transfer. Exhibit 47. Former PCC Warden William

- 20 -

Example Petition for Executive Clemency for Joseph Payne, Sr. (cont.)

Rogers testified that no warden wanted Smith at his institution after he began cooperating in Joe's case because Smith kept seeking additional special favors in return for his continued cooperation. Exhibit 48. At the hearing, when Joe's prosecutor, Commonwealth's Attorney Jack Lewis, began to explain Smith's manipulative, lying tendencies, the court cut him off, asserting it did not want to hear more cumulative testimony concerning Smith's character. Exhibit 49.

Virtually all of the inmate witnesses who testified at trial or at the habeas hearing explained that Smith's nickname was "Dirty Smitty" because he had a reputation in prison as a con man one simply could not trust. Exhibit 50 contains a summary of the relevant testimony along with the underlying transcript excerpts. At the habeas hearing, even Smith himself acknowledged that he was a lying con man:

> Q. Why do they call you Dirty Smitty?
>
> A. [T]he reason they call me Dirty Smitty is because if I went and borrowed $5 from you and all of a sudden it came time to pay and I didn't have it, why I'd be out to give you a song and dance.

Exhibit 51.

4. **Undisclosed Inducements**

Although Smith testified at Joe's trial that all he was promised in return for his testimony against both Howard and Joe was the ten-year sentence reduction he had already received, Exhibit 52, his letters to the DOC and his habeas hearing testimony

- 21 -

Example Petition for Executive Clemency for Joseph Payne, Sr. (cont.)

demonstrate the opposite. In a May 30, 1986 letter to the Manager of the Virginia DOC Interstate Corrections Compact, Smith complained:

> Further, . . . the myth that I received a sentence reduction for my cooperation and testimony in the Howard and Payne trials, is just that, a myth. **The Dept. of Corr. (internal affairs) and the Commonwealth told me I would receive a sentence reduction after each of the trials, but I only received the one.**

Exhibit 53 (emphasis added). Smith testified at the state habeas hearing that he was not "really sure if it was . . . [Investigator] Fairburn or Stokes," who, prior to Joe's trial, promised Smith he would be recommended for an additional sentence reduction. Exhibit 54.

Only three days after Smith wrote the letter claiming he had not received the second sentence reduction he was promised for his testimony against Joe, Investigator Fairburn initiated a request to PCC Warden Rogers that Smith be recommended for another sentence reduction. Exhibit 55. Ultimately, Smith received an additional five-year time cut, raising the total sentence reduction for his testimony at both trials to fifteen years. Exhibit 56. (As a result of these sentence reductions, Smith, who was serving a 40-year sentence for a series of 4 armed robberies, *see* Smith's record, Exhibit 57, was released from the custody of the DOC sometime in September, 1995).

At the hearing, Investigator Fairburn denied that Smith was ever promised an additional sentence reduction in return for his testimony against Joe. Exhibit 56 at State Habeas Hearing Tr. 591-

- 22 -

Example Petition for Executive Clemency for Joseph Payne, Sr. (cont.)

95. Remarkably, Fairburn claimed that after Joe's trial, he decided gratuitously to recommend Smith for an additional sentence reduction simply because he and Warden Rogers "felt [that Smith] should have [another] time cut." *Id.* at 592-94. Fairburn testified that Smith's letter claiming he was promised an additional sentence reduction is a lie and that it is pure "coincidence" that he decided to initiate an additional sentence reduction request shortly after Smith began complaining about not receiving what he was promised.[3] *Id.*

Internal Affairs Investigator Barrack testified that he had been in charge of the investigation of a forcible sodomy charge to which Smith had signed a sworn confession and for which Smith was indicted in Buckingham County in February 1985, just one month before Dunford's murder. Exhibit 59. Barrack testified that when he discovered that Smith was a possible witness in the Dunford murder, he recommended to the Commonwealth's Attorney in Buckingham County that the sodomy charge against Smith be *nol prossed* if Smith "agreed to testify" against Howard and Joe. Exhibit 59. The charge was in fact *nol prossed* after Smith testified against Howard, at the same time that Smith received his 10 year sentence

[3] Fairburn also admitted that in his entire career as an investigator (he is now retired), this is the only case in which he ever recommended any sentence reduction at all, let alone two reductions. Exhibit 58, State Habeas Petition Hearing Tr. 580; *see also* Exhibit 56 State Habeas Petition Hearing Tr. 591-95.

- 23 -

Example Petition for Executive Clemency for Joseph Payne, Sr. (cont.)

reduction.[4] Exhibit 61. The dismissal of the sodomy charge against Smith was not disclosed to Joe's counsel, and thus, was never presented to the jury.

III.
THE COURTS HAVE AVOIDED CONFRONTING THE OVERWHELMING <u>EVIDENCE UNDERMINING CONFIDENCE IN JOE'S CONVICTION</u>

A. <u>Powhatan County Circuit Court's Decision</u>

In a seven-page order dated February 6, 1992, Powhatan County Circuit Judge Thomas Warren summarily denied Joe's habeas petition, without citing a single page of the habeas hearing transcript. Exhibit 43. Judge Warren's order categorically stated that "[n]o credible evidence was produced at the hearing that [Smith] perjured himself at trial or that the prosecution knowingly used perjured testimony." *Id.* at ¶ 1. The order conclusorily stated that the hearing testimony of the eyewitnesses who saw Smith commit the murder -- Eddie Phillips, Zeb Artis and Frank Clements -- was "in hopeless conflict," although it did not identify the conflict. *Id.* at ¶ 4.[5] Judge Warren asserted, with no specific explanation, that

---

[4] The account of the dropping of the sodomy charge in Smith's recantation is entirely consistent with the Investigator's testimony. In the recantation affidavit, Smith stated that an Internal Affairs investigator advised him that the sodomy charge would be "take[n] care of" in return for his testimony against Howard and Payne, and that after Howard's trial but before Payne's trial, he was advised that the sodomy charge had in fact been dropped. Exhibit 60, Dec. 17, 1987, Affidavit of Robert Smith ¶¶ 20, 23.

[5] Since the state habeas court's order was issued, Joe repeatedly has defied the Commonwealth to identify in the record any "hopeless conflict" in the materially consistent eyewitness testimony of Phillips, Artis and Clements. The Attorney General's (continued...)

- 24 -

Example Petition for Executive Clemency for Joseph Payne, Sr. (cont.)

none of Joe's other inmate (or former inmate) witnesses was credible. *Id.* at ¶¶ 5-6. The order also stated, without elaboration, that "[t]he Court has absolutely no reason to believe that time cuts or any other inducements were authorized or promised that were not disclosed at trial." *Id.* at ¶ 12.[6]

The order held Smith's recantation was inadmissible hearsay, without addressing habeas counsel's claim that the "declaration against interest" exception applied or the more fundamental claim that in a habeas proceeding a court should not bar such probative evidence of innocence. *Id.* at ¶ 9. Judge Warren made no finding as to Smith's credibility at all except to note that "the jury thought Smith was a credible witness." *Id.* at ¶¶ 2, 19.

---

[5](...continued) response has been limited to citing picayune differences, six years after the fact, concerning whether Joe was wearing a robe or a towel and who initiated a conversation about cigarettes directly before the murder. Exhibit 62, Brief for the Respondent-Appellee, p.10 n.4. No one can find **any** material conflict, let alone a "hopeless conflict," in the testimony of these witnesses because none exists.

[6] This categorical statement is astonishing. It is uncontroverted that Smith was given an additional 5 year time cut that was not disclosed at trial. *See* Exhibit 35 at Bates No. 01417. The only question is whether Smith understood, prior to testifying against Payne, that he might receive such an additional benefit in return for his testimony. In order for the state habeas court to make its finding, it must have believed that

- the Commonwealth, for no good reason, took an additional 5 years off the sentence of a convicted felon who had already received a 10-year time cut in exchange for his testimony; and
- it was a pure "coincidence" that three days before the Commonwealth "unilaterally" initiated the additional time cut, the felon wrote a letter, apparently lying, about being promised just such an additional time cut.

- 25 -

Example Petition for Executive Clemency for Joseph Payne, Sr. (cont.)

This latter finding is perhaps the most troubling. It constitutes an abdication of the state habeas court's fact finding responsibilities. In a hearing whose primary purpose was to present a wealth of evidence the jury never heard undermining the credibility of the Commonwealth's uncorroborated "eyewitness," it was improper for the court to rely on the jury's verdict as a reason not to address this wealth of evidence.

B. District Court's Dismissal of Joe's Habeas Claims

After his petition for appeal to the Virginia Supreme Court was summarily denied, Joe filed a federal habeas petition in the United States District Court for the Eastern District of Virginia, Richmond Division. In addition to asserting the claims he had raised in his state habeas proceedings, Joe also moved for a federal evidentiary hearing on the grounds that the state habeas court's summary conclusions were not fairly supported by the record, and that the state court failed even to address Smith's credibility. In a written memorandum and order of June 6, 1994, the district court dismissed all of Joe's claims and denied his motion for an evidentiary hearing. *Payne v. Thompson*, 853 F. Supp. 932, 941 (E.D. Va. 1994), Exhibit 63.

As to Joe's claims that his conviction was based on perjured testimony and that the Commonwealth knew or should have known that the testimony against Joe was perjured, the district court first held that a demonstration of perjured testimony, without a showing that the prosecution knew of the falsity of the testimony in

- 26 -

Example Petition for Executive Clemency for Joseph Payne, Sr. (cont.)

question, was insufficient to warrant habeas relief. Exhibit 63, 853 F. Supp. at 936-37. Citing several pages of the 833-page state habeas hearing transcript in which the prosecutor made the unsurprising assertion that Smith did not admit to him that he was committing perjury, Exhibit 64, State Habeas Hearing Tr. 772-73, 779, 782, the district court held that the state habeas court's findings were fairly supported by the record. *Payne*, 853 F. Supp. at 937. Those cited pages from the direct and cross-examination at the state habeas hearing of Joe's prosecutor concern only his personal interaction with the Commonwealth trial witnesses. They do not in any way address the overwhelming evidence adduced at the state hearing supporting Joe's perjury claims, nor do they address either the knowledge or actions of Internal Affairs investigators and other members of the prosecution team.

Citing several more pages of the prosecutor's state habeas hearing testimony, *id.* at 763-71, 779-80, the district court held that the state habeas court's finding that it had "absolutely no reason to believe that time cuts or any other inducements were authorized or promised that were not disclosed at trial," was "fairly supported by the record." *Payne*, 853 F. Supp. at 938. Again, nothing in these cited pages demonstrates anything more than that the prosecutor himself was not personally aware of undisclosed promises and inducements made or initiated by investigators and about which much of Joe's evidence is entirely uncontroverted.

As to Joe's actual innocence claim, the district court, without discussing the evidence Joe presented, summarily held that

- 27 -

Example Petition for Executive Clemency for Joseph Payne, Sr. (cont.)

Joe "cannot meet the 'extraordinarily high' threshold standard established by *Herrera v. Collins*, 113 S. Ct. 853 (1993)] for such claims." *Id.* at 937, Exhibit 63.

C. **Fourth Circuit Denial of Payne's Appeal**

In denying Joe's appeal, the Fourth Circuit, like the district court, simply deferred to the state habeas court's conclusory "findings." Exhibit 1 at *3. The most striking thing about the court's opinion is the way Joe's probable innocence, and Smith's probable guilt, jump off the pages of the Court's own summary of the evidence.

The Fourth Circuit's description of Joe's trial suggests that there was substantial doubt as to Joe's guilt. First, it describes the tenuous nature of the prosecution's case:

> In his direct testimony [at trial], Smith acknowledged that he had been involved in the planning stages of the conspiracy [to kill Dunford], that he had multiple prior felony convictions, and that he had received a ten-year reduction in his sentence for testifying against Payne and another coconspirator; other witnesses asserted that Smith was a liar and a cheat. Two additional prosecution witnesses implicated Payne in the conspiracy to murder Dunford and testified that Payne planned to commit the murder. One of these witnesses was so unstable that the prosecutor announced to the court prior to his testimony that his mental stability was questionable. The remaining witness concluded his cross-examination by stating that **Payne withdrew from the conspiracy prior to the day of the murder**. . . .

Id. at *1 (emphasis added). The decision describes the defense case and the sense of both parties that conviction was unlikely.

> . . . Payne offered the testimony of another inmate, Frank Clements, who claimed to have seen Smith commit the murder. He further testified that Payne was taking a shower at the time of the murder. On cross-examination,

- 28 -

Example Petition for Executive Clemency for Joseph Payne, Sr. (cont.)

> however, the prosecution was able to demonstrate that Clements' testimony differed in critical respects from the testimony he had provided in the trial of one of Payne's coconspirators. Nevertheless, . . . so confident was the defense that the prosecution would fail that Payne rejected an offer—extended while the jury was deliberating in the guilt phase of the trial—to permit him to plead guilty and receive a sentence that would have been concurrent to the one he was presently serving. The jury nonetheless found Payne guilty of murder.

Id. at *1. The Fourth Circuit also recognized the reasonableness of defense counsel's "strategy" during the sentencing phase of the trial of "capitaliz[ing] on the lingering doubt the defense believed certainly must have existed in the jurors' minds." *Id.* at *2.

The Fourth Circuit's description of the evidence Joe presented in state habeas proceedings is equally compelling:

> Payne offered **copious evidence** in support of his . . . claims during the forthcoming evidentiary hearing. He presented the testimony of several inmates who asserted that they were eyewitnesses and had seen Smith commit the murder. The testimony of these witnesses was consistent to the extent that they all professed to have seen Smith approach Dunford's cell, lock it, and throw liquid into it immediately before the explosion. However, the testimony contained discrepancies concerning what Payne, Clements, and Smith were wearing the morning and whether Payne or another inmate had initiated a conversation immediately prior to the murder. Payne also presented the testimony of several inmates who claimed that Smith had boasted about committing the murder and had admitted that he intended to lie during the trial to implicate Payne in order to receive a reduction in sentence. In addition, Payne proffered a 16-page affidavit, signed by Smith, in which he fully recanted his trial testimony. Further, Payne presented evidence indicating that Smith had received an additional five-year sentence reduction, the dismissal of a forcible sodomy charge, and favorable parole consideration [none of which was disclosed to the jury]. Payne also offered **a wealth of evidence demonstrating that Smith was an appalling and known prevaricator.**

- 29 -

Example Petition for Executive Clemency for Joseph Payne, Sr. (cont.)

Id. at *2 (emphasis added).

Notwithstanding a recitation of the facts that demonstrates serious lingering doubt as to Joe's guilt, the Fourth Circuit denied Joe's appeal. As for Joe's claims of actual innocence, the Fourth Circuit, citing *Herrera v. Collins*, 506 U.S. 390, 400-02 (1993), held that such claims are more appropriately the province of executive clemency, not habeas corpus. Exhibit 1 at *3 n.2.

D. <u>**Each Court Has Passed The Buck**</u>

Each court that has reviewed Joe's case has chosen to defer to someone else rather than address what the Fourth Circuit characterized as the "copious evidence" of Joe's innocence.

The state habeas court deferred to the jury, who did not see the "copious evidence" presented at the state habeas proceeding. The federal district court deferred to the state habeas court, which deferred to the jury, who did not see the evidence. The Fourth Circuit, too, deferred to the state habeas court, which deferred to the jury, who did not see the evidence. In addition, the Fourth Circuit deferred to Governor Allen, indicating that executive clemency, not federal habeas corpus, is the appropriate forum to address Joe's innocence.

If clemency were to be denied on the grounds that the courts have already reviewed Joe's claims, then Joe would be executed without ever having had anyone take responsibility for addressing the "copious evidence" of his innocence. We urge you not to let that happen.

- 30 -

Example Petition for Executive Clemency for Joseph Payne, Sr. (cont.)

IV.
JOE'S CASE IS ONE OF THE RARE FEW WHERE CLEMENCY IS APPROPRIATE

A. Executive Clemency is the "Fail Safe" For The Condemned Man Who May Be Innocent

Joe's case is unique. Generally, when capital murder cases reach this stage, there is a substantial degree of certainty as to the condemned man's guilt, as a number of courts have reviewed the record and fully addressed the petitioner's claims. Here, by contrast, an objective review of the record and the courts' decisions raises overwhelming doubt as to Joe's guilt. The Fourth Circuit's own recitation of the facts emphasizes the "lingering doubt" that surrounds Joe's conviction and demonstrates Joe's probable innocence.

The Fourth Circuit's opinion also asserts, however, that federal habeas courts are not the "traditional forum" to address such concerns. Exhibit 1 at *3 n.2. Indeed, the United States Supreme Court has emphasized that executive clemency is the appropriate avenue for relief based on evidence suggesting the innocence of a man on death row:

> Executive clemency has provided the "fail safe" in our criminal justice system . . . . It is an unalterable fact that our judicial system, like the human beings who administer it, is fallible. But history is replete with examples of wrongfully convicted persons who have been pardoned in the wake of after-discovered evidence establishing their innocence.

Herrera v. Collins, 506 U.S. 390, 415 (1993).

Virginia Governors have provided just such a "fail safe" over the years. So far as we can tell, no one has ever been executed in

- 31 -

Example Petition for Executive Clemency for Joseph Payne, Sr. (cont.)

Virginia based solely on the uncorroborated testimony of a witness acknowledged to be unreliable. For example, in 1912 Governor William Hodges Mann commuted the sentences of Eugene Dorsey, Calvin Johnson and Richard Pines because the accomplice who testified against them had "proven himself to be unworthy of credit." *See* Governors' List of Pardons, Commutations, etc. and Reasons Therefor, March 4, 1912. In an explanation that is eerily applicable in Joe's case, Governor Mann asserted the necessity for clemency as follows:

> [The accomplice Smith] was a confessed perjurer, and the judge in sentencing him declared that he was a perjurer, and no human being can tell whether he told the truth first or last, and this is the condition which confronts my conscience and involves the lives of three men. If all these facts had been before the juries trying the cases, I would have less difficulty in reaching a conclusion, but they were not, and after careful thought I am in such a frame of mind that, while I do not think the prisoners entitled to pardon, I do not think it just to them . . ., or to the Commonwealth, which only desires to punish those certainly guilty, to permit them to be electrocuted and thus to put correction of any mistakes which may have been made out of the power of the State if the mystery which now surrounds the murder . . . shall ever be cleared up.

Id.

More recently, this same desire to punish only those "certainly guilty" and repugnance towards exclusive reliance on inmate or accomplice testimony in capital cases was the basis for Governor L. Douglas Wilder's commutation of Herbert Russell Bassette's death sentence. Bassette's conviction was based solely upon the testimony of **three** alleged accomplices. In 1992, Bassette's sentence was commuted because the unreliable testimony

- 32 -

Example Petition for Executive Clemency for Joseph Payne, Sr. (cont.)

of the three alleged accomplices was not corroborated, thus raising serious doubts as to his guilt. Exhibit 65.[7]

Joe Payne's case is one of the few arising in the Commonwealth where there is a need for the "fail safe" of executive clemency. Joe is scheduled to be executed based solely on the uncorroborated testimony of a convict who is a "known and appalling prevaricator," and is, by all accounts other than his own, the actual murderer. The state and federal habeas court decisions do not quell the lingering doubt in this case, and, if anything, suggest Joe's probable innocence. If the Commonwealth wishes to execute only those "certainly guilty," then Joe should be granted clemency.

B. <u>Nothing In The Record Dispels The Concern That Joe Is About To Be Executed For A Crime He Did Not Commit</u>

We urge you to attempt to seek some certainty in the record that Joe Payne, and not Robert Smith, actually murdered David Dunford. We submit that you will not be able to find it.

Throughout the habeas process, the responses to Joe's claims have focussed primarily on procedural arguments. Neither the pleadings in this matter nor the habeas court rulings address the fundamental contradiction in this case: On the one hand the Commonwealth readily concedes that Smith is a discredited, unreliable convict who will lie under oath whenever it suits his interest. *See, e.g.*, Exhibit 66, at 10-11 & n.5, 23. On the other

[7] Governor Wilder also commuted the death sentences Joseph M. Giarratano and Earl Washington based on evidence demonstrating the likelihood of their innocence. Exhibit 65.

- 33 -

Example Petition for Executive Clemency for Joseph Payne, Sr. (cont.)

hand, the prosecutor, the Attorney General's Office and the state habeas judge categorically aver that there is "absolutely no reason" to disbelieve the uncorroborated trial testimony procured from this congenital liar in exchange for his freedom.[8]

None of the arguments raised during the habeas process satisfactorily addresses this concern. For example, one cannot rely on the jury's verdict to allay this concern, because the jury did not hear the "copious evidence" presented at the habeas hearing. Similarly, although the state habeas judge summarily asserted that all of the witnesses who testified on Joe's behalf at the sentencing stage are inmates unworthy of belief, such a facile dismissal of the eyewitness accounts of individuals with nothing to gain from their testimony ignores the fact that the only evidence against Joe is the account of one inmate who had every incentive to lie.

Nor is Smith's account corroborated by any physical or testimonial evidence. The Commonwealth's three other inmate witnesses (each of whom was freed in return for his testimony) all claimed that Joe withdrew from any alleged conspiracy prior to the day of the murder. See Exhibit 50. In fact, **of the eleven inmate**

---

[8] We also urge you to examine the manner in which the Commonwealth procured Smith's testimony. Not only did the Commonwealth fail to charge Smith for his admitted involvement in the conspiracy to murder Dunford and give him a ten-year time cut. According to the DOC investigators, it also unilaterally gave this felon serving a 40-year sentence for a string of armed robberies an additional 5-year time cut for no reason at all. This unprecedented generosity led Fourth Circuit Judge William Wilkins, Jr. to ask at oral argument whether "the Commonwealth is now giving **freebies** to convicts."

- 34 -

Example Petition for Executive Clemency for Joseph Payne, Sr. (cont.)

witnesses to testify at the trial or the state habeas hearing, the only one to offer an account inconsistent with Smith's having committed the murder is Smith. Exhibit 67.

Finally, although there are a number of arguments in the record concerning the 1981 murder for which Joe is serving a life sentence, the facts of that case should not be used to justify Joe's execution for a prison murder he did not commit.

C. Payne Should Not Be Executed Based On The 1981 <u>Murder For Which He Is Serving A Life Sentence</u>

On February 4, 1981, Joe Payne murdered Mrs. Louise B. Winslow in a robbery of Winslow's Grocery Store in Bristow, Virginia. As the attached presentence report indicates (and as Joe readily agrees), this crime, which Joe committed with his foster brother while intoxicated, was an inexcusable act of violence. Joe immediately confessed to the crime, demonstrated remorse, and, on several occasions attempted suicide. He was charged with capital murder.

In preparation for trial, Joe's defense counsel in that case had him examined by the Forensic Unit of Central State Hospital in Petersburg, Virginia. Attached at Exhibit 68, is the August 31, 1981 letter from Joe's counsel to the Forensic Unit Administrator describing the reasons for the examination, Joe's background, and the circumstances surrounding the crime. After a thorough examination of Joe, as well as review of voluminous material provided by both the Commonwealth's Attorney and defense counsel, the State's Forensic Unit Director, Dr. James C. Dimitris, and its

- 35 -

Example Petition for Executive Clemency for Joseph Payne, Sr. (cont.)

Clinical Psychologist, Dr. Henry O. Gwaltney, concluded that Joe could be rehabilitated. Exhibit 69. Below are their conclusions:

> As a result of our examinations and review of material furnished to us, it is our opinion, with reasonable professional certainty, that Mr. Payne was under substantial emotional distress at the time of the crime. Although an individual who has sincerely attempted to support his family and achieve occupationally, he had been unable to do so and had recently lost his job due to reasons which he felt were entirely unfair. His marriage was disintegrating and his wife had definitely planned to leave him with a child that he cared very greatly about. This rejection on the job and by his wife was extremely distressing to Mr. Payne and the expectation of another child being born in the near future and his loyalty in attempt to help his brother taxed his limited resources substantially. This led to utilizing poor judgment through the excessive use of alcohol and resulting in the criminal act.
>
> Based on our entire experience with Mr. Payne, it is our opinion that with his desire and motivation, through the correctional processes available for youthful offenders, like the Southampton Correctional Center, he could be given the opportunity to develop into a more mature individual who could cope with life, as well as be given vocational and personal skills that will allow him to do so. This is based, of course, on the availability of such needed services and his willingness to be involved in taking advantage of the therapeutic and educational opportunities.

Id.

Based in part upon these findings, and the fact that Joe had no other record of violence,[9] the trial judge in the Winslow case found that Joe could not be determined a future danger, and that the appropriate sentence was life in prison.

Any argument, tacit or explicit, that it does not matter whether Joe committed the prison murder because he should have been

---

[9] Joe's only other conviction was a grand larceny charge in 1976, for which the Circuit Court of Prince William County sentenced him to a two-year suspended sentence.

- 36 -

Example Petition for Executive Clemency for Joseph Payne, Sr. (cont.)

executed for the murder of Mrs. Winslow is dangerous and unprincipled. Such a position is premised on the assumption that it is acceptable for the Commonwealth to subvert the criminal justice process and the Constitution in order to obtain executions.

D. Granting Joe Clemency Will Strengthen The Death Penalty In Virginia

Most people in Virginia favor the death penalty. Most also are likely to agree that executions should be carried out only when there is reasonable certainty as to the guilt of the condemned man. Going forward with the execution of a man who probably is innocent of the crime for which he was sentenced places the goal of performing executions over the ends of justice. By contrast, granting clemency to Joe will assure the people of Virginia that there remains a "fail safe" in the Commonwealth for the rare cases like this one where the fallibilities of our criminal justice system result in the wrongful conviction and death sentence of an innocent man. It will send a signal that the Commonwealth is strong and fair.

- 37 -

Example Petition for Executive Clemency for Joseph Payne, Sr. (cont.)

V.
CONCLUSION

We conclude with the question we started with: "Are you certain that the Commonwealth is executing the man who actually killed David Dunford?" We submit that the only reasonable answer based on the record and the habeas court decisions in this case is "No." Accordingly, we request that Joe be granted clemency.

Respectfully submitted,

Paul F. Khoury
Michael A. Rotker
WILEY, REIN & FIELDING
Washington, DC 20006

Dated: October 22, 1996

- 38 -

Example Petition for Executive Clemency for William Saunders

William Saunders

PETITION FOR EXECUTIVE CLEMENCY

ON BEHALF OF

<u>WILLIAM SAUNDERS</u>

Barbara L. Hartung
(VSB #38062)
[redacted]
Richmond, VA 23219
[redacted]

Virginia Capital
Representation Resource
Center
[redacted]
Richmond, VA 23219
[redacted]

Counsel for
William Saunders

April 23, 1997

Example Petition for Executive Clemency for William Saunders (cont.)

TABLE OF CONTENTS

Example Petition for Executive Clemency for William Saunders (cont.)

THE SENTENCE OF DEATH WAS WRONGLY IMPOSED
AND SHOULD BE COMMUTED TO LIFE WITH PAROLE.

William Ira Saunders was sentenced to death on May 3, 1990, for the robbery and murder of Mervin Dale Guill as Guill was waiting to make a drug buy. The death sentence was imposed solely on the basis of future dangerousness. Saunders v. Commonwealth, 406 S.E.2d 39, 42 (Va. 1991). Ex. 1. The Danville Commonwealth's Attorney, William H. Fuller, III, who prosecuted Saunders, the judge, James F. Ingram, who tried and sentenced Saunders after a bench trial, and the Danville Chief of Police, T. Neal Morris, have concluded that the death sentence was wrongly imposed. Their letters supporting clemency in this case are attached as Exhibits 2, 3, and 4, respectively.

Based on the unique circumstances preceding the sentencing of Mr. Saunders and based on his record while incarcerated in the subsequent seven years, Mr. Fuller, Judge Ingram, and Chief Morris now believe that a sentence of life with parole, the sentence available at the time of sentencing, is the appropriate punishment in this case. Judge Ingram states in his letter (Ex. 3):

> As a result of the defendant's post conviction conduct while awaiting sentencing in jail, I imposed the death penalty upon Saunders because there was a probability that based upon that evidence, the defendant would commit criminal acts of violence that would constitute a continuing serious threat to society.
>
> *　　　*　　　*
>
> I have had an opportunity to review William Ira Saunders' behavior while he has been an inmate on Death Row and I am satisfied that his conduct in the years following his sentencing have not borne out my belief of his future dangerousness which he demonstrated during his period of incarceration awaiting sentencing.
>
> I am of the opinion that the sentence which was imposed upon Saunders is not the correct sentence today and I believe it would

Example Petition for Executive Clemency for William Saunders (cont.)

not only be appropriate, but in the interest of justice that William Ira Saunders' sentence be reconsidered and that his death sentence be commuted to a life sentence.

The Danville Commonwealth's Attorney William H. Fuller agrees that Saunders' death sentence was based largely on his post-trial misconduct at the Danville Jail in the six month period between his conviction for capital murder and the imposition of sentence. Mr. Fuller states:

> In retrospect, despite Saunders' behavior from conviction to sentencing almost six months later, it concerns me that, had the sentencing hearing gone forward when originally scheduled, Saunders' conduct that caused him to receive the death penalty would not have occurred and would not have affected his sentence. Significantly, Saunders created no problem while incarcerated from July 20, 1989 to January 5, 1990, the date that his sentencing was originally scheduled. Thus, I am convinced that if Saunders had been sentenced on January 5, 1990, as originally scheduled, the judge would not have imposed the death penalty, based upon the evidence of future dangerousness introduced at the first penalty hearing on November 16th.

Ex. 2 at 2. * * *

> Since June of 1995, when I started reviewing this file after Saunders filed a federal habeas petition, I have felt that so long as Saunders has not been involved in violent conduct while incarcerated since receiving the death penalty, his sentence should be reconsidered. His prison record, which I have reviewed, indicates that he has not been involved in any violent conduct since he was sentenced to death on May 3, 1990.

Ex. 2 at 3.

Mr. Fuller's support for clemency in this case is based also on the substantial criminal records of the Commonwealth's witnesses in the years following Saunders' trial. Mr. Fuller writes:

> I believe there is an additional reason for re-examining Saunders' death sentence. I am concerned that several of the Commonwealth witnesses in this case have compiled the following criminal records since Saunders was convicted of capital murder.

2

Example Petition for Executive Clemency for William Saunders (cont.)

[After reviewing the convictions of three primary witnesses, Mr. Fuller concludes as follows.]

I have no doubt that Saunders committed the capital murder and that the testimony of the Commonwealth witnesses was substantially true, but I also believe that Saunders' conduct during the long delay from conviction to the second sentencing hearing was the primary reason he received the death penalty. Moreover, in view of the criminal conduct of most of the Commonwealth witnesses since Saunders' conviction, I am not comfortable with Saunders' death sentence.

Ex. 2 at 2, 3.

As set forth herein, the credibility of the Commonwealth's primary witnesses has been eroded not only by their criminal convictions but by additional events since Saunders' capital trial which raise further doubts about their trial testimony and about the imposition of a death sentence in this case. Facts not available at the time of trial raise serious concerns about the death sentence imposed in this case.

With the consent of the Attorney General's Office, Saunders is petitioning for clemency prior to the conclusion of legal proceedings in federal court[121]. In an effort to conserve the resources of all involved and to avoid further litigation[122], the parties have agreed that Saunders should seek clemency at this time. Clemency is appropriate given the rare and unusual circumstances of Mr. Saunders' case.

---

[121]Under Virginia law, no procedural mechanism permits Saunders to present this motion and the underlying facts to the Virginia state courts at this time. Clemency is the only form of state relief available. In order to permit Saunders to present this petition for clemency, the Attorney General's Office agreed to defer the federal district court hearing previously scheduled for April 24, 1997, and the District Court granted Saunders' motion for adjournment.

[122]If clemency is granted, Saunders will withdraw his federal habeas petition now pending in the U.S. District Court, Richmond Division, before the Hon. Robert R. Merhige, Jr.

3

Example Petition for Executive Clemency for William Saunders (cont.)

INTRODUCTION

Mervin Dale Guill, a 41 year old white man, was shot on July 17, 1989, as he sat in his car, waiting to make a drug buy in Danville, Virginia. A prosecution witness, Lacy Johnson, testified that he along with William Saunders was in the car with Guill. Without warning, Saunders shot Guill and robbed him. Within two days, Johnson informed the police that Saunders had shot Guill. No physical evidence connected Saunders with the shooting of Guill. The murder weapon was never recovered. Saunders' fingerprints were not found on Guill's property or on his car. Johnson's prints were found on the victim's car. Johnson also led the police to Guill's discarded wallet and papers. All the trial testimony attributing the shooting to Saunders came either from witnesses who had been with Guill prior to the shooting and who had a motive to fabricate their testimony or from a jailhouse snitch. Two of the witnesses, Lacy Johnson and Katrina Wilson, were married within three weeks of the shooting. Under then existing Virginia law, they could not testify against one another. Va. Code § 19.2-271.2. Johnson and Wilson later divorced. A jail house informant, Bernard Smith, testified to a conversation between Smith and Saunders during which Saunders admitted shooting and robbing Guill.

Since the trial concluded, Johnson has claimed responsibility for Guill's murder on several occasions. He told to his current wife, Teresa Hill Johnson, that he had killed someone and identified that individual as "the insurance man on Memorial Drive, " i.e., Dale Guill. See Ex. 5. Johnson admitted his responsibility to Candace Bowman Battle on the very night of the murder and again as recently as August, 1995. See Ex. 6. Johnson told Battle that he had "set up" Saunders for the murder. Levi Poole, a trial witness, signed a sworn affidavit that Johnson had admitted killing someone. See Ex. 7. Poole also stated that he had given false testimony at Saunders' trial but later recanted that admission when interviewed by the Commonwealth. After the state court

4

Example Petition for Executive Clemency for William Saunders (cont.)

proceedings concluded, Bernard Smith stated in a sworn affidavit that he had given false testimony at Saunders' trial. Ex. 8. Smith later recanted that recantation during an interview with the Commonwealth's Attorney. Ex. 8. Antonio Winbush submitted an affidavit stating that he had heard Johnson admit to killing someone and understood the victim to be Guill. He also stated that his wife, Katrina, formerly Johnson's wife, had admitted giving false testimony at Saunders trial. Winbush also recanted after an interview with the Commonwealth. Ex. 9. (Katrina Winbush and Lacy Johnson submitted affidavits denying these accusations.)

Saunders' death sentence was based solely on a finding of future dangerousness[123]. At the sentence phase in November, 1989, the prosecution's expert predicated his opinion on Saunders' future dangerousness on the credibility of the prosecution's witnesses. In contrast, a defense expert concluded that Saunders was not a future danger. The trial court adjourned the sentencing decision until January 5, 1990, pending review of the presentence report. On January 5, 1990, the trial court again adjourned the sentence to February 26, 1990. The court did not impose sentence until May 3, 1990--over five months after conviction.

From the time of his arrest in July 1989 until mid-February 1990, Saunders did not engage in any violent behavior. However, between February 20, 1990, and May 3, 1990, Saunders committed six acts of misconduct, including setting his bedsheet on fire, while he was in the Danville Jail awaiting sentence. These jail incidents were viewed by the court as evidence of Saunders' future dangerousness. The trial court imposed a death sentence based primarily on Saunders' post-conviction actions. See Ex. 3; Ex. 26 at 200-202 (5/3/90). The trial court rejected defense counsel's argument that the post-conviction bad acts were the direct result of the stress and

[123]The complete trial transcript is Ex. 26. References to the transcript appear as "Tr." followed by a page number.

5

Example Petition for Executive Clemency for William Saunders (cont.)

uncertainty experienced by Saunders as he awaited the court's decision on his sentence. In affirming his death sentence, the Virginia Supreme Court relied heavily on Saunders' post-conviction offenses. Ex. 1.

This clemency petition is based in part on the circumstances that surrounded Saunders' capital sentencing proceeding and on his record since the imposition of his capital sentence. Saunders has been incarcerated for almost seven years on death row at the Mecklenburg Correction Center. In that period, there has been no reoccurrence of the violent behavior that he exhibited while awaiting sentence in the Danville jail. Ex. 24. His only violent act was a self-inflicted wound during an unsuccessful suicide attempt in April, 1995. Thus, the prediction that Saunders would constitute a future danger, even when incarcerated, has proved to be erroneous. Moreover, Saunders' record at Mecklenburg provides further reason to believe that Saunders' violent behavior at the Danville jail resulted from delay over his sentencing and the stress induced by a possible death sentence. Saunders' behavior in the intervening seven years supports his trial expert's opinion that he would not constitute a future danger. The petition is also based on post-trial events and disclosures that cast substantial doubt on the trial testimony of the Commonwealth's central witnesses.

In view of these facts, the Commonwealth's Attorney who prosecuted Saunders, the judge who tried and sentenced Saunders, the Danville Police Chief who investigated the case, and petitioner, William Saunders, join in seeking executive clemency. His sentence should be commuted from death to life with the possibility of parole.

THE EVIDENCE AT THE GUILT PHASE

Viewed in the light most favorable to the Commonwealth, the evidence at trial

6

Example Petition for Executive Clemency for William Saunders (cont.)

demonstrated the following. Mervin Dale Guill, a 41 year old white man, was shot on July 17, 1989, in either the late afternoon or early evening in a parking lot in Danville, Virginia. Earlier that afternoon he had withdrawn $600 in cash, receiving five, $100 bills and five, $20 bills. Ex. 26 (Tr. 32, 11/15/89).

Between 5 and 8 p.m. on July 17th, James Eason saw a man, later identified at Guill, lying prone in a grey car in a parking lot near the Old Dutch Supermarket next to the shoe store on Memorial Drive. The car's gas cap was smoldering on the ground, and rags had been stuffed into the gas tank in an unsuccessful effort to ignite the car. (Tr. 177). As the man in the car appeared to be dead, Eason immediately called 911. The police arrived within five to ten minutes, photographed the car, and retrieved the burnt material from the gas tank. (Tr. 178). The burnt material was identified as a shirt or undergarment [Trial Ex 20A and 20B]. (Tr. 189-90).

Guill was killed by a gunshot wound to the back of the head. The bullet penetrated the brain stem causing instantaneous death. The muzzle of the gun had been in contact with the scalp when fired and powder residue was found around the entry wound. (Tr. 20). The bullet was recovered from the body and given to the forensic examiner, William Conrad. (Tr. 17). Conrad described the bullet as "a 22 caliber coated lead bullet that had been damaged. It had six lands and grooves impressed on the bullet with right hand twist." (Tr. 25). Due to damage and weight loss, Conrad could not determine if the bullet was a long rifle or a short round. (Tr. 26). The bullet was never identified by Conrad or admitted into evidence. As the gun that fired the bullet was never recovered, Conrad never compared the damaged bullet to the gun. On cross examination, Conrad admitted that <u>thousands</u> of guns in circulation could have fired a bullet of this type.

In the early morning hours of July 19th, more than a day after Guill's body was found, Lt. T. A. Brown received a phone call from Lacy Johnson asking Brown to meet him at 2

7

Example Petition for Executive Clemency for William Saunders (cont.)

a.m. on Grove Street in Danville. When Brown arrived, Johnson was accompanied by a woman named Katrina, Johnson's girlfriend. Brown brought Johnson and Katrina to the police department where he took a written statement from Johnson. (Tr. 184). Johnson named Saunders as the shooter.

Based on Johnson's information, Lt. Brown, Det. Thomas Breedlove and Johnson went to a vacant house on High Street where they found a tri-fold, brown man's wallet lying in the weeds between two houses. (Tr. 185). It contained no identification. Based on Johnson's information, some of Guill's documents were also retrieved from the sewer located on the corner of Ridge and Grove Street. (Tr. 191-192). The lab recovered some fingerprints from the Guill's documents, but <u>none</u> of the prints taken from Guill's property matched the prints of William Saunders.

At trial Johnson stated that the day before the shooting, Saunders showed Johnson three guns: a .25, a .38, and a gold .22. The .22 was about 7 inches long. All the guns had "F.I.E." stamped on them. (Tr. 114).

The next day, July 17th, Guill arrived at Katrina's apartment on Grove Street around 4:30-5 p.m. and asked Johnson to help him buy a half ounce of cocaine.[124] A half ounce cost between $700-800. As they drove by Dooley's Store on Jefferson Avenue, Johnson spotted Katrina, Saunders, and Levi Poole. Guill stopped to pick up Katrina. While Guill was talking to Poole outside the car, Saunders told Johnson, "I should rob this white mother fucker but you know him." (Tr. 121). All four got into Guill's car to continue the search for drugs. Saunders was seated behind Guill, and Katrina was behind Johnson. (Tr. 120).

---

[124]Guill was white while Johnson and the others were black.

8

Example Petition for Executive Clemency for William Saunders (cont.)

Guill pulled in at Allen's Shoe Shop about 7:30 p.m. and waited to make a drug buy. (Tr. 124, 143). Katrina left the car and started to walk home. Within "a minute or so," the shooting occurred. (Tr. 143). As Johnson talked to Guill, Guill suddenly lunged forward in the car. Johnson looked back and saw Saunders holding a gold gun in Johnson's face. Saunders got out of the car, searched Guill, and removed Guill's chain and a big cluster ring. Saunders looked at the wound in Guill's head and then brushed Guill's hair over it. (Tr. 129-30).

Johnson stated that Saunders removed Saunders' white, tank top shirt. He stuffed it into the car's gas tank, and tried to light the shirt with matches. Two to three minutes after the shooting, Saunders and Johnson left the car and crossed Memorial Drive on foot. (Tr. 143). Saunders carried Guill's gold rope chain in his hand. When the two men reached Katrina, she remarked, "I heard a noise. It sound like a shot." According to Johnson, Saunders replied, "Don't worry about it . . . I just killed that man." Saunders added, "Naw, Lacy didn't do. I did it." Saunders threw the wallet into bushes near a house on High Street. (Tr. 133). On Grove Street, Saunders threw the papers from the wallet into the sewer. (Tr. 133). At that point, Saunders began counting the money.

Saunders, Johnson and Katrina returned to Katrina's apartment. Saunders, according to Johnson, washed the blood off his hands. Everyone left the apartment for a brief period. They stopped at Dooley's to buy beer and order a pizza which was delivered to Katrina's apartment. (Tr. 138). When they got inside the apartment, Saunders was drinking beer and sniffing cocaine. Levi Poole and Saunders' brother also came by the apartment that evening. (Tr. 140). Saunders remained in the apartment until four or five in the morning. (Tr. 139).

Johnson called the police around 2 a.m. on July 19, 1989. Lt. Brown picked up Johnson who gave his account of Guill's shooting. (Tr. 142). On cross, Johnson denied giving a

9

Example Petition for Executive Clemency for William Saunders (cont.)

false police report to avoid criminal charges and denied that he delayed reporting until he could create a story to tell the police. However, Johnson admitted giving false information to the police in the past as well as false testimony when he was on trial. (Tr. 154-55). He had convictions for stealing a car, breaking and entering, grand larceny, assault and battery, and giving false information to the police. (Tr. 157). He acknowledged three felony convictions. (Tr. 165).

Johnson admitted that he had used illegal drugs and that he recognized the street signals employed to indicate drug availability. (Tr. 158). He denied telling Anthony Martin one month before Saunders' trial that he, Johnson, had spent Guill's money. He also denied bragging to Angie Johnson and Betty Brandon on the night of the shooting about robbing Guill. (Tr. 160).

Katrina Wilson Johnson corroborated much of Johnson's testimony.[125] Between 4 and 4:30 p.m., Guill arrived at her apartment and left with Johnson. (Tr. 43). As Katrina waited for their return, Saunders and James Levi Poole arrived. Saunders had a brown "leather like" bag with a finger strap. Poole took the bag, unzipped it and removed a long gold gun. (Tr. 46). Katrina had seen this gun, in the same leather bag, the day before when Saunders came to their apartment. The gun was six to seven inches long and gold in the front. (Tr. 46).

Katrina, Poole and Saunders walked to Dooley's Market on Jefferson between 5 and 5:30 p.m. Johnson and Guill arrived and parked the car. Between 5:30 and 6:00 p.m., the four got into the car and left Dooley's. Guill drove, Johnson was in the front passenger seat, Katrina sat behind Johnson, and Saunders sat behind Guill. (Tr. 48). Guill was to drive Katrina home. However, instead of driving Katrina home, Guill drove around looking for a half ounce of cocaine

---

[125]On August 4, 1989, three weeks after the shooting, Katrina Wilson then 25 years old and Lacy Johnson then 20 were married. Under Va. Code § 19.2-271.2 neither could be called to testify against the other in a criminal proceeding. They are now divorced.

10

Example Petition for Executive Clemency for William Saunders (cont.)

and ultimately pulled into the parking lot of the Old Dutch Supermarket next to the car wash. Guill parked the car and waited to make a drug buy.

Katrina left and began walking home. It was now between 7 and 7:30 p.m. As Katrina walked up High Street, she heard a noise "like a shot." (Tr. 53). Katrina then saw Saunders and Johnson walking up behind her "real fast." Four to five minutes had passed since she had left the car. (Tr. 53). When Katrina commented that she had heard a noise like a shot, Saunders grabbed her, hugged her, and admitted that he had just killed "the man," adding "Everything will be all right, just don't say nothing." (Tr. 54). As Katrina, Johnson and Saunders continued walking, Saunders repeated "a hundred, a hundred, a hundred, a hundred, a hundred." Katrina testified, "I guess he was counting the money that he had taken from Guill." (Tr. 54).

According to Katrina, all three returned to Lacy's apartment on Grove Street. That night they along with Levi Poole and Saunders' brother, Marvin, sat around drinking beer and eating pizza. Poole and Marvin Saunders left at an unspecified time. Saunders remained until 3:30 or 4 a.m., then went home. (Tr. 58).

On cross examination, Katrina stated that she married Johnson on August 4, 1989. However, she denied that they had married to gain the protection of the marital privilege and insisted that they had been engaged to marry since March, 1989. (Tr. 65-66).

James Levi Poole testified about events prior to and after the shooting. On July 17th, he and Saunders went to Katrina's apartment. Saunders had a leather pouch that contained a .22 gun with a long barrel. Poole took the gun out, looked at it, said "Naw, that's five years for me," and returned the gun to Saunders. (Tr. 76). Poole was on parole at the time. (Tr. 77). Poole, Saunders and Katrina went to Dooley's Store where they met Johnson and Guill. Poole described the gun as chrome, then corrected himself stating that it was gold. (Tr. 76). Johnson,

11

Example Petition for Executive Clemency for William Saunders (cont.)

Katrina and Saunders left with Guill while Poole stayed behind. (Tr. 79). Later that night, around 7 or 7:30 p.m., Poole went to Katrina's apartment. He saw Johnson, Katrina, Saunders, and Saunders' brother. (Tr. 80). Poole talked for about 10 minutes, ate some pizza, and he left about 8 or 9 p.m. (Tr. 82).

On cross examination, Poole admitted telling defense counsel that he had never seen Saunders with a gun. Poole admitted telling defense counsel that Johnson had made some statements to Poole about the robbery of Guill. (Tr. 84-85). But at trial Poole denied that Johnson had made any statements about the robbery and claimed only that "[S]omebody told me he .. this .. this the way it happened." (Tr. 84, 86).

At trial, Shanta Chandler Thompson stated that she had been at the car wash on Union Street on July 17, 1989, between 7:30 and 8 p.m. Thompson never heard any gun shot. (Tr. 171). Thompson saw Katrina come from the side of Old Dutch and then cross the street proceed up High Street. (Tr. 168-69). About two minutes later, Thompson saw Johnson and an individual she identified at trial as Saunders cross the street in front of the carwash and proceed up High Street. (Tr. 169). Thompson stated that Saunders was <u>wearing a black T-shirt and shorts</u>. Thompson stated that she had no doubt about the individuals she saw that evening. (Tr. 171). Defense counsel had been provided with Thompson's pretrial sworn statement to the prosecutor (Tr. 174). However, defense counsel never cross-examined Thompson on her inability to identify Saunders when she first talked to the detective. In fact, Thompson had looked at photographs and "narrowed them down to two pictures." After viewing the photographs, she subsequently identified Saunders in a six person, line-up on August 29th. Defense counsel never filed any <u>Wade</u> motion challenging Thompson's identifications of Saunders and failed to challenge her identification on cross-examination.

12

Example Petition for Executive Clemency for William Saunders (cont.)

The Commonwealth called Bernard Smith, then nineteen years old and held on charges in the Danville City jail. Smith saw Saunders with two guns in June or July. One was a .38 and the other was a gold .22 about nine to ten inches long. (Tr. 88). After Saunders was arrested on the capital murder charge, Saunders and Smith were held in the same jail. (Tr. 90-91). On an unspecified date, Saunders told Smith that Johnson had snitched on him and he wanted someone to knock him off. (Tr. 89). Later Saunders told Smith that he had shot Guill in the back of the head with a .22 by the car wash on Memorial Drive. (Tr. 91). Guill had been looking for one half ounce of cocaine. (Tr. 93). Saunders shot Guill because Guill would not give Saunders his money. Saunders took Guill's jewelry and money. Johnson and some girl had been with Guill and Saunders at the time. According to Smith, Saunders said Johnson had told Saunders not to shoot Guill because Lacy knew Guill. After these two conversations, Smith contacted the police. (Tr. 95). Smith talked to Det. Breedlove and then to the prosecutor, William Fuller. (Tr. 99). He was released from jail on August 31, 1989, and had no subsequent arrests. (Tr. 100).

Smith had prior convictions for shoplifting, assault, drunk in public, disorderly conduct and abusive language. (Tr. 98-99). Smith had been convicted of burglary in Pittsylvania County but had not yet been sentenced. He also admitted that in August, when he talked to Saunders, he had been convicted on the felony charge in Pittsylvania and that sentence was pending. Smith denied cooperating with the Danville police to help himself. (Tr. 103). While Smith was out on bond on the Chatham burglary, he had been charged with assault in Danville. His grandmother had signed the bond on the burglary case but refused to do so on the assault case. On August 28, 30 and September 1, 1989, Smith spoke to the police and prosecutor about Saunders' statements. (Tr. 103-04). He had been released on bond on August 31, 1989.

The defense presented several witnesses at the guilt phase of the trial. Betty

13

Example Petition for Executive Clemency for William Saunders (cont.)

Brandon, 26 years old and then in jail on pending charges, lived at 808 Grove Street on the night of the shooting. Brandon saw Johnson, Saunders, Poole, and other people at her apartment as well as Katrina's on the night of the shooting. (Tr. 215). The very night of the shooting Johnson bragged that he, Poole and Saunders had robbed Guill. Johnson had received Guill's money, and he showed Brandon some money that night. Johnson was using cocaine when he talked to Brandon. He had a bread bag with cocaine in it and was offering cocaine to everyone present. (Tr. 216-17). Brandon saw Johnson and Katrina doing drugs. On the night of the robbery, Brandon bought two, $25 dollar bags from Johnson. (Tr. 221-22). Johnson told her that he had followed Guill on a bike that day. After Guill offered Johnson a ride, they picked up Saunders, Katrina and Poole. (Tr. 223). The group robbed Guill and left his car. Guill was later found dead at the Old Dutch. (Tr. 224). On cross examination, Brandon acknowledged prior convictions for writing bad checks.

Anthony Martin, a 19 year old high school student, had a conversation with Johnson about a month and a half before the trial. When Martin told Johnson, "I heard you shot this man," Johnson had responded, "Naw, I just spent the dead man's money." (Tr. 229). Johnson did not tell Martin who shot Guill. (Tr. 231).

Sandra Mease, 27 years old, stated that she had known Dale Guill for ten or eleven years and had dated him. She had also dated Saunders but not at the same time. (Tr. 233-34). On one occasion, Guill had asked her to sell him drugs, and she had refused. When asked if Johnson sold drugs, Mease said "yes." The Commonwealth objected and the objection was sustained. (Tr. 234). On cross-examination Mease, known as "Missy," stated that she and Guill were only friends and did not having a dating relationship. (Tr. 235, 240). Saunders did not know that she had been seeing Guill. (Tr. 239). Mease knew nothing about the shooting of Guill. (Tr. 241).

Margie Saunders, Saunders' mother, testified that he had been living with her off

14

Example Petition for Executive Clemency for William Saunders (cont.)

and on at the time of the shooting. Ms. Saunders produced one of Saunders' shirts. (Def. Ex. 3). The shirt was not the same size as the shirt recovered from the gas tank. (Tr. 225-26).

At the guilt phase, the circumstances surrounding Saunders' arrest and his post-arrest statement were never presented to the court. Ex. 10. Saunders had been arrested on July 20, 1989, at his sister's apartment on 338 North Ridge Street in Danville, Virginia. Although the police searched the apartment, they did not recover any evidence connected to the robbery of Guill--no guns or bullets, no money, no jewelry, and no other possessions or papers.

After his arrest, Saunders gave a statement. Ex. 10. He had been with Katrina and Poole at Dooley's Market on Jefferson sometime after 2:30 p.m. on July 17, 1989, when Johnson and an unknown, white male pulled up. While the man talked to Poole, Johnson spoke to Saunders and Katrina and told them to get in the car. All four drove off (Guill and Johnson in the front, Saunders and Katrina in the back) looking for a half ounce of cocaine for Guill. They drove to Peyton Place, to the north side, and then across the bridge to the car wash on Memorial Drive. They parked at the car wash, and Johnson went into a building. Johnson came back and said he could not get anything. Guill stated that he would go to Greensboro for cocaine. Guill dropped everyone off at Katrina's apartment on Grove Street, and Saunders never saw him again. Saunders said they did not park at the lot beside Old Dutch and Allen's Shoe Shop while he was with them. In his statement, Saunders denied any knowledge of the shooting or of Guill's wallet or papers. He stated correctly that his fingerprints would not be found on those items.

At the conclusion of the guilt phase, defense counsel argued that the witnesses were not credible. Johnson and his then girlfriend Katrina Wilson had concocted a story exonerating Johnson and attributing all criminal acts to Saunders. As added protection, Johnson married Katrina several days after the shooting to prevent her testifying against him at any trial. Johnson and

15

Example Petition for Executive Clemency for William Saunders (cont.)

Katrina persuaded their friend Thompson to back up their story about the time of these events. (Counsel failed to argue that Thompson said Saunders had been wearing a black shirt, when according to the other testimony Saunders had placed his white shirt in the car's gas tank.) Johnson had a prior conviction for giving false evidence to the police. (Tr. 256). Smith gave false testimony about Saunders' admissions to obtain favorable treatment on his pending charges. However, Smith's story conflicted with Johnson's. Smith stated that Saunders had demanded the money and Guill had refused. This directly contradicted Johnson's description of the shooting as sudden and unexpected. (Tr. 259). Poole gave inconsistent descriptions of the gun. (Tr. 259). Saunders' fingerprints were not found on any of Guill's possessions although, according to Johnson, Saunders was the last one to handle Guill's papers. No physical evidence connected Saunders to the shooting. (Tr. 260). Given the nature of the testimony and the lack of credibility of the witnesses, guilt had not been established beyond a reasonable doubt. (Tr. 260).

In rebuttal summation, the prosecutor argued that Johnson was completely credible. Johnson's account was confirmed by Katrina and Shanta Thompson. (Tr. 268). (The prosecutor, like defense counsel, failed to note that Thompson said Saunders had been wearing a black shirt. If the others were to be believed, Saunders did not have any shirt by the time Thompson saw him.) The prosecutor argued that Guill was shot for his money and because he was white. (Tr. 266). He admitted that without Johnson there would have been no case against Saunders. (Tr. 271). Smith was credible because his pending sentence on the Chatham burglary conviction was outside the control of the Danville prosecutor's office. "An offense that I have no control over. He has been made no promises." (Tr. 272). Since Smith had been in jail, he could have learned the details of the shooting only from Saunders. (Tr. 272).

Based on this testimony and evidence, the court found Saunders guilty of capital

16

Example Petition for Executive Clemency for William Saunders (cont.)

murder in the commission of a robbery, of robbery, and of the use of a firearm in the commission of a felony. (Tr. 275).

THE EVIDENCE AT THE SENTENCE PHASE

The sentencing phase of the trial began on November 16, 1989, and was ultimately continued to May, 1990. Viewed in the light most favorable to the Commonwealth, the evidence demonstrated the following.

A. Evidence Presented On November 16, 1989

Bernard Smith, James Jones, and Saunders went to Chatham, Virginia, on the night of June 1, 1989, and broke into a Western Auto store using a crowbar. Saunders handed Smith six guns from the store, and Saunders took three guns, a .22, a .25, and a 9 mm.[126] The .22 was gold color and had long barrel. Ex. 26 (Tr. 11). The police recovered the six guns from Smith's house. Smith pled guilty to this offense and was awaiting sentence. (Tr. 12). Smith saw Saunders with the .22 and the .25 after the break-in. (Saunders was charged and later convicted of burglary and grand larceny based on these facts.) While in jail, Saunders told Smith about shooting Guill. Saunders also claimed that he had shot a man in Washington, D.C. over some money and drugs. (Tr. 14).

Elton Pruitt, the owner of the Western Auto Store, confirmed that on June 1, 1989, nine guns were taken along with a pair of binoculars. (Tr. 6). One gun was an FIE brand .22 with two cylinders for a .22 magnum and for a .22 long rifle. The .22 long rifle cylinder was in the firearm when it was stolen. The barrel was about 5-3/4" and the gun was brass plated. (Tr. 7).

[126]Defense counsel failed to establish that Saunders had been arrested at the scene of the Chatham robbery and that no guns were recovered from him at that time. Counsel made no effort to introduce evidence concerning the facts of Saunders' arrest in Chatham. Ex. 14, 15, 16.

17

Example Petition for Executive Clemency for William Saunders (cont.)

Both Katrina Wilson and Lacy Johnson testified at the sentencing phase. Katrina had overheard Saunders admit that he had stolen the guns from a shop in Chatham. On the day Guill has shot, Katrina asked Saunders if he had ever done anything like that before, and he responded, "Plenty of times." With prompting, Katrina stated that Saunders said that he had shot a man in Washington, D.C. and had taken his "reefer" the weekend before Guill was shot. (Tr. 22-24).

Johnson repeated his prior testimony that Saunders had three guns the day before the shooting. Saunders reported that he and Smith had stolen the guns from Chatham. (Tr. 29). Johnson was with Katrina when Saunders said he had shot someone "plenty of times." Saunders also said that he shot a drug dealer in D.C. the weekend before Guill's murder and took the dealer's drugs and money. (Tr. 29). According to Johnson, Saunders shot Guill because he was white and Saunders hated white people. (Tr. 30). Saunders had tried to get Johnson involved in devil worship using the bones of a black cat to get "powers." (Tr. 30).

On cross examination, Johnson admitted giving false information to the police and acknowledged his prior felony conviction. (Tr. 33). On redirect, Johnson explained the false information charge. He had initially denied any involvement with a stolen car. However, when the other participants blamed him, Johnson gave a statement to the police and testified against them. (Tr. 34).

The Commonwealth introduced Saunders' prior record: two statutory burglary convictions in 1987; petit larceny on November 26, 1988, recorded in the General District Court; receiving stolen merchandise on October 27, 1988, recorded in the General District Court; disorderly conduct and resisting arrest on March 11, 1989, in the General District Court; disorderly conduct in front of a school and misdemeanor assault and battery on a police officer on March 19, 1988, in General District Court. (Copies of these records appear at Ex. 11). The pre-

18

Example Petition for Executive Clemency for William Saunders (cont.)

sentence report was also admitted. This concluded the Commonwealth's evidence of future dangerousness.

An examination of the underlying facts of these prior offenses demonstrates that Saunders' record consisted largely of property crimes and not violent offenses. The 1987 statutory burglary convictions were transferred from the Danville Juvenile and Domestic Relations Court to the Circuit Court. Both convictions were for breaking into the Sunrise Mart at night with the intent to commit larceny. Saunders with another stole a case of beer valued at $57.44 on one occasion and a case of beer valued at $96.00 on the other occasion. He received a five year suspended sentence with 12 months on the Danville City Farm to be followed by 12 months probation.

Saunders' Danville General District Court records include a misdemeanor conviction for stealing a sweat shirt and some T-shirts with a total value of $30.45. (Nov. 26, 1988). He had misdemeanor conviction for buying a stolen bicycle (Oct. 27, 1988). He was convicted of disorderly conduct in front of a junior high school and resisting arrest (March 11, 1989). He had a misdemeanor charge of disorderly conduct and misdemeanor assault and battery on a police officer (March 19, 1989). The records also revealed that Saunders was without an attorney on each of the charges in the Danville General District Court. On several of the charges, including the misdemeanor assault charge, no prosecutor appeared in Court on the charges, indicating their minimal nature.

At the initial sentencing phase in November, 1989, Saunders presented several witnesses in mitigation. Friends and family members described Saunders as quite, polite, and respectful. He had not exhibited violent behavior, animosity to white people, or belief in witchcraft and magic powers. (Tr. 89-104, 113, 123-125).

One witness was Robert E. Turner, IV, who met Saunders when Turner worked at

19

Example Petition for Executive Clemency for William Saunders (cont.)

the W.W. Moore, Jr., Detention Home in Danville. Saunders had been sent to the facility at age 17 after convictions for breaking and entering and petit larceny. In a report dated April 22, 1987, Turner, stated that Saunders was not a behavioral problem, was "very well behaved," and had adjusted to the "secure setting" of the detention home. Although Saunders had appeared to be depressed on several occasions, Turner had several conferences with him and Saunders "appeared to get much better." (Tr. 49).

Dr. Paul Mansheim, a psychiatric expert appointed by the Court to assist defense counsel, was unable to predict that Saunders would commit dangerous acts in the future. Mansheim had reviewed Johnson's statements, Johnson's claim that Saunders shot someone in D.C., Johnson's charge that Saunders hated white people and was involved in devil worship, and Johnson's prior criminal record before reaching this conclusions. Mansheim concluded that Johnson's testimony was suspect given his prior record of giving false testimony to the police. (Tr. 54). Mansheim also viewed Johnson's and Wilson's sudden marriage with suspicion in view of Virginia's law on marital privilege. The fact that their testimony reported the same inculpatory statements by Saunders provided an additional basis to believe their testimony was contrived. (Tr. 55). Mansheim had reviewed the testimony of Bernard Smith concerning Saunders' alleged admissions and had reviewed Smith's prior record. Smith's testimony was also suspect given his upcoming sentencing and large number of prior charges. Smith had a significant incentive to help the prosecution. (Tr. 57).

Mansheim had reviewed Turner's report which indicated that Saunders was well behaved, socialized with others, responded well to female authority figures, presented no behavior problems, and could benefit from counseling. (Tr. 59).

Mansheim confronted Saunders with his alleged admissions concerning devil

20

Example Petition for Executive Clemency for William Saunders (cont.)

worship and the killing in Washington. Saunders denied making such statements. (Tr. 53, 56). He also denied any prejudice against white people. (Tr. 57). Mansheim's interview with Saunders revealed that Saunders had responded well when he lived with his uncle between February 1984 and August 1986. Saunders had no juvenile record during that period. (Tr. 60).

Mansheim concluded that Saunders would function well under circumstances where he had few choices and others were providing him with direction. (Tr. 61). His criminal record indicated that he accepted responsibility for his actions and pled guilty. Based on his criminal record, Mansheim could not predict that Saunders would commit a dangerous act. (Tr. 61). His only prior allegedly violent crime had been assaulting a police officer. On that offense, Saunders had received a short sentence (60 days, 45 suspended, 15 to run concurrently with disorderly conduct), which indicated that the offense was not serious. (Tr. 62-63). A penitentiary would provide the necessary structured environment. (Tr. 65-66). Mansheim could not predict future dangerousness or violent acts by Saunders. (Tr. 93). The offense of conviction demonstrated only that Saunders had been dangerous on one occasion and did not mean he would be so again. (Tr. 96).

William Saunders, then 20 years old, testified at the sentencing phase. Saunders denied any animosity to white people, denied that he would ever kill anyone or kill on the basis of race, denied any devil worship involving cats, and denied making statements about devil worship to anyone. (Tr. 130-31, 134). Saunders denied killing anyone in D.C. or telling anyone that he had done so. (Tr. 133). He specifically denied any conversation with Bernard Smith in which he told Smith about killing someone. (Tr. 134). Katrina, Johnson and Smith had not told the truth. (Tr. 135). Saunders stated that he had been well-behaved in school and while in the W.W. Moore Detention Home. He acknowledged periods of depression while at the facility. (Tr. 131). While

21

Example Petition for Executive Clemency for William Saunders (cont.)

at his uncle's house, he lived under strict rules and believed that he could do so again. He had been well-behaved while confined in the Danville City Jail on these charges. While at the City Farm, Saunders had studied the Bible and had received eight certificates for Bible study while in jail. (Tr. 136). Saunders believed he could improve in a penitentiary setting. (Tr. 133). Saunders acknowledged his prior convictions but stated that he believed he could straighten himself out. (Tr. 149) Saunders saw no point in "straightening out" if he got the death penalty. (Tr. 150).

On rebuttal, the Commonwealth called Levi Poole and Dr. Arthur Centor. On one occasion, Saunders had been cutting Poole's hair and as he did so told Poole that he would shoot him if he were white. Saunders then said he was just kidding. (Tr. 152). Poole also stated Saunders had suggested killing a black cat, throwing its bones in the river, in order to get "powers." On cross, Poole admitted that Saunders may have been joking. (Tr. 154)

Dr. Arthur Centor, a forensic clinical psychologist, provided rebuttal testimony for the Commonwealth.[127] Defense counsel failed to object to Centor's testimony as the Commonwealth's expert. Centor had reviewed the statements of Johnson, Katrina and Smith; the statements of Poole were "mentioned" to him. (Tr. 161). Based on material provided by the

---

[127]In August, 1989, shortly after Saunders was charged, defense counsel moved for a competency examination pursuant to Va. Code Ann. §§ 19.2-169.1 and 19.2-169.5. In response, the court granted the motion for a competency examination and sua sponte without motion by defense counsel, also appointed Centor pursuant to Va. Code § 19.2-264.3:1 to examine Saunders on "the issue of mitigation or aggravation of the offenses." Centor thus became the expert assigned to assist Saunders in the examination of evidence in mitigation of the offense in the event of a conviction. Centor's subsequent behavior when reporting his results reflected his belief that this was his role. As required by statute, he sent his report finding Saunders competent to stand trial to the Court, the prosecutor, and defense counsel. A full report stating his findings on mitigating and aggravating circumstances was sent only to defense counsel and in doing so Centor cited the requirements of Va. Code §§ 19.2-169.5 and 19.2-264.3:1(D).

22

Example Petition for Executive Clemency for William Saunders (cont.)

prosecutor and the defense and based on his examinations of Saunders, Centor testified that Saunders had a high probability of future dangerousness provided the witnesses' statements were credible. (Tr. 160). Given those statements, Centor had changed his initial opinion, provided to defense counsel, that Saunders would not be a future danger. Thus, Centor reported to defense counsel by letter on November 9, 1989, that Saunders did show a high probability for future acts of violence.

On cross-examination, Centor said that when he first interviewed Saunders in August 25, 1989, he had a complete copy of Saunders' criminal record, unidentified statements of some prosecution witnesses, and the police offense report. Based on these materials, he sent a letter report to the trial judge on August 28, 1989, indicating that Saunders was competent to stand trial. On that same date, Centor had sent a complete report to defense counsel and listed various mitigating factors: no history of prior violent criminal acts, no indication of a disruptive or abusive family life, a potential for average intellectual functioning, and denial of drug and alcohol abuse. When balanced against the aggravating factors of the offense and his prior criminal record, Centor had concluded that Saunders did "not show a high probability of future dangerousness." (Tr. 167).

Centor's opinion at trial, predicting future dangerousness, was contingent on a finding that the witnesses were credible. However, Centor admitted that he had never reviewed Johnson's criminal record and was unaware that Johnson had a conviction for giving false information to the police. Centor conceded that this fact would effect his opinion of the witness's credibility. (Tr. 171). As to Smith, Centor had been told about Smith's then pending charge but not about any prior offenses. (Tr. 171).

On redirect, Centor stated that three factors had caused him to change in his opinion to a prediction of future dangerousness: i) the nature of the offense here combined with statements

23

Example Petition for Executive Clemency for William Saunders (cont.)

about a prior murder in Washington, D.C., (ii) Saunders' reported belief in invulnerability through the practice of witchcraft, and (iii) Saunders' alleged statements showing racial prejudice. (Tr. 176-78). Defense counsel made no objection to this testimony.

The November sentencing phase concluded with these witnesses. The court ordered the preparation of the pre-sentence report, and the sentence date was set for January 5, 1990.

B. Postponement Of The Capital Sentencing

On January 5, 1990, the trial court advised counsel and Saunders that the court required additional time before imposing sentence. The sentence was adjourned to February 26, 1990. Ex. 26 (Tr. 5, 5/3/90). Throughout this six month period, Saunders was held in the Danville City Jail as he had been since his arrest in July, 1989. He had only one disciplinary offense for "using vulgar or back talk toward and [sic] officer or non-inmate" on September 7, 1989. Ex. 12.

On February 20, 1990, Saunders set his bedsheet on fire to protest a search of his cell. He was charged with arson. Sentencing on the murder conviction was deferred until the arson charge was resolved. Saunders entered a guilty plea to the arson offense on March 22, 1990. (Tr. 3/22/90). Sentencing on the capital murder conviction was adjourned to May 3, 1990.

C. Evidence Presented On May 3, 1990

At the May 3rd sentencing proceeding, the Commonwealth presented evidence of six instances of misconduct by Saunders during the nearly six month period that he was held pending sentence in the Danville City Jail. Ex. 26 (5/3/90, Tr. 5-6).

Eight members of the Danville Sheriff's Department testified about the February 20, 1990, incident when Saunders attempted to burn his bedsheet. The officers were searching each

24

Example Petition for Executive Clemency for William Saunders (cont.)

cell for a missing spoon, and Saunders objected to the way the search of his cell was conducted. (Tr. 17, 34) Saunders threatened to burn his bedsheet after the officers left and, in fact, tried to light it as Deputy Bryant Booth was leaving. Booth stomped it out. Booth then found a second sheet burning on the concrete catwalk outside the cell. Saunders took responsibility. (Tr. 18). Saunders then refused to leave his cell to be placed in isolation. Seven or eight officers in riot gear and nightsticks entered Saunders' cell. As Saunders struggled, his hands and legs were tied and he was taken to isolation. (Tr. 25). Saunders stated he had set the fire to protest against the manner in which the officers had treated his cell during the search. He had been angry but did not intend to hurt anyone. (Tr. 44-45).

Three separate incidents occurred during weekend in April. On April 28, 1990, inmate Kent Douglas Wells accused Saunders of removing a jar of skin cream from Wells' cell. Saunders' refused to return the cream and, without provocation according to Wells, hit Wells in the face. (Tr. 68) Wells stated that three other inmates started to beat Wells until Officer Booth responded. (Tr. 70-71). The same day, April 28, 1990, Saunders' cell was searched pursuant to a routine search for contraband. The head of a razor with the blade intact and covered with tape was found in the rim of the commode. (Tr. 80). A TV antenna was discovered in the drain opening of the sink. (Tr. 84).

The next day, April 29, 1990, inmate Bobby Dale Jackson, who was in the same cellblock as Saunders, was attacked by inmate Dobbins. Saunders joined in and hit Jackson with a mop handle. Dobbins and Saunders threatened to kill Jackson if he told the guards. Jackson immediately reported the incident. (Tr. 91). Jackson acknowledged that the jail was overcrowded in April. (Tr. 92).

On April 30, 1990, in response to Saunders' participation in the April 28th and 29th

25

Example Petition for Executive Clemency for William Saunders (cont.)

incidents over the weekend, the officers decided to move him to isolation. Saunders initially agreed to cooperate and then changed his mind. (Tr. 95). He had been held in isolation from February to mid-April 1990. (Tr. 97, 117). After some discussion, Saunders went voluntarily to the isolation unit. (Tr. 100). However, when he entered the cell with Deputy Stokes, he jumped on the commode and tried to pull the light fixture down. Stokes grabbed Saunders around the waist, and they both fell. (Tr. 101-102).

Other officers then entered the cell since it was not clear what was happening. One of them, Michaels, hit Saunders on his leg with a nightstick. They left Saunders in the cell. Saunders removed the plastic covering from the fluorescent fixture and took out one of the bulbs. He broke the light bulb and broke the plastic cover into two sharp pieces about 12" and 16" long. Saunders pulled down the rest of the lights and refused to relinquish the plastic pieces. (Tr. 108, 112).

Frank B. Fuller, Jr., who had spoken with Saunders on several occasions and had prepared the pre-sentence report in his capital case, met with Saunders in his isolation cell. After a lengthy discussion with Fuller, Saunders handed over the broken light bulb and broken plastic. Saunders told Fuller that he had been moved to isolation for no reason, that he had gone voluntarily, and once there he had been jumped by Booth, Michaels and Hopkins who then beat his legs with a blackjack. (Tr. 140-41). Saunders had grabbed the plastic pieces and threatened to kill the three officers in retaliation. (Tr. 140, 150). Saunders surrendered the plastic pieces to Fuller.

Frank Fuller confirmed that the Danville City Jail had no windows, no natural light, no outside ventilation, and no outdoor recreation yard. Saunders had been held there for over nine months, believed he was not getting fair treatment at the jail, and wished to be moved. (Tr. 147).

On May 2, 1990, Deputy Mark L. Harraway smelled smoke and observed burned

26

Example Petition for Executive Clemency for William Saunders (cont.)

paper in Saunders' commode. Saunders admitted setting the paper on fire and had stated "he wanted to take and burn up all the paper, so he could flush the commode." (Tr. 153).

The defense presented no witnesses, and Saunders did not testify. (Tr. 156).

The prosecutor argued that based on the evidence at trial, the presentence report, his prior criminal record, and these recent post-conviction jail incidents Saunders would be a future danger even if incarcerated and the death sentence should be imposed. (Tr. 159-169).

Defense counsel maintained that the post-conviction jail incidents were the direct result of six months incarceration while the court determined whether a death sentence or a life sentence would be imposed. This had been a very stressful period for Saunders. All the jail incidents had occurred after the original January sentencing date. Setting aside Guill's murder, Saunders had no history of serious violent behavior. Given his young age, 19 at the time of the offense, he could be expected to benefit from a life sentence. Counsel emphasized that the Commonwealth's primary witness had significant credibility problems. Moreover, the defense psychiatrist had not found a probability of future dangerousness. (Tr. 169-181).

The court imposed a sentence of death based solely on future dangerousness. (Tr. 204). The court credited the testimony of Dr. Centor but specifically excluded any reliance on alleged admissions by Saunders to unadjudicated crimes, i.e., killing in Washington, D.C. (Tr. 197). The court relied on Saunders' prior convictions, on testimony that Saunders had stolen the gun used in the murder, and on his apparent lack of remorse for Guill's murder. (Tr. 199). The post-trial jail incidents were determined by the court to be strong evidence of future dangerousness. (Tr. 202-203).

Before imposing the death sentence, the Court stated:

I think that your conduct since trial, however, borders on near

Example Petition for Executive Clemency for William Saunders (cont.)

> incredible and unbelievable. I think that I must tell you, in all sincerity, Mr. Saunders, I have yet to comprehend, after hearing the evidence today, of some of the things that you've done, while awaiting sentencing on a capital murder, defy any conclusion, except to convince anyone who may have heard some of those things, that not only is there a probability of continuing criminal acts of violence in the future, but you've continued to commit acts of violence, while awaiting sentencing. Certainly, the mitigating factors and things that the Court has attempted to balance, in determining the appropriate sentence here, are so out-weighed by the actions and whatever motivated you to do them, since then, as to give the appearance of a very angry and hostile person, who really has . . . well, I think it can only be said, in the form that you just simply don't have any regard for life, or other peoples' property, and this is alarming.

Tr. 200 (5/3/90).

* * *

> I'm afraid that this evidence that the Court has heard today, absolutely reeks of aggression, hostility, rage, uncontrollable conduct, at best . . . but I don't think that it can be denied that it loudly exclaims dangerousness, not only from your own mouth, but from the things that you have done. . . . . [Y]ou do constitute a danger to all around you . . . be it friend, cellmate, guard or any other person in authority.

Tr. 201-202 (5/3/90).

The court imposed the death sentence for capital murder, a term of life imprisonment for the robbery, two years for use of a firearm, and one year for the arson conviction. (Tr. 206).

The Virginia Supreme Court relied heavily on evidence of Saunders' post-conviction, pre-sentence offenses when affirming the death sentence. The Court related each of the six incidents at length and concluded that "this evidence was uniquely probative of future dangerousness." Saunders v. Commonwealth, 406 S.E.2d 39, 45-46 (1991).

NEW AND UNDISCLOSED EVIDENCE IMPEACHING THE CREDIBILITY OF THE COMMONWEALTH'S WITNESSES

Since the time of Saunders' capital murder trial, the credibility of the

28

Example Petition for Executive Clemency for William Saunders (cont.)

Commonwealth's witnesses has been seriously undermined by the release of previously undisclosed statements made to the Commonwealth's agents and by the discovery of statements by Johnson admitting his part in the robbery and murder of Dale Guill. In addition, Smith and Johnson--the principal witnesses against Saunders--have compiled significant criminal records since his trial providing further reason to view their testimony with caution. Ex. 2. These are persuasive reasons to reevaluate the appropriateness of a death sentence in this case.

A. Bernard Smith

As set forth above, Bernard Smith testified at Saunders' capital murder trial that Saunders had made a jailhouse confession to Smith in August, 1989. Smith's two, typed pretrial statements dated August 28, 1989, had been provided to Saunders' defense counsel before trial. (Ex. 13). During his federal habeas investigation, Saunders obtained Smith's sworn affidavit that his pretrial and trial statements had been fabricated.[128] Ex. 8. Smith's trial allegations that Saunders admitted shooting Guill with a gold .22 gun taken when Smith and Saunders robbed a Western Auto store in Chatham, Virginia, on June 1, 1989, were inconsistent with Smith's statement to the police made on June 2, 1989. (Ex. 14). In that June, 1989, statement, Smith said he--not Saunders--had broken the store window, taken the guns, and made off with the guns before the police arrived. (Ex.14). Further support for claims that Smith fabricated his testimony can also be found in the post-sentence investigative report dealing with the Western Auto burglary. That report stated that Saunders had been apprehended by Officer James Austin in a nearby car moments after the burglar alarm sounded. (Ex. 15 at 2A). The arrest warrant shows that Saunders was

[128]The Attorney General's Office later submitted Smith's sworn statement dated March 28, 1996, recanting the allegations and statements contained in his 1995 affidavit given to current counsel. Ex. 8.

29

Example Petition for Executive Clemency for William Saunders (cont.)

arrested at June 1, 1989 at 5:35 a.m. (Ex. 16). None of the warrants or reports indicate that any guns were found on or seized from Saunders at the time of his arrest. These documents refuted Smith's claim that Saunders escaped that evening with three guns, one of which was later used to murder Guill.

On March 27, 1997, Saunders obtained for the first time transcripts of taped interviews of Bernard Smith conducted by the Commonwealth's Attorney and others on August 28, 1989, August 30, 1989, and August 31, 1989. See Ex. 17. None of these pretrial statements had been provided to Saunders' defense counsel. See Ex. 18.

Smith's August 28th statement contains the following statements that are either inconsistent with or directly contradicted his trial testimony. Smith stated, as he later did at trial, that Saunders said he shot Guill because Guill would not give him the money (Ex. 17, 8/28/89 at 9) and that he used one of the guns from the Western Auto burglary, i.e., Chatham (at 9). Contradicting Smith's later trial testimony, Saunders did <u>not</u> say what gun was used, only that he had a <u>.38</u> (at 23). At trial, Smith testified that Saunders said he had shot Guill with <u>a long, gold .22</u>. According to Smith's pretrial statements, Saunders did not say how many times he shot Guill. After he shot Guill, Saunders said he left, but Saunders did not say where he went (at 10). Moreover, Smith stated that Saunders did <u>not</u> say anything about taking Guill's money. Saunders did <u>not</u> describe what he did after he shot Guill, and Saunders gave Smith no other details of the shooting (at 16, 17). When Guill was shot, Lacy and a girl were with Saunders. Saunders did not say who the girl was or if she was anybody's girlfriend (at 12). Smith reported that Saunders never said he planned to shoot Guill (at 16). Smith was asked about any other details of the shooting and said <u>he had told everything Saunders said</u> (at 24). This conversation with Saunders had occurred about two weeks prior to Smith's August 28th interview with the Commonwealth's Attorney. (at

30

Example Petition for Executive Clemency for William Saunders (cont.)

18).

Two days later, on August 30, 1989, Smith gave a second taped interview. Smith stated, in part, that Saunders had offered him a .22 gun if Smith were released. Saunders was mad at Johnson because Johnson had "snitched" to the police. Saunders would tell his brother where to find the .22, and the brother would then give it to Smith (Ex. 17, 8/30/89 at 1). The .22 was described as a long, gold gun taken during the Chatham robbery (at 2). Saunders never said how he had used the gun, only that it was accurate (at 2). Smith should use the gun to shoot Johnson and throw the gun in the Dan River when he was finished (at 2). Saunders never told Smith where the gun was. Upon Smith's release, Saunders would direct his brother to give the gun to Smith or Saunders would tell Smith where to find it (at 3). When asked why Saunders wanted the gun thrown in the river, Smith responded: "So they wouldn't find the evidence, the gun, I guess it was the gun that killed the man with [sic]. Dale." (8/30/89 at 3)(emphasis added). Saunders never told Smith that he shot Guill with the gold .22. Yet Smith testified to that fact and more at trial.

The next day, August 31, 1989, Smith was interviewed again and reported that the day before Saunders had offered him $25,000 to shoot Johnson. Smith was to receive the gold .22 gun from Saunders' brother to carry out the deed.

The Commonwealth's Attorney stated that on August 30, 1989, he informed Smith's attorney of Smith's cooperation in the murder investigation and of Smith's willingness to locate the .22 gun. Ex. 19. The Pittsylvania prosecutor was notified and on the prosecutor's recommendation the judge released Smith on a $1,000 recognizance bond on August 31. After Smith's release, Fuller discussed Smith's efforts to locate what Fuller described as "the murder weapon" "on several occasions." Ex. 19 at 2-3. (As set forth at trial and in prior pleadings, the weapon was never recovered.) These facts were not known to defense counsel, and they provided a basis for

31

Example Petition for Executive Clemency for William Saunders (cont.)

impeaching Smith's trial testimony.

Smith's trial testimony directly contradicted his pretrial statements. Smith testified that during their joint incarceration Saunders told Smith that he had shot Guill in the back of the head with the .22 "that came from the store" because Guill "wouldn't give him the money, or something, so he shot him." Ex. 26, Tr. at 91. Smith stated that "after [Saunders] shot him, he got his jewelry and his money, and left." Tr. at 92. To get the jewelry and money, "he went in his pocket." Ibid. After Saunders shot Guill, "he was talking to him." "Move mother fucker, some shit like that . . . something." Ibid. Saunders told Smith that he took "some jewelry and money." Ibid. Smith added "Lacy told him not to do it 'cause he [Lacy] know [Guill]." Ibid. After several leading questions by the prosecutor, Smith stated that Saunders shot Guill because "he was white." Tr. at 96.

On cross examination, Smith stated that all his conversations with Saunders had occurred <u>before</u> he contacted the police. Tr. 99-100, 104. Smith denied that he had acted to "get in the good graces of the police" or that he had any selfish interest. Tr. 102-103. Smith maintained that no one had made any promises and that "I didn't ask them for no help." Tr. 103.

A review of defense counsel's cross examination of Smith confirms that counsel had not been provided with Smith's pretrial interviews. Smith was never questioned about his prior inconsistent and contradictory statements. Smith never acknowledged that he had been acting as an agent for the Commonwealth. All of these facts, unknown at the time of trial, provided further bases to attack Smith's credibility.

Comparing Smith's pretrial statements to his trial testimony leads to only one conclusion. Smith gave false testimony at Saunders' trial. Smith's testimony was critical to Saunders conviction since his testimony appeared to provide independent confirmation of the facts

32

Example Petition for Executive Clemency for William Saunders (cont.)

and details of the murder from Saunders himself.

Since Saunders' trial in 1989, Smith has been convicted of eleven misdemeanor offenses. He has five felony convictions in Danville, Martinsville, and Chesterfield County. Ex. 2 at 2-3.

B. Lacy Johnson

Johnson's testimony has been suspect from the beginning. Facts and witnesses revealed to Saunders after the conclusion of his state proceedings demonstrate that Johnson certainly lied about his role in the robbery/murder of Guill. He was not an innocent and unsuspecting eyewitness to a murder. At a minimum Johnson was an accomplice and could have been the triggerman.

On February 6, 1996, the Commonwealth provided Saunders with a copy of Det. Breedlove's handwritten notes on the case. Ex. 20. The notes revealed two facts previously unknown. First, Johnson had taken two polygraph examinations and "passed" only part of the examination concerning whether he shot Guill. Second, a previously unidentified witness, Kevin McMoore, had told the police that Johnson admitted to McMoore on the day after the robbery that he and Saunders had planned to rob Guill. However, according to McMoore's statement, Johnson did not know that Guill would be shot.

In March, 1997, Saunders received the four page polygraph report from the July 26, 1989, and August 10, 1989 examinations of Johnson. Ex. 21. On both dates, the Commonwealth's own polygraph examiner recorded deceptive responses by Johnson. On July 26, Johnson was asked "Did you know in advance Saunders was going to shoot Dale [Guill]?," and his response was deemed deceptive in two separate examinations on that date. Johnson offered an explanation which the examiner concluded "could have caused the deceptive responses." The explanation was that

33

Example Petition for Executive Clemency for William Saunders (cont.)

while at Dooley's Market, Saunders had stated that he ought to rob Guill. However, on August 10, 1989, the examiner conducted an additional "continued" examination. Johnson's negative responses to the following three questions were judged deceptive:

5. Other than what you told me, was anything said about taking Dale's money?

7. Did you plan with Saunders to take Dale's money?

10. Are you hoping an error will be made on this test?

Unlike the prior examination, the examiner did not conclude that Johnson's explanations could account for the repeated deceptive responses. Ex. 21.

The polygraph results alone demonstrate that Johnson was lying about his role in the robbery of Guill. The police department's own polygraph examiner had concluded on three separate examinations that Johnson gave deceptive responses when asked about his knowledge of a plan to rob Guill and his part in a plan to rob Guill. Furthermore, he was deemed to be deceptive on question 10, "Are you hoping an error will be made on this test?". The only possible conclusion was that Johnson was lying about his role in the robbery of Guill. Nevertheless, at trial Johnson presented himself as an unsuspecting eyewitness to Guill's murder. In fact, Johnson was at a minimum an accomplice in the robbery/murder and perhaps the shooter.

In the years since Saunders' conviction, Johnson on several occasions has admitted that he -- not Saunders -- shot Dale Guill. The most recent admission was reported to current counsel by the Attorney General's Office in a letter dated February 6, 1996. Ex. 5. That letter recounts a relatively recent claim by Johnson that he shot Dale Guill:

> On January 11, 1996, another statement was taken from Teresa Johnson [Lacy Johnson's wife]. In this statement she admitted lying in her first [December 27, 1995] statement to the police because she said Lacy had assaulted her and she was afraid of him. She also orally stated that four or five months ago Lacy Johnson said he shot

34

Example Petition for Executive Clemency for William Saunders (cont.)

the insurance man on Memorial Drive.

A second individual, Candace Bowman Battle, stated in a sworn affidavit that Johnson came to her on the very night of Guill's murder in 1989. Johnson told Bowman that he had just killed a man and thrown the gun in the Dan River. In 1994, Johnson told Battle that he had married Katrina to avoid going to jail. And in August, 1995, Johnson admitted to that he had "set the whole thing up, he set [Saunders] up, and he was not going to jail for nobody." Ex. 6. Johnson later denied Battle's allegations in an affidavit submitted by the Commonwealth in the federal court proceedings.

A third individual, a prosecution witness, Levi Poole, stated in a sworn affidavit that he heard Johnson admit to his then wife, Katrina, that he had killed someone. Ex. 7. In that same affidavit, Poole also admitted giving false testimony at Saunders' trial when he said Saunders had a long, gold .22 gun. According to Poole, Johnson had the gold gun about a week before the murder. Under questioning by the Commonwealth, Poole later recanted this admission concerning his trial testimony but not the statement attributed to Johnson. Ex. 7.

A fourth individual, Antonio Winbush, who married Katrina after she divorced Johnson, stated in a sworn affidavit that he had heard Johnson on several occasions admit that he had killed someone. Ex. 9. In the context of that conversation, Winbush understood Johnson to be referring to Dale Guill. Winbush also stated that Katrina had admitted giving false testimony at Saunders' trial. Winbush later recanted these statements. Ex. 9. The Commonwealth also submitted affidavits from Johnson and Katrina refuting these allegations.

Finally, in the years since Saunders' trial, Johnson has compiled a significant criminal record. According to Commonwealth's Attorney Fuller, Johnson has more than 30 felony convictions, mainly for burglary and larceny, along with six misdemeanor convictions. Ex. 2.

35

Example Petition for Executive Clemency for William Saunders (cont.)

A death sentence cannot be based on the testimony of Lacy Johnson.

C. Levi Poole

As noted above, Poole submitted an affidavit recanting portions of his trial testimony (Ex. 7), but later recanted the recantation after an interview by the Commonwealth. Poole has also compiled a significant criminal record since Saunders' trial. He has been convicted of 26 misdemeanors in Danville, three felonies in other jurisdictions, and nine misdemeanors in the Danville Juvenile and Domestic Relations District Court. Ex. 2.

In light of the record of criminal convictions held by Bernard Smith, Lacy Johnson, and Levi Poole, Commonwealth's Attorney Fuller has serious reservations about Saunders' death sentence:

> I believe there is an additional reason for re-examining Saunders' death sentence. I am concerned that several of the Commonwealth's witnesses in this case have compiled the . . . criminal records [above] since Saunders was convicted of capital murder.

Ex. 2 at 2.

Commonwealth's Attorney Fuller has concluded that:

> [I]n view of the criminal conduct of most of the Commonwealth witnesses since Saunders' conviction, I am not comfortable with Saunders' death sentence.

Id. at 3.

> Therefore, I believe that justice would best be served by commuting Saunders' death penalty to a life sentence to be served consecutively with the life sentence he receive for robbery.

Id. at 3-4.

D. Statements Of Other Witnesses

Evidence from other witnesses supports a conclusion that Johnson had a role in the

36

Example Petition for Executive Clemency for William Saunders (cont.)

robbery/murder. Statements given to Det. Breedlove by Betty Brandon on August 3, 1989, and Angie Johnson on July 24, 1989, report Johnson's admission that he robbed Guill with Saunders. See Ex. 22, 23. The names of these witnesses, but not their complete statements, had been provided pretrial on November 7, 1989, by the Commonwealth's Attorney. The pretrial disclosure indicated that Johnson had talked about robbing a guy with Sanders. The complete statements were provided to Saunders on March 27, 1997. Their statements support the conclusion that Johnson lied about his role in the offense.

Angie Johnson stated that Lacy Johnson offered her cocaine of the night of the shooting if she would bring him drug customers. She observed Lacy using cocaine and saw "a lot of cocaine" on the table in Katrina's apartment, some of it bagged up and some in an open bag. Lacy told her how he and Saunders robbed Guill of $700. Angie saw Levi Poole, Katrina, and Eric McMoore in the apartment. Ex. 23.

Brandon stated that she received cocaine from Johnson on the night of the shooting. Later that evening Johnson came by with a bread bag containing cocaine. Johnson said he had stolen $700 from a man and used it to buy the cocaine. Johnson knew the man because Katrina had been selling the man sex for money.[129] Ex. 22. Brandon testified for the defense and stated that on the night of the shooting, Johnson bragged that he had robbed Guill along with Poole and Saunders. Johnson said he took Guill's money. Johnson had a large quantity of cocaine that evening. He sold some to Brandon, who observed Johnson and Katrina doing drugs. Ex. 26, Tr. 215-224.

At trial, Saunders also presented the testimony of Anthony Martin who reported that

[129]This allegation did not come out at trial. If true, it provided a motive for Johnson to shoot Guill. Johnson testified that he and Katrina had been engaged to be married since March, 1989, and were married at the time of Saunders' trial.

37

Example Petition for Executive Clemency for William Saunders (cont.)

a month and a half before trial, Johnson admitted spending Guill's money. At trial, Johnson denied that he had planned to rob Guill, denied that he had told anyone that he had spent Guill's money, and denied that he used cocaine at Katrina's apartment on the night of the shooting. Ex. 26, Tr. at 125-27, 138-40, 154, 159, 164.

D. A Review Of All The Evidence Demonstrates That Johnson Took Part In The Robbery And May Have Shot Guill

A review of the evidence presented at trial in conjunction with all the facts and statements revealed or discovered since the trial demonstrates that Johnson, not Saunders, probably shot Guill and then named Saunders as the shooter. No physical evidence connected Saunders to Guill's murder. No money, jewelry or papers belonging to Guill were ever recovered from Saunders. Johnson led the police to what little physical evidence was found. Saunders' fingerprints were not on any of Guill's property, but Johnson's fingerprints were found on Guill's car. The "long, gold .22" was never recovered by the police. There is no proof that the gun stolen from the Western Auto store even killed Guill. Moreover, several witnesses placed a significant quantity of cocaine as well as money in Johnson's possession on the night of Guill's murder. It is reasonable to assume that the shooter got the bulk of Guill's money and property. Moreover, Johnson has repeatedly claimed responsibility for the shooting in the years since the murder. An unbiased assessment of the facts demonstrates that Johnson was the probable shooter in the robbery homicide. Under Virginia law, only the "triggerman" may be sentenced to death.

The evidence conclusively demonstrates that Johnson was at least an accomplice in the robbery/murder and lied at trial. Johnson acknowledged his participation to various witnesses at the time of the murder. The police department's own polygraph tests confirmed what he told those witnesses and confirmed that his denials of involvement were false. Johnson was seen with the

38

Example Petition for Executive Clemency for William Saunders (cont.)

proceeds of the robbery on the night of the shooting. Furthermore, Katrina Wilson Johnson cannot be viewed as a reliable witness given her sudden marriage to Johnson after the shooting and her own involvement in these events. Her apparent confirmation of Johnson's account must be dismissed or viewed with considerable suspicion.

The independent confirmation of Johnson's testimony provided by Bernard Smith at trial was a fiction. Smith's initial statement to the police reported that Saunders shot Guill with a .38. In that first interview, Smith could provide none of the details he later gave at Saunders' trial. Moreover, Smith's initial police interviews provide reason to believe that Smith was truthful when he later admitted that he lied at Saunders' trial. One need only compare Smith's August 1989 interviews to his November 1989 trial testimony to confirm that he gave false testimony.

And as stated by Commonwealth's Attorney Fuller, the extensive record of convictions compiled by Smith, Johnson, and Poole since Saunders' trial provides yet another reason to reconsider the sentence in Saunders' case. A man should not be convicted, much less put to death, based on the testimony of these witnesses. Clemency should be granted in this case.

SAUNDERS' RECORD WHILE ON DEATH ROW

Even if despite all the facts, one concludes that no doubt has been raised concerning Saunders' conviction for capital murder, clemency should be granted as to his sentence. The prediction that Saunders would be a danger even if incarcerated was incorrect.

Judge Ingram has stated that Saunders' post-conviction behavior was the reason the death sentence was imposed. After reviewing Saunders' disciplinary record at Mecklenburg, Judge Ingram has concluded that the death sentence is not warranted in this case:

As a result of the defendant's post conviction conduct while

39

Example Petition for Executive Clemency for William Saunders (cont.)

> awaiting sentencing in jail, I imposed the death penalty upon Saunders because there was a probability that based upon that evidence, the defendant would commit criminal acts of violence that would constitute a continuing serious threat to society.
>
> Had Saunders not behaved as he did from the time of his conviction until the time of his sentencing, I would not have imposed the death penalty on January 5, 1990, as originally scheduled, or thereafter.
>
> I have had an opportunity to review William Ira Saunders' behavior while he has been an inmate on Death Row and I am satisfied that his conduct in the years following his sentencing have not borne out my belief of his future dangerousness which he demon- strated during his period of incarceration awaiting sentencing.
>
> I am writing this letter because I believe that the judicial system which imposed this sentence upon Saunders cannot rectify this situation at this time, but that executive clemency is the only alternative which can ensure justice in this case.

Ex. 3.

Commonwealth's Attorney Fuller reached the same conclusion after reviewing the circumstances which led to the imposition of a death sentence and after reviewing Saunders' record since he has been at Mecklenburg.

> In retrospect, despite Saunders' behavior from conviction to sentencing almost six months later, it concerns me that, had the sentencing hearing gone forward when originally scheduled, Saunders' conduct that caused him to receive the death penalty would not have occurred and would not have affected his sentence. Significantly, Saunders created no problem while incarcerated from July 20, 1989 to January 5, 1990, the date that his sentencing was originally scheduled. Thus, I am convinced that if Sanders had been sentenced on January 5, 1990, as originally scheduled, the judge would not have imposed the death penalty, based upon the evidence of future dangerousness introduced at the first penalty hearing on November 16th.

Ex. 2 at 2.

* * *

Since June of 1995, when I started reviewing this file after Saunders

40

Example Petition for Executive Clemency for William Saunders (cont.)

> filed a federal habeas petition, I have felt that so long as Saunders has not been involved in violent conduct while incarcerated since receiving the death penalty, his sentence should be reconsidered. His prison record, which I have reviewed, indicates that he has not been involved in any violent conduct since he was sentenced to death on May 3, 1990.
>
> Therefore, I believe that justice would best be served by commuting Saunders' death penalty to a life sentence . . .

Ex. 2 at 3.

In the nearly seven years that Saunders has been held on death row, he has not repeated the violent behavior that occurred prior to his sentencing. His infractions have been generally minor violations of prison rules. Contrary to Judge Ingram's fears at the time of sentencing, there have been no injuries to prison staff or to other inmates.

The following summary of Saunders' disciplinary record is based on reports provided to Saunders current counsel by Mecklenburg Correctional Center. Ex. 24 (Offense reports in chronological order).

- On May 21, 1992, Saunders was charged with disobeying a direct order and received a verbal reprimand. The offense was covering his cell window.
- On June 20, 1993, Saunders was charged with using vulgar or insolent language toward an employee and received 15 days cell restriction. The offense was prompted when he stood in the doorway of another's cell and was ordered to move.
- On June 24, 1993, Saunders was charged with failing to follow institutional count procedures and received general detention. The offense consisted of failing to stand for count.
- On July 4, 1993, Saunders was charged with "aiding and abetting another to be in an unauthorized area" and received 30 days loss of radio, suspended for 90 days of good

41

Example Petition for Executive Clemency for William Saunders (cont.)

behavior. The offense was permitting another inmate to enter his cell.

- On July 23, 1993, Saunders was charged with disobeying a direct order and received a verbal reprimand. The offense was covering his cell window.

- On July 23, 1993, Saunders was charged with failing to follow institutional count procedures and received fifteen days cell restriction. The offense was failing to stand for count.

- On July 28, 1993, Saunders was charged with "gathering around or approaching any person in a threatening or intimidating manner" and received 30 days loss of commissary. The offense consisted of using loud, vulgar language, making threatening statements, and pointing a finger at a guard while the guard supervised a cell shakedown.

- On July 29, 1993, Saunders was charged with delaying, hindering or interfering with an employee in the performance of his duties and received 15 days cell restriction. The offense was throwing food into the pod area.

- On August 27, 1993, Saunders was charged with failing to follow institutional count procedures and received 15 day cell restriction. The offense was failing to stand for count.

- On September 25, 1993, Saunders was charged with delaying, hindering or interfering with an employee in the performance of his duties and received 15 days cell restriction. The offense was throwing paper from the cell food slot.

- On November 2, 1993, Saunders was charged with failing to follow institutional count procedures and received 15 days loss of recreation. The offense was failing to stand for count.

- On November 13, 1993, Saunders was charged with behavior that presents a

42

Example Petition for Executive Clemency for William Saunders (cont.)

threat to self and the institution and received prehearing detention and 30 days loss of TV. The offense was possession of intoxicants.

- On January 12, 1994, Saunders was charged with delaying, hindering, or interfering with an employee in the performance of his duties and received 10 days loss of recreation. The offense was failing to enter his cell promptly.

- On April 17, 1995, Saunders was charged with two offenses of delaying, hindering, or interfering with an employee in the performance of his duties. The first offense occurred when Saunders threw pieces of paper and carton of milk into the pod area. The second offense occurred three hours later when Saunders meal tray was found in the pod hallway. The punishment was 20 days loss of recreation on each offense.

- On June 22, 1995, Saunders was charged with disobeying a direct order and received 20 days loss of recreation. The offense was refusing to be cuffed to order to be moved to another pod.

- On June 23, 1995, Saunders was charged with a disobeying direct order and received 30 days loss of recreation. The offense was refusing to uncover his cell window.

- On July 21, 1995, Saunders was charged with "threatening bodily harm" and received prehearing detention. The offense was cursing a guard after the guard allegedly cursed at Saunders. He received 30 days loss of recreation.

- On September 19, 1995, Saunders was charged with threatening bodily harm based on his remark to a guard that he would throw his food tray at him. The punishment was 30 days loss of recreation.

- On January 8, 1996, Saunders was charged with two offenses for disobeying a direct order and received prehearing detention. The first offense was based on Saunders' refusing

43

Example Petition for Executive Clemency for William Saunders (cont.)

to return a magazine to another inmate. The second offense was refusing to be cuffed for a cell search twenty five minutes after the first offense. The resolution of the charges was not noted.

- On April 13, 1996, Saunders was charged with delaying, hindering, or interfering with an employee in the performance of his duties and received 20 days loss of commissary. The offense was throwing his food tray into the pod hallway.

- On January 17, 1997, Saunders was charged with disobeying a direct order and received 30 days loss of recreation. The offense was covering his cell window.

Saunders has inflicted injury only on himself while at Mecklenburg. On November 13, 1994, containers of blood were found in his cell, and he was placed on 30 minute security checks. (This was not a disciplinary offense.) On April 5, 1995, Saunders was found in a pool of blood and sent to South Hill Hospital. He was seriously injured from self-inflicted wounds in a suicide attempt. (This was not a disciplinary offense).

Based on a seven year record, Judge Ingram, Commonwealth's Attorney Fuller, and Chief of Police Morris have concluded that the reasons that supported a death sentence in Saunders' case have proved to be incorrect. Saunders' expert at the trial had stated that Saunders did not demonstrate a probability of future dangerousness. The Commonwealth's expert at the trial had found a probability of future dangerousness <u>only if</u> the Commonwealth's witnesses were credible. As has been argued and demonstrated above, the Commonwealth's central witnesses against Saunders were not credible and their subsequent criminal records only serve to highlight doubts about their trial testimony. Saunders' post-conviction offenses prior to his capital sentencing were certainly due to the stress and uncertainty as he awaited the Court's decision. He has not repeated that behavior. Saunders' death sentence should be commuted.

44

Example Petition for Executive Clemency for William Saunders (cont.)

CLEMENCY IS APPROPRIATE IN THIS CASE

Executive clemency is the appropriate avenue for relief where the state provides no procedural mechanism within the judicial system for the review of a conviction or sentence based on new facts or changed circumstances. Virginia Governors have provided this "fail safe" mechanism over the years.

Doubts about a defendant's guilt and a justified skepticism about accomplice testimony have provided a basis for commuting a death sentence. In 1992, Governor L. Douglas Wilder commuted the death sentence of Herbert Russell Bassette where Bassette's conviction was based solely on the testimony of three alleged accomplices. Governor Wilder commuted the death sentences of Joseph M. Giarratano and Earl Washington based on evidence demonstrating the likelihood of their innocence.

In November, 1996, Governor George F. Allen commuted the death sentence of Joseph Patrick Payne based on the unreliability of the sole eyewitness to the murder and substantial evidence indicating Payne's innocence.

William Saunders' case presents equally serious questions about the credibility of the witnesses against him. In addition, he was subjected to the unusual stress of waiting nearly six months to learn what sentence would be imposed. As demonstrated, he has not repeated the violent behavior that led to the death sentence. Moreover, the Commonwealth's Attorney who prosecuted him, the judge who tried him and sentenced him to death, and the Chief of Police whose office investigated the case have all concluded that a death sentence is not appropriate in this case. Saunders' case is certainly unique in generating support for clemency from the very individuals who originally sought his conviction and imposed the death sentence. The case is also unusual as application of clemency is being made with the consent to the Attorney General's Office prior to the

45

Example Petition for Executive Clemency for William Saunders (cont.)

conclusion of the court proceedings.

46

Example Petition for Executive Clemency for William Saunders (cont.)

CONCLUSION

For all these reasons, we urge you to commute William Saunders' death sentence and to impose a sentence of life with the possibility of parole, the sentence available when he was sentenced in May, 1989.

Respectfully submitted,

Barbara L. Hartung, VSB 38062
[redacted]
Richmond, Virginia 23219
[redacted]

Virginia Capital
Representation Resource Center
[redacted]
Richmond, Virginia 23219
[redacted]

Counsel for William Saunders

April 23, 1997

47

<5> CLEMENCY CAMPAIGN AND PROMOTIONAL STRATEGIES

Clemency Campaign

Jamie and Gladys Scott were each sentenced to serve life sentences in a Mississippi prison after being convicted of a 1993 armed robbery. Three teenage boys testified—in exchange for lighter sentences—that the Scott sisters had them rob two men at gunpoint after the sisters lured the men to an isolated roadside.

Having exhausted all of the sisters' appeals, the appointed public defender continued to work on their case and prepared pardon applications on their behalf.

The sisters' family started a website, dubbed "Free the Scott Sisters," where they posted regular updates about the sisters and their case. Over a period of time, news about their case spread, via African American radio programs, social networking websites, and blogs, attracting advocacy groups and activists to the sisters' clemency campaign.

When Jamie Scott's health started to decline due to a kidney ailment requiring regular dialysis, advocates for the sisters contacted the Mississippi NAACP, who then organized several highly publicized rallies at the Capitol Building in Jackson, Mississippi, drawing the support of the Mississippi ACLU and other activists. The prosecutor who tried the case and one of the men who was robbed also supported the sisters' release.

Because of Jamie's medical condition, there was a large push to release her.

Then-Governor Barbour suspended the sisters' sentences with the conditional provision that Gladys donate a kidney to her sister Jamie—an idea that Gladys originally proposed in a petition for early release.

On July 4, 1990, in the small town of St. John, Missouri, Stacey Lannert, age eighteen, shot her father to death while he laid passed out drunk on the sofa. When Stacey later confessed to killing her father, she alleged mental, physical, and sexual abuse by him, claiming that she killed him to protect her younger sister, Christy, from suffering a similar fate.

At trial, the prosecution claimed that Stacey murdered her father because she wanted money. Stacey, on the other hand, claimed that her father had sexually abused her from the age of eight, and that reports she made of the abuse to her guidance counselor, babysitter, and psychiatrist were ignored and never reported to the proper authorities.

Stacey's attorney wanted to present a Battered Spouse Syndrome defense (BSS), but the court wouldn't allow the defense to bring in experts to testify, as case law stated that such evidence can only be admissible if the defendant lawfully acted in self-defense or defense of another. Defense counsel did not show that Stacey's actions were based on self-defense, therefore the expert testimony and instructions to the jury on the BSS defense were not permitted.

The jury found Stacey guilty of first degree murder—rejecting the alternative defense that she suffered from a mental disease or defect—and sentenced her to life imprisonment without the possibility of parole.

After sentencing, some jurors expressed outrage that facts of sexual and physical abuse were never introduced at the trial. The trial judge, commenting on the case, said, "The sentence is severe for a 20-year-old. It is also somewhat surprising considering the evidence of sexual abuse by the victim's father…[A] conventional life sentence would be more appropriate from a comparison standpoint."

After exhausting all of her appeals, Stacey petitioned for either a pardon or a commutation to reduce her sentence to life, with the possibility of parole after fifteen years.

In her petition and in letters of support, Stacey was described as a model prisoner, active in many different community projects as well as helping other survivors of incest and abuse. During her imprisonment, she trained service dogs for the handicapped. Stacey also served as president for the Outreach program, an organization that brought troubled teens into prison for a wake-up call.

Stacey was the focus of a great deal of public support, with numerous websites collecting electronic signatures from the public, in support of her clemency petition. Among her supporters were Nancy Grace, Oprah, and the lead detective in her case, James Wethington.

In 2009, outgoing Missouri Governor Matt Blunt commuted Stacey's sentence, and that of another woman convicted under similar circumstances, stating, "After an exhaustive review of the facts in both cases, I am commuting the sentences of Stacey Lannert and Charity Carey, who suffered extensive abuse before they took action against the men who raped them and subjected them to other horrible physical and emotional abuse."

Stacey's sentence was reduced to twenty years, making her eligible for immediate parole.

After her release, Stacey and her sister, Christy, started Healing Sisters, a website and non-profit organization focused on ending sexual abuse in America.

As these two stories show, there was one key psychology principle at work: social proof. It is the principle of majority rules. When there are a lot of people doing something, other people tend to believe it must be the right thing to do. Marketers and salespeople exploit the principle of social proof all the time by using testimonies from celebrities who endorse their products or services.

The level of social proof generated in the two cases just discussed also softened the opposition. In Stacey's case, the lead detective was a supporter of hers from the very beginning of the case. In the Scott sisters' case, the prosecutor, as well as one of the men who was robbed, supported their release.

The levels of social proof these two cases generated are extremely difficult and should not be looked at as a means to your own victory, because doing so would be setting yourself up with an unreasonable expectation. Very few cases attract the media or public's interest. However, you can still use the principle of social proof to your advantage in your own campaign, on a smaller scale. Before addressing that, it is best to soften your opposition with a direct approach.

Softening the Opposition

It is important that you make every attempt possible to neutralize anyone who may oppose your request for clemency. As discussed in Chapter 2, the sentencing judge and prosecutor will be contacted and asked to give an opinion about you and your case. That is why you should attempt to neutralize them first, by sending them each a letter as well as a copy of your clemency application.

Modify the letter you wrote to the governor or clemency board, addressing it to the judge and using everything you wrote before, with a new ending—an ending that asks for a letter of recommendation instead of for clemency. Do the same with a letter to the prosecutor. Mail these at the same time you mail your original application.

Next, if asking for a commutation or other relief, you should publish a public apology to neutralize any opposition from victims. If you are requesting a pardon, based on actual innocence, you would ask for public support instead of apologizing for a crime you did not commit. Such a public announcement should be made in the appropriate section of the newspaper in the county where you were convicted. The notice should run for a week or two. It may be possible to get this done without payment if you write to the editor of the newspaper, explaining what you want to do and that you are without the funds to pay for a public notice.

Your public apology must be brief. You should state the date of the offense, the offense you were convicted of, the sentence you received, and then give a humble and sincere apology, as if offering it to a friend or family member who was deeply hurt and offended by your behavior.

Psychological Principles of Influence

There are six universal principles that are used in sales and advertising to influence the decisions of others: social proof, liking, reciprocation, commitment and consistency, authority, and scarcity. These principles will be of benefit to you once you gain an understanding of how you can apply them in your campaign. Below is a brief summary of each principle.

- ***Social Proof***
  As we discussed earlier, people often look for social cues to determine whether some behavior is acceptable or unacceptable in a certain situation. When people see or hear of others they know doing something, they tend to follow suit.

- ***Liking***
  This principle is obvious. We associate with people we like, and our associations with either good things or bad things influence how others feel about us. And we tend to agree and comply with the requests of people we know and like. We like those who have similar backgrounds, interests, and support us, compliment us, make us laugh and are fun to be around, and who are physically attractive. If people like you, they will support you and comply with your requests. If they don't, they wont.

- ***Reciprocation***
  If you do something for someone, he or she will feel obligated to return the favor. You can see this principle working, in one way or another, in all professional and personal relationships. If a relationship or interaction becomes unbalanced, the person giving the most will feel as though they are being taken advantage of and will soon become resentful. By knowing that this principle works below a conscious level, you should enter into every social interaction giving, not looking for what you are going to get, because whatever you give will be returned. Of course, this principle can and will be abused by others, so you should look to the person's prior relationships before becoming too involved with him or her. You will learn much about people by the social proof they generate in their life.

- ***Commitment and Consistency***
  Once someone has made a choice or taken a stand, he or she will feel personal and interpersonal pressures to maintain consistency with that previous commitment. Instead of letting their beliefs guide their actions, people often observe their actions in order to determine their beliefs. This is why the foot-in-the-door technique is effective—most people who have first complied with a small request or made a minor purchase will also comply later with a larger request or purchase.

- ***Authority***
  This principle is based on the importance people give to information from authority figures, experts, professionals, or celebrities. Studies have shown that people tend to obey authority figures even when the authorities' requests made no sense or conflicted with the test subjects' own personal beliefs. This is why expert witnesses are used at trials, and why advertisers use celebrity endorsements or testimonies from experts in their ads.

- ***Scarcity***
  People tend to value things more when they are rare and hard to get. When people fear they may miss out, they will give an opportunity or object more value. Advertisers use this principle all the time with "limited time only" offers.

These six principles are used every day to influence people's decisions. And they obviously have scores of applications in clemency campaigns. But this information will not be nearly as useful without an understanding of how we determine our own value and the value of those with whom we wish to form alliances.

Attracting Support

It is a universal human trait to seek out people who provide us with feelings and benefits we ourselves desire, and avoid those who cause costs to our reputation or pocketbook.

What follows is a list of visual, behavioral, and social cues that convey value when displayed to others, which will help you attract support to your clemency campaign.

> ***Visual Cues***
> We are judged on the basic and most fundamental of things, one of these being our appearance. We automatically make a value assessment whenever we first see someone. For the purposes of attracting support, it is important that you make a good first impression.
>
> Although being a prisoner will limit you somewhat, it is no excuse for not making use of what is available to look your best. There are a few small things you can do to make a big difference in how you appear to others. For example, if you are well-groomed, smile, and carry yourself with confidence, you will make good impressions. You may feel insecure about how you look, and think that there is nothing you can do to change, but this is not true. If you are willing to make a few changes, you can make significant improvements to your appearance. One of the easiest and most fundamental things to affect a change is your hairstyle. For the purposes of your clemency campaign, you want to look like an average citizen, up to date but not flashy or flamboyant. The best example of this look is a hairstyle worn by one of the anchors from your local news channel, whose styles fit the time period and are inoffensive to residents of your region. If you have facial hair, consider shaving it off, as psychological studies have shown that many people feel it connotes untrustworthiness.
>
> Whatever choices you make about your appearance, when you take pictures for promotional material/media and to send with your clemency application, take extra care with your grooming to look your best for the circumstances. Displaying a friendly smile will be invaluable to your future efforts, because smiling conveys openness, friendliness, and confidence.
>
> ***Behavioral Cues***
> Your behavior while in prison is a reflection of how you would behave on the outside, after your release. As you will remember from the Stacey Lannert story, she conveyed her value through the lifestyle she lived in prison, training dogs and working with children in an outreach program. Do likewise. Start

cultivating a lifestyle that conveys certain positive traits you possess, such as social intelligence, kindness, sincerity, love and commitment, orientation to family, confidence, generosity, ambition, charisma, love of fun, positive attitude, creativity, sense of humor, unreactivity, resourcefulness, independence, leadership qualities, etc.

Social Cues
It is important to develop and maintain interpersonal relationships. Family and friends can be of great help to you, writing letters of support and discussing your cause with others. The more people who spread your name and discuss your cause, the more attention it will receive, resulting in your accumulation of valuable resources that are paramount to running a successful campaign. You need people who will vouch for your character, enabling others to believe that supporting your cause is the right thing to do. In doing so, you generate social proof, attracting yet more supporters to your campaign.

We will discuss, in the next section, a few ways to generate social proof via social media for those who have outside resources. If you do not have any family or friends, you may want to consider placing an online pen pal ad to meet people.

Campaign Platform and Promotional Strategies

To start building a campaign platform, it will be necessary for you to have outside assistance from family and/or friends—people who can set up a website, electronic petition to gather signatures of support, social network profiles, a blog, etc. There is a virtually unlimited number of things that can be done when mounting a campaign for your freedom.

As mentioned earlier, if you do not have any family or friends, you may want to consider an online pen pal ad to meet people who may be willing to help you. There are also many businesses that exist solely to assist prisoners, and will charge a reasonable price to set up some kind of social platform for you (e.g., website, social network profile, electronic petition, blog, etc.). It may, however, be more practical and economical for you to start a letter-writing campaign instead, in which you send letters to people in positions to help you, such as your state representatives, senators, community leaders, pastors, and known activists. This is what the Scott sisters' family and friends did, and it brought them great success.

Every campaign will be different, with its own unique set of facts and circumstances. What works for someone else may not necessarily work for you. Of course, financial resources play a major part in any campaign. This is where the money you have saved—instead of spending it frivolously—can be used.

Here is a list of some tools to consider using in your campaign.

Websites
A website can be used to present information about you and your cause, post updates about your case, attract supporters, and collect donations. Particularly

if you have evidence of actual innocence, a website is ideal for presenting that evidence for the world to see, in the form of images, documents, and text. But if you do not have someone with experience and skills to set up and maintain a website, as well as to respond to the e-mails that will come in response to your online presentation, it will not be helpful.

Petition Websites

Your free-world supporters can create a petition to collect electronic signatures from public. These petitions are free and easy to set up, and require no effort to maintain. When you reach the desired number of signatures, the supporter who set up the petition can print the full petition and mail it to the governor or clemency board. Most of these sites offer services to promote your petition for you, at a price as low as a few dollars a day, encouraging people to put their names to your cause.

Online Social Networks

You can have a profile set up on an online social network to convey your personality via displays of your positive traits. Most social networks are free and allow you to link to websites, petitions, and blogs. But you will be a pebble in a pond without someone to publicize and maintain it on a near-daily basis. Many of these networks offer paid services to promote yourself to large numbers of members, as well.

Blogs

A blog can be used to post small amounts of information about you and your cause, but its main purpose is as a place for stories and anecdotes that give visitors an impression of who you are. You can post images to a blog also, which is useful if you draw or paint. Blogs are almost always free, easy to set up, and do not need to be maintained on a daily basis. The most effective use for a blog in a clemency campaign is for posting writings and other content that convey positive traits you want people to know you possess. If you are writing, use stories and anecdotes from your life that are touching, embarrassing, interesting, or humorous, making sure that whatever you blog about effectively displays your individual humanity, so the visitors to your blog will be able to view you as a *person*, not merely a prisoner. Refer to the principles outlined in the Social History, Self-development and Personal Transformation, and Goals sections of Chapter 4 for a reminder of how best to accomplish this.

Blogs that are updated frequently stand the best chance of being found and read. If you cannot keep a blog regularly updated with new content, you should post at least four or five entries—stories, anecdotes, drawings, etc.—that together give a solid impression of who you are as a person. You can still link to this blog from other websites and social media tools, making it an extension of your overall platform.

Promotional Ads

You can publicly spread your name and promote your cause via classified ads, online banner ads, billboards, and online pen pal/legal ads.

To those proclaiming innocence, there are also websites that give free ads and pages for presenting the facts and evidence in your case.

Demonstrations

Your supporters can hold vigils, fundraisers, and petition-signing drives, as well as conduct TV, radio, and Internet interviews on your behalf. They can also create flyers/pamphlets to pass out at public events, promoting your online platform.

There is no limit to the number of things you and your supporters can do, if you have the resources.

In this chapter we discussed clemency campaigns and promotional strategies. The prisoner who has the most supporters and financial resources will be able to take advantage of the tools available. The prisoner who has few supporters and no financial resources will be limited. However this does not mean the prisoner cannot run a successful clemency campaign, because it is not the size of the dog in the fight, it is the size of the fight in the dog. Stay focused and do not let setbacks or slow progress discourage you.

<6> SOCIAL INTELLIGENCE, COMMUNICATION SKILLS, AND CLEMENCY HEARING

Social Intelligence

People possessing social intelligence have a deeper understanding of how to gain and maintain a high social status, demonstrating their value to others and intuitively avoiding lower-value behavior. They have the ability to infer what others are thinking and feeling, by reading nonverbal cues. This ability lets them respond to the thoughts and emotions of others in the most useful and appropriate manner. Nothing about social interactions is confusing to those who are socially intelligent. Instead, everything is obvious, giving them an advantage throughout the social interactions they engage in.

Social intelligence is not difficult to acquire, it only takes practice—regular observation of people interacting. In time, the keen observer will be able to trust that everything is as he or she intuitively perceives them to be.

We all see things, but because we do not have a clear, logical frame of reference, we dismiss what we perceive as unreliable assumptions. More often than not, we fail to see things because our perception is clouded by expectations. And one of the most powerful expectations is formed by a desire to see a particular outcome realized.

For example, suppose Johnny is issued a conduct violation for destroying the mattress in his prison cell. He is called into the office of the disciplinary officer to give a statement. As Johnny begins talking, the officer turns her body toward him, giving him her full attention. When he explains to her that the mattress was already ripped open when he moved into the cell, she scratches her head, rubs her eye, shifts her body, looks away to pick up a pen, and starts writing. Johnny continues to talk until she interrupts him by reading her finding of guilty. He is sanctioned: sixty days without contact visits, ninety dollars for the cost of a new mattress.

Angry and reactive, Johnny heads from the disciplinary office directly to the phone, determined to get a visit before his visiting restrictions start. He dials his girlfriend's number several times before she finally accepts the call. Johnny explains his situation and asks her to come visit. She hesitates, then says, "I'll… try to come up, but… I can't make any promises… My car hasn't been running right… But I do miss you."

On visiting day, Johnny skips recreation, showers, shaves, fixes his hair just so, and waits to be called for his visit. But his girlfriend never shows up. Johnny tries to call and find out why she didn't show up, but she never answers. Feeling rejected and agitated, he goes to eat dinner, has a disagreement with another prisoner that ends with flying fists. Off to segregation goes Johnny.

Suppose Johnny were socially intelligent. Reading the disciplinary officer's nonverbal cues—eye blocking, body shifts, and so on—he would have stopped talking instead of wasting time and energy trying to convince her. After her finding of guilty, he would have remained unreactive, said with a smile, "Thank you for your time," and gone back to his cell. There, he would have made a written request to appeal the decision, since, on the day he moved into the cell, an officer made a record of the mattress's poor condition. Johnny's conduct violation would most likely have been dismissed and expunged at a later date.

When he asked his girlfriend to visit and she said, "I'll... try to come up," he would have interpreted her response to mean, "No, I don't feel like visiting you," and gone to recreation instead of pinning his hopes on her coming to see him.

Johnny would have recognized that since his girlfriend wasn't going to get to see him for sixty days, she should have found a way to come visit him. Why? Because when we love and care about someone, sixty days without seeing them is a very long time. Her response wasn't appropriate for the situation.

In both examples, the disciplinary officer and the girlfriend gave signals of disinterest. Through nonverbal cues, people will unconsciously indicate disinterest with avoidance or distancing behavior, such as avoiding eye contact, turning or leaning away, crossing their arms, blocking their eyes, and other tactics. Through verbal cues, people show their disinterest by using many pauses and being hesitant to commit, avoiding absolutes, and giving short noncommittal responses like, "I'll... try to send you some money but I can't make any promises," or, "I'll... try to visit but can't say for sure I'll make it." Disinterested people will infrequently answer their phone when you call, and respond to your letters in an irregular fashion.

Even when receiving indicators of disinterest, socially intelligent people will remain unreactive, work to preserve comfort with those being interacted with, and pretend not to notice giveaway nonverbal cues during the communication. Socially intelligent people use their skills to meet people. They create opportunities and use as many resources as possible to help them accomplish their goals in life, instead of wasting time and energy interacting with those who are not interested in them or their causes.

Communication Skills

We communicate every day with our words, with the tone of our voice, and with our body language. But before we even open our mouths, people form impressions of us based on our body language: postures, hand gestures, and facial expressions.

Poor posture is one sign people interpret as indicative of low confidence. But it can be corrected with a basic posture exercise known as the wall stance.

To do this exercise, find a wall and stand with your back against it. Your heels, buttocks, and shoulders need to be touching the wall.

Slide your hand behind your back and make sure there isn't a lot of room between the small of your back and the wall. Stay in this position for at least a minute.

Now walk around, maintaining this posture. It will feel strange until you get used to it and commit it to memory. Do this exercise daily, until the body posture becomes habitual. You should consciously check yourself from to time to make sure your body is in alignment and you are not slouching. This will speak volumes about you to officials at your clemency hearing, without you having to say one word out loud.

There is a simple way to read the body language of others as well as be aware of our own: the limbic system, a complex network in the brain, which controls our basic emotional responses. When we feel threatened—whether physically or psychologically—the limbic system alerts the nervous system to alleviate the threat. The body responds in one of three ways: freeze, flight, or fight. If you watch an animal respond to a potential threat, the first thing it will do is hold still, listening intently. Once the threat is fully realized, the animal either flees (takes flight) or turns to fight. These three responses can be perceived in human behavior, through nonverbal cues, also called *tells*.

For the purposes of this book, only flight response is of interest. It is most apparent in people's avoidance, distancing, and pacifying behaviors. Having already dealt with the first two, we will move on to the subject of pacifying behavior.

When people feel anxious, the limbic system automatically alerts the nervous system to pacify the discomfort. And since the face and neck are physical locations with many, many nerve endings, people are apt to touch or rub these areas in response to the limbic system's signal.

If you are paying attention, in real time, you will see these tells immediately proceeding something you say or do to make the person you are speaking with uncomfortable. As their discomfort increases, you will see a flurry of these tells, which will let you know when to adjust your body language, eye contact, tone of voice, or words, to preserve or restore comfort with the person being interacted with.

Through practice, honing your observation skills to read tells, you will intuitively know how to lead a conversation to get the outcome you want.

Our voices are our identities. They tell people (literally and figuratively) who we are, how we feel about ourselves, and what we believe. Five of the most common problems people have when speaking with others are: talking in a low or soft voice, talking too rapidly, talking in a monotonous voice, using pausers, and talking in a manner that makes statements sound like questions. The following will help you identify which one of these problems, if any, you have when talking with others, along with simple exercises to correct it.

Talking in a Low or Soft Voice

If you are soft-spoken, the problem you may have is that the volume of your voice sounds louder in your head than it actually is.

A thought exercise may correct this problem. Close your eyes and picture a large volume knob. Visualize turning the volume up a little over halfway. Now practice talking at this volume whenever you engage someone in conversation. If it's someone you talk to daily and they notice the change, you will know you have corrected the problem.

Talking Too Rapidly

If you talk very rapidly, you are probably hard to understand and give others the impression that you are nervous, lack confidence, and believe you must get everything out before people stop listening and ignore what you have to say. To address this problem (and to make better impressions in the process), consciously slow down and speak in a calm, slow voice. To yourself, practice saying in an even-paced, commanding voice, "I am comfortable, confident, and command the attention of others when I speak." Do this exercise daily until you get the results you want.

Talking in a Monotonous Voice

If you speak in an unvarying tone, turn on your TV or radio and find someone who has a dynamic voice you like. Pay close attention to it—its volume, pitch, speed, rhythm, and inflections put on certain words.

Now find a story or piece of writing, and practice reading it out loud while modeling the voice of the person you would like to sound like. Continue to practice this until you develop a dynamic and compelling voice of your own, which pulls people in, commanding their attention.

Pausers

Is your speech littered with "um"s, "er"s, "like"s, "you know"s, or other meaningless conversational filler? People use these pausers in an unconscious attempt to hold the attention of others while trying to think of what to say next, or to try to elicit understanding or agreement. Either purpose conveys insecurity.

To correct this problem, you will need to develop comfort with the momentary pauses that arise during conversation. Being consciously aware of the message of insecurity you are sending to others should be enough of a motivator for you to eliminate most pausers from your speech.

Statements That Sound like Questions

Do you raise your voice at the end of declarative statements? If so, your statements sound more like questions, a habit that makes you sound unsure of yourself and what you declare to be factual.

To correct this problem, take a declarative statement and practice saying it with confidence, as if you believe every word without question.

As you focus on your posture, body language, and voice, you will notice a day-to-day difference in the impressions you make on others, by seeing how they respond to you, as well as make a good impression at your clemency hearing.

Frames, Frame Control, and Reframing

Frames are the contexts in which people perceive a person, thing, or situation. They are ways of looking at the world. Controlling a frame means keeping the subject (or point of view) going in the direction a person wants it to go, during an interaction, to get the outcome he or she wants. The person who controls the frame controls the interaction.

It is possible to change one's own frame, a frame set by someone else, or a frame that has been allowed to develop in a certain conversation or situation. This change is referred to as *reframing*, which means to transform the meaning of something by putting it into a different context than the one it was originally.

Understanding how to set a frame, how to control it, and how to reframe or, if necessary, take over another's frame, will be of great help in the context of your clemency hearing. With such knowledge, you will be able to guide the hearing so that you generate social proof (everyone's attention will be focused on you), make a good impression, demonstrate high self-esteem, and maintain the overall focus on your positive self-development.

In the next section, we will see how to prepare for a clemency hearing, and how to use these tools to your benefit.

Clemency Hearing

The purpose of a clemency hearing is for state officials to review physical evidence supporting innocence (if this is the claim you are making), to make credibility determinations of witnesses, and to make a personal assessment of the prisoner asking for clemency relief, to determine whether he or she has been rehabilitated and can be released without posing a threat to society.

You will need to prepare a tight eight- to ten-minute routine, one that presents all information the governor or clemency board will be expecting to hear from you (refer back to Chapters 2 – 4). Think of your routine in terms of a framed picture. What do you want this picture to convey about you? How do you want others to perceive it?

Put the story you told in your personal letter (refer to Chapter 4) into that frame, only as a shorter version.

When you have your brief version written down, you will need to rehearse it. Practice how you will deliver it at your hearing. You *must* rehearse it out loud, over and over, focusing on your delivery, until it feels natural and is congruent with your body language, tone of voice, and facial expressions. At your hearing, you will be expected to answer questions. This will be your opportunity to set your desired frame, which should serve to answer all the questions the interviewer will likely ask you—what you did, how you did it, and why—before he or she has a chance to ask them. Anticipating these questions and the answers you will provide for them allows you to control the frame throughout your hearing, predetermining what and how content is presented.

The purpose of setting your own frame, and controlling it, is to fully tell your story without being interrupted. Once a question is asked, answer it, and immediately go into your story. As long as you are talking and moving from subject to subject, giving more and more relevant details about yourself, the interviewer will allow you to keep speaking. At the same time, you are conveying your personality, demonstrating your value, and focusing the attention of the entire room on you, generating social proof. Attention follows value. If all eyes are on you and everyone is interested in what you have to say, the interviewer knows it would be rude, and possibly counterproductive to interrupt.

If you do happen to be interrupted by a question, answer it, and lead back to the point at which you were interrupted. However, if the question asked seems to be intended to clarify or move your story along, give an answer, then stop addressing the subject being discussed, and move on to the next. In this way you control the information and how it is being presented. Do not bring a subject up again unless explicitly asked about it.

It is inevitable that certain questions will be asked, and, if not answered appropriately, will lead to a bad impression being made. But if you can anticipate what these questions will be, you can come up with a contingency plan. For example, if you were to be asked, "How much time served is enough for this crime?" an appropriate answer would be, "Enough time has been served when the emotional or psychological issue that led to the crime being committed has been found and corrected." Then you would give information that demonstrates how you identified your issues, what you did to address them, and what the process of correcting them consisted of. One thing to remember is to *always* take responsibility for your behavior. The moment it seems as though you are placing blame—on your mother, absent father, drugs, alcohol, the victim, whoever—they will use it as justification to deny your clemency application.

When you refer to the victim(s) in your case, use their first name. When you refer to a victim by his or her first name, it shows that you are identifying a person, not a distant stranger or object. Also, when recounting details of your crime, never refer to the plural pronoun *we*. Doing so suggests that you and the victim(s), or you and your codefendant(s), were in mutual agreement, it suggests a togetherness, whereas use of the singular pronoun *I* suggests you're acknowledging responsibility for your own behavior.

When you finish your presentation, simply thank the officials for the opportunity to speak and for their careful consideration of your application, then be quiet. Wait and watch for any tells from those overseeing, as well as from those attending, the hearing, to determine how your presentation was received. Stay confident, maintain eye contact, and nod to anyone who gives you eye contact.

Conclusion

You may refer to the appropriate appendix for the timeline, if any, your state adheres to when determining the outcome of clemency proceedings.

Obtaining clemency relief is difficult, and the relief you seek may not be immediately forthcoming. No matter the outcome of this stage, take what you have learned, using the tools you have gained from this book to fully apply yourself to future endeavors. As you do, you will accomplish the goals you set. You *will* secure another chance at freedom.

APPENDIX

At the time of publication, the contact information listed in the following pages was correct. Offices do move, however, and phone numbers may change, so you are encouraged to verify the details before making contact by phone or mail.

ALABAMA

Applicable Forms of Executive Clemency

The governor of Alabama only has the authority to grant reprieves and commutations from the death penalty. The authority granted to the Alabama Board of Pardon and Paroles by the state legislature does not include commutations or conditional pardons. Therefore the sole relief available to most Alabama prisoners is parole.

Eligibility

After a prisoner's sentencing, the Board prepares a file, calculating the earliest date parole may be granted by law.

Section 15-22-28 of the Alabama Administrative Code states, "The Board shall not grant parole to any prisoner who has not served at least one third or 10 years of his sentence, whichever is the lesser, except by unanimous affirmative vote of the Board."

If the Board denies parole and schedules the next consideration more than three years from the denial, the review committee may consider an earlier scheduling, but such review may not start earlier than twenty-four months after the Board's initial denial of parole.

After serving a minimum of five years, a prisoner may initiate contact with the institutional parole officer, or with the Board's central office, and ask for a review of the prisoner's progress, to determine if the eligibility to schedule an earlier parole consideration has been met.

Rescheduling may be granted for: a prognosis of imminent death, a recommendation from the prosecuting attorney or sentencing judge in the prisoner's case, or other circumstances that demonstrate a likelihood of the prisoner's success on parole. Cause, however, cannot be justified simply because the prisoner has been following the rules while incarcerated. If, after an inquiry or investigation, the officer or agent is persuaded that an earlier consideration for parole would be appropriate, the matter will be referred to the review committee by that officer or agent's submission of a report detailing the reasons for the recommendation.

Application Process

Prisoners do not apply for parole consideration through an administrative request, considerations are determined by the eligibility criteria mentioned above.

On set dates, the Board holds public hearings for parole considerations. Prisoners are not required to retain counsel, although they may do so if they choose. Prisoners are afforded an opportunity to give reasons why they should be granted parole. Write to the address below for more information.

Alabama State Board of Pardons and Parole
301 South Ripley Street
Montgomery, AL 36130
Telephone: (334) 242-8700

ALASKA

Applicable Forms of Executive Clemency

The governor of Alaska has the authority to grant pardons, reprieves, commutations, and to suspend and remit fines and forfeitures, in whole or in part, for any offense against the State of Alaska or the Territory of Alaska.

Eligibility

All prisoners are eligible to apply, but certain conditions must be met in order for an application to be considered. No application regarding the conviction or sentence for which clemency is being sought will be considered prior to judgment and commitment, during an appeal, or during any form of postconviction relief.

Application Process

Prisoners start the process by first completing an Eligibility Determination Form and sending it to the Alaska Board of Parole Office. When eligibility is determined, a clemency application form will be provided to the prisoner. Requests for Eligibility Determination Forms should be requested from and submitted to the Alaska Board of Parole.

When an eligibility determination is made, and an actual clemency application is sent back to the Board Office, the application is investigated, and a summary is prepared and submitted to the governor's Executive Clemency Advisory Committee (ECAC).

The ECAC consists of the lieutenant governor, the attorney general or a representative from the department of law, and a public member. The Committee meets as often as necessary to review pending applications.

Following the consideration and review of an application, the ECAC prepares a summary and recommendation, and submits it to the governor, along with the prisoner's entire file. The governor then reviews the case, makes a decision, and notifies the prisoner of the decision. The entire process, from the time of submission of an application to a decision by the governor, often takes up to one full year, but may take longer, depending on the circumstances.

Some Factors to Consider

The Board considers the entire history of a prisoner during the clemency process, and prisoners are required to sign waivers permitting the Board's investigation of their employment and personal history (and medical conditions, if pertinent).

The comments of the sentencing judge, prosecuting attorney, and victim(s) are solicited and considered, when available, by the ECAC and the governor.

In a commutation application, the amount of time the prisoner has already served is of particular importance.

Eligibility Determination Forms

The clemency process may be started by requesting Eligibility Determination Forms from the address below.

Attention: Clemency Determination
550 West 7th Avenue, Suite #601
Anchorage, AK 99501

ARIZONA

Applicable Forms of Executive Clemency

The governor of Arizona has the authority to grant pardons, reprieves, and commutations after conviction for any offense, except impeachment. These may be granted upon conditions, restrictions, and limitations the governor deems proper.

Eligibility

A prisoner must have served a minimum of two years on the current offense(s), and may not be within one year of his or her parole eligibility (or mandatory release date for sentences longer than three years) to be considered for a commutation of sentence. The only exceptions are special orders by the court, sentences of three years or less, or imminent danger of death. Future sentences (consecutive terms) will not be considered for reduction.

Application Process

The Board of Executive Clemency has exclusive authority to recommend reprieves, commutations, paroles, and pardons. No reprieve, commutation, or pardon may be granted by the governor unless it has first been recommended by the Board.

All applications are presented to the chairman of the Board, and the Board will send the application with its recommendation to the governor. The file will include documentation of the victim(s) or any family of the victim(s) having been notified.

After a hearing providing the victim(s), the prosecuting attorney, and the presiding judge an opportunity to be heard, the Board may make a recommendation to the governor for commutation of sentence after finding, by clear and convincing evidence, that the sentence imposed is clearly excessive based on: the nature of the offense, the record of the prisoner, and a substantial probability that, when released, the prisoner will conform his or her conduct to the requirements of the law.

Any unanimous Board recommendation for a commutation that is not acted on by the governor within ninety days from the date submitted will automatically become effective.

The clemency process may be started by requesting forms from the address below.

Arizona Board of Executive Clemency
1645 West Jefferson, Suite #101
Phoenix, AZ 85007
Telephone: (602) 542-5656

ARKANSAS

Applicable Forms of Executive Clemency

The governor of Arkansas has the authority to grant pardons, reprieves, and commutations after conviction. The governor relies on the recommendation of Arkansas's Post Prison Transfer Board (PPTB), and will not review a clemency application that hasn't previously been reviewed by the PPTB.

Eligibility

All prisoners are eligible to apply, but certain conditions must be met in order for an application to be considered. A prisoner who is denied clemency will not be eligible to reapply for four years from the date of denial. If the prisoner is serving a sentence of life without parole for a crime other than capital murder, the eligibility for reapplication is six years from the date of denial. If the prisoner is serving a sentence of life without parole for a capital murder conviction, he or she may not reapply for eight years from the date of denial.

Application Process

Grounds for which a clemency application may be granted are: to correct an injustice that occurred during a prisoner's trial, to reduce an excessive sentence, a life-threatening medical condition, or the prisoner's exemplary institutional adjustment and the ends of justice having been achieved.

At least four Board members will individually review a prisoner's clemency application and vote to recommend that clemency be granted, denied, or scheduled for a hearing (a hearing is required for all death penalty cases). After its review or hearing, the Board will submit to the governor a report detailing its investigation, any relevant information about the prisoner, and its recommendation to grant or deny clemency.

Once the governor sets an execution date in a death penalty case, any clemency application in that case must be filed no later than forty days before the scheduled execution date. A late application will not be accepted. Once an execution date is set, the Institutional Release Service Office notifies the prisoner and his or her attorney of the deadline. If the fortieth day is a Saturday, Sunday, or a holiday, an application filed on the next business day will be accepted.

The clemency process may be started by obtaining an application from the Institutional Release Officer (IRO) at the applicant's prison, or by writing to the address below.

Assistant for Executive Clemency
Office of the Governor
State Capitol Building
Little Rock, AR 72201
Telephone: (501) 682-8184

CALIFORNIA

Applicable Forms of Executive Clemency

The governor of California has the authority to grant pardons, reprieves, and commutations after conviction, notwithstanding if a prisoner applying for a commutation has been convicted of two or more felonies in separate proceedings. In such an instance, a majority of the California Supreme Court must vote to approve the governor's grant of clemency.

Eligibility

All prisoners are eligible to apply for a commutation of sentence. Any other form of clemency is dependent upon the circumstances of each particular case.

Application Process

The clemency process is started by sending a letter to the governor's office requesting clemency forms. The letter should include: prisoner's name (including any aliases) and DOC ID number, the county and case number of conviction, the date and circumstances of the offense(s), the date of prisoner's commitment to the Department of Corrections, and the reason why clemency is being requested.

The governor's Legal Affairs Staff will review the letter and send the prisoner Application for Executive Clemency and Notice of Intention to Apply for Executive Clemency forms. When the Application and Notice of Intention forms are received, the prisoner must complete the Application for Executive Clemency and have it notarized. The Notice of Intention to Apply for Executive Clemency must be sent, via regular or certified mail, to the district attorney of the county where the prisoner was originally convicted.

The Acknowledgment of Receipt portion of the Notice of Intention form must be completed and signed by the district attorney. The Application and the Notice of Intention forms must then be submitted to the governor's office.

When the formal Application is received, the governor refers it to the Board of Prison Terms (BPT). The BPT will conduct an investigation to determine if the prisoner meets the standards set forth in California Penal Code, Section 485.05, which states, "During the period of rehabilitation the person shall live an honest and upright life, shall conduct himself or herself with sobriety and industry, shall exhibit a good moral character, and shall conform to and obey the laws of the land."

When the investigation is completed, the case is presented to the executive board of the BPT to decide if a recommendation to the governor for a commutation would be appropriate. The prisoner is notified when the BPT's executive board is considering his or her case, and given the opportunity to forward any additional information.

The prisoner is not permitted to attend the hearing. The Application, investigation report, and the board's recommendation, thereafter, are sent to the governor. Notification of the hearing's result is also sent to the prisoner.

The governor reviews the information and decides whether to grant or deny the prisoner's clemency application. There is no specific length of time for the completion of the clemency process.

The clemency process may be started by requesting forms from the address below.

Legal Affairs Secretary
Governor's Office
Sacramento, CA 95814
Telephone: (916) 445-1841

COLORADO

Applicable Forms of Executive Clemency

The Colorado Constitution, Article IV, Section 7, states, "The governor shall have the power to grant reprieves, commutations and pardons after conviction for all offenses except treason, and except in case of impeachment, subject to such regulations as may be prescribed by law relative to the manner of applying for pardons, but be shall in every case where he may exercise this power, send to the general assembly at its first session thereafter, a transcript of the petition, all proceedings, and reasons for his action."

Eligibility Restrictions

A prisoner who has committed a violent crime against a peace officer (i.e., assault on a law enforcement officer, riot, etc.) is not eligible.

A prisoner applying for clemency must be in a facility of confinement such as a prison, jail, community placement, private or public contract facility, or out-of-state facility. If the prisoner is within fifteen months of parole eligibility, he or she is not eligible to apply for clemency.

A prisoner serving a single life sentence must have served one third of his or her sentence, or ten full years, whichever is less. If serving a life sentence with consecutive sentences which have been adjusted by the Department of Corrections, or legislative action, he or she must serve ten full years before being eligible for a commutation.

A prisoner serving a sentence other than that mentioned in this section must serve one third of his or her actual sentence, or ten full calendar years, whichever is less.

If a prisoner was convicted of any code of penal discipline class I or II violation(s) within a two year period prior to submitting an application, or is housed in administrative segregation, he or she is not eligible for a commutation.

No prisoner is eligible for a commutation who was on probation at the time the crime being proposed for a commutation was committed.

Any parole violator who has been charged with and convicted of a new crime is not eligible to apply for a commutation, but is eligible to apply for a commutation of the new sentence provided he or she meets the current eligibility criteria.

A prisoner who has pending charges or appeals, or has not exhausted all other judicial remedies, is not eligible for clemency review.

Waiver of Ineligibility Criteria

The governor and the Department of Corrections' director may grant a waiver of ineligibility criteria in cases involving a medical emergency, or for compelling cases that demonstrate catastrophic medical and/ or mental health issues, or a unique situation (i.e., heroism, severe sentence disparity, or rehabilitation).

A prisoner may reapply after four years from receipt of official notification of a denial from the governor or the governor's clemency coordinator. Cases not reviewed, or tabled, are terminated within one year of the date of application.

Application Process

A prisoner may start the application process for a commutation with the assistance of a Department of Corrections' case manager. He or she must complete an Executive Clemency Advisory Board (ECAB) Application Eligibility Criteria for Commutation of Sentence & Character Certificate.

The attachments to be included with an application are: a personal letter to the governor stating specific reasons and circumstances for requesting clemency; a Performance Review Summary (PRS) conducted within the ninety days prior to the prisoner's clemency request; an Admission Data Summary and Diagnostic Summary completed at the time of the prisoner's arrival at DOC; psychological and psychiatric reports that include diagnostic information from clinical staff or contractors; reports of disciplinary actions and sanctions (including investigative reports, if applicable); the prisoner's most recent time computation; a current FBI record of arrest; detainers and notifications requests, or other pertinent law enforcement communications; any pre-sentence investigation report and/ or offense report; any reports of adjustment to community placement (if applicable); a current report containing a diagnosis, prognosis, and recommendations of any existing serious medical or mental health issues; as well as any additional documents, references, or exhibits that would assist the governor in making an informed decision.

Copies of the completed application are sent to the sentencing judge and district attorney in the judicial district where the conviction was obtained. Colorado law requires that the ECAB obtain comments from the appropriate judge and the district attorney, if applicable; ECAB makes every attempt to contact victim(s) or family member(s) associated with the crime.

Clemency applications are routinely reviewed by ECAB for recommendation. The governor has final discretion to grant, refuse, or table any clemency application.

An application may take six to twelve months to process. The prisoner's case manager will process the prisoner's application with the assistance of the Department of Corrections' offender services. The governor's clemency coordinator will notify the prisoner of the governor's final decision.

The clemency process may be started by requesting forms from an institutional case manager, or requesting the forms from the address below.

Executive Chambers
136 State Capitol
Denver, CO 80203
Telephone: (303) 866-2471

CONNECTICUT

Applicable Forms of Executive Clemency

The Connecticut Board of Pardons and Paroles has the authority to grant pardons, and commutations, conditioned, provisional or absolute, after conviction for any offense against the State of Connecticut.

Eligibility

A prisoner serving a sentence of eight years or more may apply to the Board if he or she has served five years. If serving a sentence of less than eight years, the prisoner may apply to the Board after serving half of his or her sentence.

Application Process

The Board holds two hearings per year for prisoners: one in May and one in November. The deadline for the May docket is March 15th, and September 15th for the November docket.

The prisoner must describe specific reasons why clemency should be considered. He or she must also describe and submit evidence of extraordinary circumstances or specific exemplary conduct supporting the request for clemency. A prisoner should specify the type of clemency being sought, in the "Premise for Clemency" section of the application.

A panel of the Board prescreens applications in a businesslike fashion, selecting for further proceedings only those of merit. The applications selected are examined carefully, personal interviews are conducted, and claims are thoroughly investigated. The Board will also hold a formal hearing, which the prisoner may attend.

The clemency process may be started by requesting forms from the address below.

Pardon Unit
Board of Pardons and Paroles
55 West Main Street, Suite 520
Waterbury, CT 06702

DELAWARE

Applicable Forms of Executive Clemency

The Delaware Constitution, Article VII, Sections 1 and 2, states, "The governor shall have the power to remit fines and forfeitures and to grant reprieves, commutations of sentence and pardons, except in cases of impeachment; but no pardon... shall be granted, nor sentence commuted, except upon the recommendation in writing of a majority of the Board of Pardons, after full hearing The Board of Pardons shall be composed of the chancellor, lieutenant governor, secretary of state, state treasurer and auditor of account."

The Board of Pardons is a separate entity that has the authority to make recommendations to the governor for or against pardons, reprieves, commutations of sentence, and executive clemency. The governor may not grant a pardon or commutation in the absence of a recommendation from the Board. The governor is not bound to accept the Board's recommendation but exercises an independent judgment in all cases.

Eligibility

All prisoners are eligible to apply for a commutation of sentence. Any other form of clemency is dependent upon the circumstances of each particular case.

Application Process

Applications for a pardon or commutation are made in writing through the Secretary of State's Office, who acts as the secretary of the Board. The Board meets monthly and hears every application it receives. Prisoners may, and are encouraged to, represent themselves before the Board when their cases are scheduled for presentation. The hearings are public. Any person with an interest in the matter will normally be given an opportunity to speak. Decisions of the Board are often made in executive session where discussion and debate of the record may occur. The result is recorded and filed in the Secretary of State's Office, who in turn notifies the governor.

The Board requires those applying for a pardon or commutation to notify the judge who imposed the sentence, the attorney general, the chief of police having jurisdiction over the place where the crime occurred, and the superintendent of the Delaware State Police. This requirement may be met by writing a letter, stating that a petition for a commutation is being filed with the Secretary of State's Office and that the petition will be heard at the earliest date, as determined by the Board of Pardons. The letter must also include: prisoner' name and DOC ID number, current address, date of birth, offense(s) and date of conviction(s), and the applicant's reason(s) for applying for a pardon or commutation. A notarized affidavit of mailing must also accompany the letter, listing the names and addresses of each person notified.

The attorney general is responsible for notifying victim(s) and/or their family member(s) when a prisoner applies for a pardon or commutation. The attorney general will present the position of the victim(s). The Board requests that a legal representative from the attorney general's office attend all sessions of the Board.

The clemency process may be started by requesting forms from the address below.

Secretary of State's Office
401 Federal Street, Suite 3
Dover, DE 19901

FLORIDA

Applicable Forms of Executive Clemency

The Florida Clemency Board has the authority to grant pardons, reprieves, and commutations, and to remit fines and forfeitures. The Board, which is composed of the governor and three cabinet members, makes all final decisions regarding the granting of clemency. All forms of clemency may be granted, subject to various conditions. If the conditions are violated or breached, clemency may be revoked, returning the prisoner to his or her status prior to being granted conditional clemency relief.

Eligibility

A prisoner must have served one third of his or her sentence (or have served one half of the sentence, if serving a minimum-mandatory sentence) before being eligible for a commutation of sentence. Any other form of clemency is dependent upon the circumstances of each particular case.

Application Process

A Request for Review form must be filled out and submitted with copies of certified court documents concerning the conviction he or she is seeking a commutation of sentence for. The court's documents consists of the charging instrument (known as the state attorney information, or indictment), judgment and sentence, and all supporting information. These documents may be obtained from the clerk of the court in the county where the offense occurred.

When the request for Review is accepted, the Florida Parole Commission is required to review the case and provide an advisory recommendation for consideration to the Clemency Board. The prisoner will be notified as to whether the recommendation from the Parole Commission is favorable or unfavorable.

A formal hearing before the Clemency Board will not be scheduled unless the Request for Review is granted by the governor and one Board member, at which time the case will be referred to the Parole Commission for a full background investigation, report, and recommendation.

Any prisoner denied a Request for Review may not apply for another review for at least five years from the date of denial.

The clemency process may be started by requesting a Request for Review form from the address below.

Office of Executive Clemency
4070 Esplanade Way
Tallahassee, FL 32399
Telephone: (850) 488-2952

GEORGIA

Applicable Forms of Executive Clemency

The Georgia State Board of Pardons and Paroles has the authority to grant pardons, reprieves, and commutations after conviction for any offense against the state of Georgia.

Eligibility

All prisoners are eligible to apply. There is no minimum amount of time that a prisoner must serve before applying for a commutation of sentence. Any other form of clemency is dependent upon the circumstances of each particular case.

Application Process

The Board has not developed a standardized clemency application. It only requires that a prisoner make his or her request for clemency in writing, providing: name and DOC ID number, current address, offense(s) and date of conviction(s), and the reason(s) why clemency should be granted.

The Georgia State Board of Pardons and Parole consists of five members, appointed by the governor and confirmed by the senate. A panel of the Board prescreens clemency applications in a businesslike fashion, selecting for further proceedings only those of merit. The applications deemed meritorious are forwarded to the Board for review and decision.

For a clemency application to be granted, a majority vote (at least three of the five members) is required. Hearings are not open to the public. However, the Board encourages friends, family, and supporters of the prisoner to send correspondence in favor of clemency to assist with the Board's consideration. It takes several months for a prisoner to be notified of the Board's decision to grant or deny clemency.

The clemency process may be started by submitting a clemency application to the address below.

State Board of Pardons and Paroles
Balcony Level, East Tower
2 Martin Luther King, Jr. Drive, Southeast
Atlanta, GA 30334
Telephone: (404) 656-5651

HAWAII

Applicable Forms of Executive Clemency

The governor of Hawaii has the authority to grant pardons and commutations after conviction for any offense against the State of Hawaii.

Eligibility

All prisoners are eligible to apply. There is no minimum amount of time that a prisoner must serve before applying for a commutation of sentence. Any other form of clemency is dependent upon the circumstances of each particular case.

Application Process

The State of Hawaii has not developed a standardized clemency application. It only requires a prisoner to make his or her request for clemency in writing, providing: name and DOC ID number, current address, offense(s) and date of conviction(s), and the reason(s) why clemency should be granted.

The Hawaii Paroling Authority (HPA) reviews the application and prepares a report. This report and the HPA's recommendation are forwarded to the governor for review and decision.

The clemency process may be started by submitting a clemency application to the address below.

Paroles and Pardons Administrator
Hawaii Paroling Authority
1177 Alakea Street, Ground Floor
Honolulu, HI 96813
Telephone: (808) 587-1293

IDAHO

Applicable Forms of Executive Clemency

The Idaho Commission of Pardons and Parole has the authority to grant pardons, reprieves, and commutations for many offenses, but not for murder, voluntary manslaughter, rape, kidnapping, lewd and lascivious conduct with a minor child, nor manufacture or delivery of a controlled substance. In such cases, the Commission may only make a recommendation to the governor. No commutation of these offenses will be effective until approved by the governor. Any recommendation not approved within thirty days of the commutation hearing is deemed denied.

Eligibility

All prisoners who have been committed to the Department of Corrections for at least twelve months are eligible to apply for a commutation of sentence. Any other form of clemency is dependent upon the circumstances of each particular case. The Commission will consider any prisoner's commutation request only once per twelve month period. The Commission may consider petitions at any time, but hearings are usually scheduled during January, April, July, and October. The prisoner will not be present at a consideration hearing. A petition must be received by the Commission office on or before the first day of a quarterly session.

Application Process

A prisoner must request a Petition for Commutation form from the Commission. The form must be signed and completed according to the instructions on the form. It is limited to four pages and will be returned without consideration if longer.

The Commission's review and consideration of a petition will be conducted in executive session. Any review may be continued if additional information is needed, or if further consideration is called for. At the session's conclusion, the prisoner will be sent written notice of the Commission's decision.

The Commission schedules hearings at its discretion. Notice of a commutation hearing will be published in a newspaper of general circulation in Boise, Idaho, once a week for four consecutive weeks, immediately prior to the scheduled hearing. The prosecutor from the county in which the crime was committed will be notified.

The decision of the Commission, and supporting documents regarding a commutation, will be filed with the secretary of state. All written material considered during the decision-making process is a matter of public record, excluding information about any victim(s) and the prisoner's pre-sentence investigation report. Any dissenting votes will be a matter of public record.

The clemency process may be started by requesting either Petition for Pardon or Petition for Commutation forms from the address below.

Idaho Commission of Pardons and Parole
P.O. Box 83720
Boise, ID 83720
Telephone: (208) 334-2520

ILLINOIS

Applicable Forms of Executive Clemency

The governor of Illinois has the authority to grant pardons, reprieves, and commutations after conviction for any offense against the State of Illinois.

Eligibility

All prisoners are eligible to apply for a commutation of sentence. Any other form of clemency is dependent upon the circumstances of each particular case.

Application Process

The clemency process is started by requesting forms from the Illinois Prisoner Review Board. When the Board receives a petition for executive clemency, it is reviewed to ensure compliance with all the filing guidelines, such as sending a copy of the petition to the sentencing judge (if the judge is no longer on the bench, a copy is to be send to the chief judge in the county of conviction) and to the state's attorney in the county of conviction. If the petition is in compliance, the prisoner will be sent a docket number. He or she will also be notified in writing if additional information is required for completion of the petition.

An incomplete petition must be completed within ninety days or it is discarded. A late but completed petition is placed on the next available hearing docket. The prisoner is afforded the opportunity to have a public or non-public hearing. The Board's recommendation is forwarded to the governor within sixty days following that hearing. When the governor's decision is made, the Board will notify the prisoner. If denied clemency, the prisoner must wait one full year before reapplying, absent compelling new information.

The clemency process may be started by requesting forms from the address below.

Illinois Prisoner Review Board
319 East Madison, Suite A
Springfield, IL 62701
Telephone: (217) 782-7273

INDIANA

Applicable Forms of Executive Clemency

The governor of Indiana has the authority to grant pardons, reprieves, and commutations after conviction for any offense against the State of Indiana, except in cases of treason or impeachment, for which authority resides with the general assembly.

Eligibility

A petition for a commutation of sentence of a prisoner sentenced under IC 35-50 ("New Code"), who has been sentenced to a period of time in excess of ten years, may be considered after he or she has served one third or twenty years of the sentence, whichever comes first. A prisoner serving a life sentence ("Old Code") may be considered after he or she has served ten years.

Any other form of clemency is dependent upon the circumstances of each particular case.

A prisoner who has served his or her minimum sentence and is eligible for parole consideration is not eligible for clemency consideration.

A prisoner's petition will not be considered if he or she does not have a clear institutional record (i.e., no major conduct violations, and no more than two minor violations) for the twelve months immediately preceding the hearing.

Application Process

The clemency process is started by requesting forms from the Indiana Parole Board. The Board meets monthly to examine the merits of petitions for clemency. It reports its conclusions and recommendations to the governor in each case considered. Four months are usually required after receipt of eligible petitions before they can be considered at hearing. This allows adequate time to schedule appearances and to prepare necessary background information.

Statements of the sentencing judge and the prosecuting attorney must be included in the petition for clemency. If either is deceased or otherwise unavailable, then a statement from the successor(s) in office will be accepted. If either or both parties decline to make a statement, this fact will be noted in the petition along with the name and office of the person(s) contacted to make a statement.

An investigation of the attitudes and opinions of the community in which the crime occurred, of the victim(s) or relatives and friends of the victim(s), or friends of the prisoner may be required by the Board prior to making its recommendation to the governor.

The prisoner will be notified when and where appearances will be held, and informed of the final action taken by the governor on the petition for clemency.

The clemency process may be started by requesting a Petition for Clemency form from the address below.

Indiana Parole Board
302 West Washington Street, Room E321
Indianapolis, IN 46204

IOWA

Applicable Forms of Executive Clemency

The governor of Iowa has the authority to grant pardons, reprieves, and commutations after conviction for any offense against the State of Iowa.

Eligibility

All prisoners are eligible to apply for a commutation of sentence. Any other form of clemency is dependent upon the circumstances of each particular case.

Application Process

The clemency process is started by requesting forms from the governor's office. The governor considers the entire history of a prisoner during the clemency process, and prisoners are required to sign waivers permitting the governor's investigation of their employment history, medical and mental health issues, and personal history.

The prisoner is strongly encouraged to provide letter of recommendation from the sentencing judge, prosecutor, minister (if applicable), and any other reputable persons in the community who can attest to the moral character of the applicant. When the investigation is completed and the governor's decision is made, the prisoner will be notified.

The clemency process may be started by requesting an application from the address below.

Governor's Office
State Capitol Building
Des Moines, IA 50319
Telephone: (515) 281-5211

KANSAS

Applicable Forms of Executive Clemency

The governor of Kansas has the authority to grant pardons, reprieves, and commutations after conviction for any offense against the State of Kansas.

Eligibility

All prisoners are eligible to apply for a commutation of sentence. Any other form of clemency is dependent upon the circumstances of each particular case.

Application Process

The Kansas Parole Board is responsible for processing and reviewing applications for executive clemency. The law requires that the sentencing court and prosecuting attorney be notified of the application, and that a notice be published in the official county paper. The Board reviews pertinent records, reports, and other available information. Should a personal interview with the prisoner be required, he or she will be notified.

Upon full review the Board will submit a report, along with all information received, to the governor. The prisoner will be notified when the governor renders a decision.

The clemency process may be started by requesting Application for executive Clemency forms from the address below.

Kansas Parole Board
Landon State Office Building
900 Southwest Jackson, 4th Floor
Topeka, KS 66612
Telephone: (785) 296-3469

KENTUCKY

Applicable Forms of Executive Clemency

The governor of Kentucky has the authority to grant pardons, reprieves, and commutations, and to remit fines and forfeitures for any offense against the State of Kentucky, except in cases of treason or impeachment.

Eligibility

All prisoners are eligible to apply for a commutation of sentence. Any other form of clemency is dependent upon the circumstances of each particular case.

Application Process

There is no formal application that is specific for a commutation of sentence. A prisoner may return a completed Application for Pardon along with a written request for a commutation, listing the extenuating circumstances supporting the request.

The governor's deputy counsel reviews all applications and forwards them to the governor for final decision.

The clemency process may be started by requesting Application for Pardon forms from the address below.

Office of the Governor
700 Capitol Avenue, Suite 100
Frankfort, KY 40601
Telephone: (502) 564-2611

LOUISIANA

Applicable Forms of Executive Clemency

Upon favorable recommendation of the Louisiana Board of Pardons (BOP), the governor may grant pardons, reprieves, and commutations, and remit fines and forfeitures for any offense against the state of Louisiana.

A first-time offender convicted of any non-violent crime, aggravated battery, second degree battery, aggravated assault, mingling harmful substances, aggravated criminal damage to property, purse snatching, extortion, or illegal use of weapons or dangerous instrumentalities, who has never previously been convicted of a felony, will be pardoned automatically upon completion of his or her sentence, without a recommendation by the BOP or any action by the governor.

Eligibility

All prisoners are eligible to apply for a commutation of sentence. Any other form of clemency is dependent upon the circumstances of each particular case.

Application Process

The clemency process is started by requesting application forms from the BOP. A prisoner is required to attach a current master prison record and Time Computation/Jail Credit worksheet, and provide the signature of a classification officer verifying the conduct of the prisoner as set forth in the master prison record. No other information should be submitted until the prisoner is given notice that a hearing has been granted.

On the first Tuesday of each month, the BOP considers applications to determine whether to grant or deny the applicant a hearing. The Board consists of five electors appointed by the governor and confirmed by the senate. All actions of the Board require the favorable vote of at least four Board members.

A prisoner may be denied a hearing based on seriousness of the crime, insufficient time served on the sentence, proximity to parole or good-time date, institutional disciplinary reports, probation or parole unsatisfactory or violated, past criminal record, or any other reason determined by the Board.

If a prisoner is denied, he or she will be notified in writing of the reason(s) for denial, and may not reapply for two years from the date of denial.

If a prisoner is granted a hearing, he or she must provide \ the BOP office with proof of advertisement within ninety days from the date of notice granting a hearing. Advertisement must be published in the official journal of the parish where the offense occurred. This ad must state: "I, [prisoner's name, document number—Department of Correction number, state], have applied for clemency for my conviction for [crime] which occurred [day/month/year], in [parish/county], Louisiana. If you have any comments or wish to communicate with the Board of Pardons please call (225) 342-5421." The ad must run for three days within a thirty-day period, without expense to the Department of Public Safety and Corrections, Corrections Services, or the BOP. During this time, the prisoner may submit additional information (i.e., letters of recommendation, certificates of achievement, and employment/residence agreement).

After receipt of all required documents, the Board will set the matter for a public hearing. Thirty days prior to the set date, the Board will give written notice of the date, time, and place to the district attorney, the sheriff of the parish in which the prisoner was convicted, and the superintendent of police in the parish of New Orleans. The victim(s) and their spouse or next of kin will also be notified, unless the Board is advised that such notification is not desired.

The district attorney, the victim(s), their spouse or next of kin, and any other individuals who desire to do so, will be given a reasonable opportunity to attend the hearing. The district attorney or his or her representative, victim(s), family of the Victim(s), and a victim advocacy group, may appear before the BOP via telephone from the local district attorney's office.

Only three individuals in favor (to include the prisoner), and three in opposition (to include the victim(s)/family) will be permitted to speak at the hearing. However, there is no limit on written correspondence, either in favor of or against the prisoner's clemency request.

After the hearing, the BOP will notify the prisoner that a favorable recommendation was denied or no action was taken by the governor. The prisoner may reapply one year from the date of the denial or notice of no action.

The office of the governor will notify the prisoner if any clemency relief is granted. The prisoner may reapply for additional relief four years from the date of the notice granting relief.

The clemency process may be started by requesting application forms from the address below.

Louisiana Board of Pardons
Department of Public Safety and Corrections
P.O. Box 94304
Capitol Station
Baton Rouge, LA 70804
Telephone: (225) 342-5421

MAINE

Applicable Forms of Executive Clemency

The governor of Maine has the authority to grant pardons, reprieves, and commutations, and to remit penalties and forfeitures for any offense against the State of Maine (except in cases of treason and impeachment), with certain conditions, restrictions, and limitations as the governor may deem proper.

Eligibility

A prisoner seeking a commutation of sentence must have served at least one half of his or her original sentence (not including "good time"), or a minimum of one year of the sentence, whichever is longer. He or she must also have written confirmation, from the warden or superintendent of the penal institution where the prisoner is serving time, that the minimum time-served requirement has been met. A prisoner seeking to rectify alleged errors in the judicial system, or who is serving a life sentence, will not be heard. Any other form of clemency is dependent upon the circumstances of each particular case.

Application Process

The clemency process is started by requesting Petition for Executive Clemency forms from the Department of the Secretary of State. The prisoner must attach a certified copy of the charging instrument (known as the indictment, information, or complaint), judgment and commitment form, and docket sheet for each conviction for which clemency is being sought. These documents may be obtained from the clerk of the court in the county where the offense occurred.

Upon receipt of a completed Petition and required documents, the pardon clerk will request a background check from the state Bureau of Investigation and the Department of Motor Vehicles. The pardon board will review the petition and either grant or deny a hearing, giving notification to the prisoner in writing.

If the prisoner is granted a hearing, the Division of Probation and Parole of the Department of Corrections (DPP) will conduct a thorough background investigation and present its findings to the board of executive clemency. The investigation will include a personal interview between the prisoner and a member of the staff from DPP.

Prior to the hearing, the prisoner must publish in a newspaper a legal notice announcing that a pardon or commutation hearing will be held. The specific requirements of the legal notice will be provided to the prisoner by the Department of the Secretary of State.

Following the hearing, the board will make its recommendation to the governor, who will accept, reject, or modify it. The prisoner will be notified in writing of the governor's decision.

The clemency process may be started by requesting Petition for Executive Clemency forms from the address below.

State of Maine
Governor's Board on Executive Clemency
101 State House Station
Augusta, ME 04333
Telephone: (207) 624-7752

MARYLAND

Applicable Forms of Executive Clemency

The governor of Maryland has the authority to grant pardons, reprieves, and commutations, and to remit fines and forfeitures for any offense against the State of Maryland, except in cases of treason and impeachment.

Eligibility

All prisoners are eligible to apply for a commutation of sentence. Any other form of clemency is dependent upon the circumstances of each particular case.

Application Process

The Maryland Parole Commission has not developed a formal application for a commutation of sentence. It only requires a prisoner to submit his or her request for clemency in writing, providing: name and DOC ID number, current address, offense(s) and date of conviction(s), and the reason(s) why clemency should be granted.

The Commission reviews the application and prepares a report. This report and the Commission's recommendation are forwarded to the governor for review and decision.

The clemency process may be started by submitting a clemency application to the address below.

Maryland Parole Commission
6776 Reisterstown, Suite 307
Baltimore, MD 21215
Telephone: (410) 585-3200

MASSACHUSETTS

Applicable Forms of Executive Clemency

The governor of Massachusetts has the authority to grant pardons, reprieves, and commutations for any offense against the State of Massachusetts, except in cases of impeachment.

Eligibility

All prisoners are eligible to apply for a commutation of sentence. Any other form of clemency is dependent upon the circumstances of each particular case.

Application Process

To aid the Advisory Board of Pardons (ABP) in reviewing commutation petitions and in making its recommendations to the governor, the governor has established guidelines. Any other form of clemency will be considered upon its own set of facts and circumstances.

A prisoner seeking a commutation bears the responsibility of demonstrating, by clear and convincing evidence, that he or she has made exceptional strides toward self-development and self-improvement and would be a law-abiding citizen; or is suffering from a life-threatening illness or has a severe and chronic disability which would be mitigated by release from prison; or further incarceration would be grossly unfair due to his or her participation in the offense; or the severity of the sentence received in relation to the sentence(s) received by codefendant(s); or there is a history of abuse suffered by the prisoner at the hands of the victim that significantly contributed to or brought about the offense.

The governor will consider a petition for a commutation that meets these guidelines and has an unanimous recommendation from the ABP. If a petition receives a majority, but not a unanimous recommendation, the governor may act on it, or return it for further action by the ABP. If the governor disagrees with the ABP's recommendation, he or she may deny relief, but will state, where appropriate, the action the prisoner should take to maximize the potential for a favorable consideration in the future.

When the ABP recommends that a petition be denied and the governor does not render a decision within a hundred and twenty days of the ABP's recommendation being submitted, it will be presumed that the governor concurs with the ABP and the petition will be denied, notifying the prisoner in writing.

The ABP's report and recommendation to the governor must include a summary of the evidence presented at any public hearing, including the support the prisoner received in the institution, in the community, the nature and extent of the opposition to the petition, and the names and addresses of those in support and in opposition; an institutional progress report showing responsible use of available rehabilitative programs; a description of realistic community correctional and parole programs available to continue the prisoner's rehabilitation, if applicable; a plan for reintegrating the prisoner into normal community life, if applicable; and the ABP's vote and recommendation.

The governor will make a final decision to grant clemency, or return the petition to the ABP for further action or to request more information. The prisoner will be notified in writing of the final decision.

The clemency process may be started by requesting clemency forms from the address below.

The Commonwealth of Massachusetts
Governor's Council
State House, Room 184
Boston, MA 02133
Telephone: (617) 725-4015

MICHIGAN

Applicable Forms of Executive Clemency

The governor of Michigan has the authority to grant pardons, reprieves, and commutations for any offense against the state of Michigan, except in cases of impeachment.

Eligibility

All prisoners are eligible to apply for a commutation of sentence. Any other form of clemency is dependent upon the circumstances of each particular case.

Application Process

Within sixty days of receiving a clemency application, the Michigan Parole Board must conduct a review to determine if it has merit.

If the Board determines that it does, the judge and the prosecutor in the sentencing county will be asked for their position on the application. If neither objects, a public hearing will be held. After the hearing, the Board will send the application, a transcript of the hearing, and its determination of merit to the governor's office for a final decision.

If the Board determines that the application does not have merit, the Board will send the application and its determination of "no merit" directly to the governor's office for a final decision. The prisoner will be notified when a final decision is rendered.

The clemency process may be started by requesting clemency forms from the address below.

Michigan Department of Corrections
Office of the Parole Board
Pardons and Commutations Coordinator
P.O. Box 30003
Lansing, MI 48909
Telephone: (515) 335-1426

MINNESOTA

Applicable Forms of Executive Clemency

The Minnesota Board of Pardons (BOP) has the authority to grant pardons, reprieves, and commutations after conviction for any offense against the State of Minnesota. The BOP consists of the governor, the attorney general, and the chief of justice of the state supreme court.

Eligibility

All prisoners are eligible to apply for a commutation of sentence. Any other form of clemency is dependent upon the circumstances of each particular case. However, prisoners must fully exhaust all judicial remedies prior to seeking any form of clemency from the BOP.

Application Process

A commutation will not be granted unless there is some new information that the court did not consider or which makes a prisoner's case unusual or extraordinary. A commutation will not be granted merely because a prisoner is sorry for his or her crime; is dissatisfied with the actions of the court or paroling authority; has adjusted well in confinement; or has made great academic or personal achievements or alleges complete rehabilitation. These facts may, however, be persuasive if coupled with new information, but can not stand alone as the basis for a commutation.

The clemency process is started by submitting an Application for Pardon/Commutation to the MBP. A prisoner must provide proof that all judicial remedies have been exhausted. A form providing this information will be included with the Application for Pardon/Commutation packet.

An Application for Pardon/Commutation packet may be obtained by making a written request to the address below.

Administrative Coordinator
Minnesota Board of Pardons
1450 Energy Park Drive, Suite 200
St. Paul, MN 55108
Telephone: (651) 642-0284

MISSISSIPPI

Applicable Forms of Executive Clemency

The governor of Mississippi has the authority to grant pardons, reprieves, and commutations, and to remit fines and forfeitures for any offense against the State of Mississippi.

A first-time nonviolent offender who has never previously been convicted of a felony will be pardoned automatically upon completion of his or her sentence, without a recommendation by the Mississippi Board of Pardons (MBP) or any action by the governor.

Eligibility

All prisoners are eligible to apply for a commutation of sentence. Any other form of clemency is dependent upon the circumstances of each particular case.

Application Process

A prisoner must request an Application for Clemency form from the office of the governor. The form must be signed and completed according to the instructions on the form. It must also be accompanied by a separate letter stating the extenuating circumstances which support the basis for the clemency request.

The governor's legal counsel will review the application and notify the prisoner of its receipt and sufficiency.

If the governor determines that an application merits further inquiry, he or she will refer it to the MBP to conduct an investigation.

Following the Board's investigation and recommendation, the governor will render the final decision, notifying the prisoner in writing.

Clemency process may be started by requesting clemency forms from the address below.

Office of the Governor
Legal Division
P.O. Box 139
Jackson, MS 39205
Telephone: (601) 359-3150

MISSOURI

Applicable Forms of Executive Clemency

The governor of Missouri has the authority to grant pardons, reprieves, and commutations after conviction for all offenses (except in cases of treason or impeachment), with certain conditions, restrictions, and limitations as the governor may deem proper.

Eligibility

All prisoners are eligible to apply for a commutation of sentence. Any other form of clemency is dependent upon the circumstances of each particular case.

Application Process

All applications for pardon, commutation of sentence, or reprieve will be referred to the Missouri Board of Probation and Parole for investigation. The Board is responsible for investigating each case and making a recommendations to the governor.

When a clemency application is received from a prisoner, the Board will determine if existing file material is sufficient to make an informed recommendation to the governor. If necessary, the Board may order an investigation to include further information.

Upon receipt of the investigative report, the Board reviews the information to determine an appropriate recommendation. Shortly after, a letter of recommendation is prepared and submitted to the governor, along with the investigative report and all material submitted by the prisoner. The governor will render the final decision, notifying the prisoner in writing.

The clemency process may be started by requesting Application for Executive Clemency forms from the address below.

Missouri Board of Probation and Parole
3400 Knipp Drive
Jefferson City, MO 65109

MONTANA

Applicable Forms of Executive Clemency

Upon favorable recommendation of the Montana Board of Pardons and Parole (MBPP), the governor may grant pardons, reprieves, commutations, and remit fines and forfeitures for any offense against the State of Montana.

Eligibility

All prisoners are eligible to apply for a commutation of sentence. Any other form of clemency is dependent upon the circumstances of each particular case.

Application Process

The Board may recommend a pardon for a prisoner who can satisfactorily prove innocence of a crime for which he or she is serving time; has demonstrated an extended period of exemplary performance; submits newly discovered evidence showing complete justification or nonguilt on the part of the prisoner; or can satisfactorily prove extraordinary mitigating or extenuating circumstances exist.

The Board may recommend a commutation for a prisoner who can prove by overwhelming evidence that the prisoner is innocent of a crime for which he or she was convicted; has demonstrated an extended period of exemplary performance; submits evidence discovered subsequent to the conviction that clearly shows that prisoner was completely justified in committing the crime; can satisfactorily prove that further incarceration would be grossly unfair; or extraordinary mitigating or extenuating circumstances exist.

The Board may also recommend to the governor that a respite or a remission of fines or forfeitures be granted.

When considering an Application for Executive Clemency, the Board will consider the nature of the crime, the comments of the sentencing judge, the prosecuting attorney, the community, and the victim(s) and family of the victim(s) regarding clemency for the prisoner, and whether release would pose a threat to the public safety.

The clemency process may be started by requesting Application for Executive Clemency forms from the address below.

State of Montana
Board of Pardons and Parole
300 Maryland Avenue
Deer Lodge, MT 59722
Telephone: (406) 846-1404

NEBRASKA

Applicable Forms of Executive Clemency

The Nebraska Board of Pardons (NBP) has the authority to grant pardons, respites and reprieves, and commutations, and to remit fines and forfeitures after conviction for any offense against the State of Nebraska, except in cases of treason or impeachment. The Board is composed of the governor, the secretary of state, and the attorney general.

Eligibility

All prisoners are eligible to apply for a commutation of sentence. Any other form of clemency is dependent upon the circumstances of each particular case.

Application Process

When an application is filed, the Board makes a thorough investigation of the case to determine whether it should be accepted for a hearing, and if accepted, the Board sets the case for a public hearing, notifying the prisoner in writing.

Public hearings are held quarterly, usually in March, June, September, and December of each year. Specific dates are determined following each meeting for the next quarterly meeting.

If a hearing is granted for a prisoner, the Board has the right to proceed without his or her attendance. An attorney for the prisoner and any other witnesses who wish to testify, in support or in opposition to the application, may be present. A notice will appear in the state and county newspaper. The press may attend.

The Board may grant a hearing to hear testimony, to receive written statements, and other information pertaining to the case, that supports or opposes the prisoner's clemency request. It is not, however, the purpose of the hearing to retry the case, or to determine guilt or innocence of the prisoner.

When the Board renders a final decision, the prisoner will receive written notification.

The clemency process may be started by requesting clemency forms from the address below.

Nebraska Board of Pardons
P.O. Box 94754
Lincoln, NE 68509
Telephone: (402) 471-2156

NEVADA

Applicable Forms of Executive Clemency

The Nevada Board of Pardons has the authority to grant pardons, reprieves, and commutations, and to remit fines and forfeitures after conviction for any offense against the state of Nevada, except treason and in cases of impeachment.

The Board consists of nine members—the governor, the seven justices of the Nevada Supreme Court, and the attorney general. A majority vote is required to grant clemency. The governor cannot be outvoted—he or she must be part of the majority voting in favor of the clemency action.

Eligibility

All prisoners are eligible to apply for a commutation of sentence (A sentence of death or a sentence of life without parole may not be commuted to a sentence which would allow parole.). Any other form of clemency is dependent upon the circumstances of each particular case.

Application Process

Certain conditions must be met in order for an application to be considered. No application for a pardon will be considered prior to judgment and commitment, while the prisoner is under indictment for another crime, or during the course of an appeal from the conviction or sentence for which clemency is being sought. Similarly, no application for clemency will be considered while application is being made for any form of postconviction relief, including a sentence reduction motion, or federal habeas corpus motion.

An application of a prisoner who is eligible for a hearing before the Board, must be accompanied by a recommendation from the Director of the Department of Corrections.

If an application is accepted for review, a complete background investigation will be conducted and a report will be submitted to the Board, detailing all of the prisoner's criminal history, character, and other information deemed relevant.

A typical hearing before the Board lasts approximately twenty to thirty minutes. A prisoner is permitted to have witnesses (i.e., friends, family, supporters) testify in favor of his or her clemency request. The hearing will be open to the public.

A prisoner is usually notified of the Board's decision within eight weeks from the submission of the application, although a decision could take up to six months.

The clemency process may be started by requesting clemency forms from the address below.

Executive Secretary
Nevada Board of Pardon
1445 Hot Springs Road, Suite #108-B
Carson City, NV 89711
Telephone: (775) 687-8278

NEW HAMPSHIRE

Applicable Forms of Executive Clemency

The governor of New Hampshire has the authority to grant pardons, reprieves, and commutations, and to remit fines and forfeitures for any offense against the State of New Hampshire, with certain conditions, restrictions, and limitations as the governor may deem proper.

Eligibility

All prisoners are eligible to apply for a commutation of sentence. Any other form of clemency is dependent upon the circumstances of each particular case.

Application Process

There are no written rules or regulations governing the clemency process. A prisoner may return a completed Petition for Pardon, along with a written request listing the reason(s) supporting the request.

Subsequent to the receipt of the petition, a criminal records check will be done and a report from the prisoner's institution will be obtained.

When the petition has been submitted and documents have been compiled, the governor and executive council will review the petition to determine whether it should be accepted for a hearing, and, if accepted, a hearing will be set. If no hearing is granted, the governor will render a final decision, notifying the prisoner in writing.

The clemency process may be started by requesting Petition for Pardon forms from the address below.

Office of the Attorney General
State of New Hampshire
33 Capitol Street
Concord, NH 03301
Telephone: (603) 271-3658

NEW JERSEY

Applicable Forms of Executive Clemency

The governor of New Jersey has the authority to grant pardons, reprieves, and commutations after conviction for any offense against the State of New Jersey, with certain conditions, restrictions, and limitations as the governor may deem proper.

Eligibility

All prisoners are eligible to apply for a commutation of sentence. Any other form of clemency is dependent upon the circumstances of each particular case.

Application Process

A prisoner must answer all questions on the Petition for Executive Clemency form. If more space is needed for any answer, additional pages may be attached. The prisoner must attach documentation to substantiate the information contained in his or her Petition (i.e., copies of diplomas, certificates of achievement, marriage certificate, etc.). When the Petition is completed, it must be forwarded to the chief executive officer at the correctional facility where the prisoner is confined.

Upon receipt of the Petition and supporting documentation, the New Jersey State Parole Board will conduct an investigation and submit a report and recommendation to the governor. The prisoner will be notified in writing when the governor renders a final decision.

The clemency process may be started by requesting Petition for Executive Clemency forms from the address below.

Clemency Investigator
New Jersey State Parole Board
P.O. Box 862
Trenton, NJ 08265
Telephone: (609) 292-4257

NEW MEXICO

Applicable Forms of Executive Clemency

The governor of New Mexico has the authority to grant pardons, reprieves, and commutations after conviction for any offense against the State of New Mexico, except treason and cases of impeachment.

Eligibility

A full pardon, directed at providing outright release from incarceration, will be considered (in a case of wrongful conviction) only after all appeals have been exhausted, and new facts have been presented which clearly attest to a wrongful conviction, uncontested by the prosecuting attorney involved in the original prosecution. Affidavits from the case's prosecutor and presiding judge must accompany the pardon request.

A commutation of sentence will normally be considered only in cases of unusual meritorious service by the prisoner. Examples of unusual meritorious service include saving the life of a member of the Department of Corrections, or that of another prisoner; assistance in stopping an insurrection that threatened the administration's control of an institution; or risk of life or serious bodily harm in securing, or attempting to secure, the release of a hostage.

Requests for clemency after instances of unusual meritorious service must be accompanied by an affidavit from the supervising authorities at the institution where the prisoner is confined.

Application Process

A prisoner should identify, in a cover letter, the type of clemency for which he or she is requesting consideration.

When a petition is received, the New Mexico State Parole Board will examine the application to determine whether it meets the criteria for consideration. If it does not, the Board will notify the prisoner and the governor, and no further action will be taken. If the application meets the criteria discussed in the "Eligibility" section, the Board will call for a field investigation by the Department of Corrections. A request for appropriate reports and case materials will be directed to the warden of the institution holding the prisoner.

The Board may also request the sentencing judge and the case's prosecuting attorney to provide pertinent input, including a recommendation for or against a commutation.

The Board will review all reports and other material, then submit a summary report and recommendation to the governor's pardons and parole committee. Shortly thereafter, that committee will submit its recommendation to the governor. The prisoner will be notified in writing when the governor renders a final decision.

The clemency process may be started by requesting clemency application forms from the address below.

Pardons and Paroles
Office of the Governor
State Capitol Building
Santa Fe, NM 87503
Telephone: (505) 476-2265

NEW YORK

Applicable Forms of Executive Clemency

The governor of New York has the authority to grant pardons, reprieves, and commutations after conviction for any offense against the State of New York (except treason and cases of impeachment), with certain conditions, restrictions, and limitations as the governor may deem proper.

Eligibility

Absent compelling and exceptional circumstances, a commutation of sentence will be considered only if the prisoner's term or minimum period of imprisonment is more than one year, with at least one half of his or her minimum period of imprisonment served, and the prisoner will not become eligible (or is ineligible) for parole within one year of the date of his or her application. Any other form of clemency is dependent upon the circumstances of each particular case.

Application Process

There is no formal application for a commutation of sentence. A written request for a commutation will cause a review and compilation of necessary information to determine eligibility and if there is a need for further investigation.

To receive a commutation, the prisoner has the burden of demonstrating, by clear and convincing evidence, that he or she has made exceptional strides in self-development and improvement, and has made responsible use of available rehabilitative programs and has addressed treatment needs. The prisoner must show that a commutation is in the interest of justice, consistent with public safety and the rehabilitation of the prisoner, that he or she is suffering from a terminal illness or has a severe and chronic disability which would be substantially improved by release from incarceration and such release is in the interest of justice and consistent with public safety, or that further incarceration would constitute gross unfairness because of the basic inequities involved.

The governor will request a report concerning the prisoner's performance and behavior from each institution at which he or she has been confined, as well as recommendations from the prosecuting attorney and sentencing judge concerning the clemency application.

The governor may also request medical and psychiatric reports and evaluations, and the opinion of the parole board, in order to make an informed decision concerning a prisoner's application. When the governor renders a final decision, the prisoner will be notified in writing.

The clemency process may be started by requesting clemency forms from one of the addresses below.

The Governor of the State of New York
Executive Chamber
State Capitol
Albany, NY 12224

or

Director, Executive Clemency Bureau
New York State Division of Parole
97 Central Avenue
Albany, NY 12206
Telephone: (518) 485-8953

NORTH CAROLINA

Applicable Forms of Executive Clemency

The governor of North Carolina has the authority to grant pardons, reprieves, and commutations after conviction for any offense against the State of North Carolina (except cases of impeachment), with certain conditions, restrictions, and limitations as the governor may deem proper.

Eligibility

All prisoners are eligible to apply for a commutation of sentence. Any other form of clemency is dependent upon the circumstances of each particular case.

Application Process

There is no formal application that is specific for a commutation of sentence. A prisoner is only required to make his or her request for a commutation in writing, providing: name and DOC ID number, current address, offense(s) and date of conviction(s), and the reason(s) why clemency should be granted.

The clemency process may be started by submitting a request for a commutation, or by requesting clemency forms from the address below.

Executive Clemency Office
4294 Mail Service Center
Raleigh, NC 27699
Telephone: (919) 715-1695

NORTH DAKOTA

Applicable Forms of Executive Clemency

The governor of North Dakota has the authority to grant pardons, reprieves, and commutations, and to suspend and remit fines and forfeitures for any offense against the State of North Dakota, except in cases of impeachment.

Eligibility

Prisoners who are eligible for parole are not eligible to apply for a commutation of sentence. Any other form of clemency is dependent upon the circumstances of each particular case.

Application Process

The North Dakota Pardon Advisory Board (PAB) meets on the first Tuesday of the months of April and November. A prisoner should request application forms ninety days prior to the PAB meeting. Applications must be returned to the PAB ten weeks prior to the PAB's next meeting.

The sentencing judge and the case's prosecuting attorney will be notified of a prisoner's commutation of sentence request. The institutional offender services program staff will conduct an investigation and produce a sentencing report. This information, along with the application and the responses of the judge, the prosecuting attorney, and any victim(s), will be forwarded for review by the PAB members six weeks prior to their meeting.

The prisoner will be notified immediately of the PAB's recommendation to the governor. The governor's office follows up by sending a letter notifying the prisoner of the governor's final decision. If a commutation is granted, the governor may reconsider the decision any time before the prisoner is released from the facility. The governor may also reconsider a decision on a clemency application if the reconsideration is made within thirty days of the initial decision. A decision made on reconsideration may not be reviewed by any court.

The clemency process may be started by requesting clemency application forms from the address below.

Office of the Governor
State of North Dakota
600 East Boulevard Avenue
Bismarck, ND 58505
Telephone: (701) 328-2200

OHIO

Applicable Forms of Executive Clemency

The governor of Ohio has the authority to grant pardons, reprieves, and commutations after conviction for any offense (except treason and cases of impeachment), with certain conditions, restrictions, and limitations as the governor may deem proper.

Eligibility

All prisoners are eligible to apply for a commutation of sentence. Any other form of clemency is dependent upon the circumstances of each particular case.

Application Process

A clemency application, once received, will be reviewed for completeness and to assure that it contains all the required documents. A prisoner must provide copies of the indictment or bill of information, as well as the judgment entry of conviction and sentence for each crime for which clemency is requested. These documents can be obtained from the sentencing county and may require a payment for copying fees. An incomplete application will be returned.

Ohio Revised Code Section 2967.07 requires a "thorough investigation into the propriety of granting a pardon, commutation or reprieve" after an application has been filed. The Ohio Parole Board will use any available pre-sentence investigation or offender background investigation on the prisoner and will supplement those investigations if necessary. A parole officer may contact the prisoner for an interview or the completion of a questionnaire.

The parole officer will also contact the sentencing judge, prosecuting attorney, and arresting agency in the county/city in which the prisoner was convicted, to obtain their opinion concerning the application for clemency.

A complete application will be submitted to the Parole Board members for review. They will decide by majority vote if the application contains sufficient merit to warrant further consideration at a hearing. If the Board members do not decide vote to conduct a hearing, the application will be forwarded to the governor with a recommendation to deny the clemency request.

If the Board members determine that an application warrants further review at a hearing, the prisoner will be notified of the date and time of the clemency hearing. An interview will be conducted, at the institution where the prisoner is confined, prior to the hearing date.

Either following the application review or a hearing, the Parole Board will determine, by at least majority vote, whether to submit a favorable or unfavorable recommendation to the governor.

The final decision for granting or denying clemency is solely that of the governor. The prisoner will be notified in writing of the governor's final decision.

The clemency process may be started by requesting clemency application forms from the address below.

Ohio Parole Board
770 West Broad Street
Columbus, OH 43222
Telephone: (614) 752-1200

OKLAHOMA

Applicable Forms of Executive Clemency

The governor of Oklahoma has the authority to grant pardons, reprieves, and commutations after conviction for any offense against the State of Oklahoma (except cases of impeachment), with certain conditions, restrictions, and limitations as the governor may deem proper.

Eligibility

All prisoners are eligible to apply for a commutation of sentence. Any other form of clemency is dependent upon the circumstances of each particular case.

Application Process

Once an application is received, a local criminal record check and investigation will be conducted. After the investigation, the application will be submitted to the Oklahoma Pardon and Parole Board for their consideration on the next available docket (the Board meets once a month). If a prisoner's application receives a favorable recommendation from a majority of the Board members, the recommendation will be forwarded to the governor's office for a final decision. The prisoner will be notified in writing of the Board's recommendation and the governor's final decision.

The clemency process may be started by requesting clemency application forms from the address below.

General Counsel, Attn: Pardons
First National Center
120 North Robinson Avenue, Suite 900W
Oklahoma City, OK 73102
Telephone: (405) 602-5863

OREGON

Applicable Forms of Executive Clemency

The governor of Oregon has the authority to grant pardons, reprieves, and commutations, and to remit fines after conviction for any offense against the State of Oregon, with certain conditions, restrictions, and limitations as the governor may deem proper.

Eligibility

All prisoners are eligible to apply for a commutation of sentence. However, if a prisoner qualifies under ORS 137.225, the governor will not consider the application unless a petition to set aside a conviction has been filed and denied. Any other form of clemency is dependent upon the circumstances of each particular case.

Application Process

The governor regards executive clemency as an extraordinary remedy of last resort, and will not consider an application based upon a wrongful conviction where the prisoner has not fully exhausted his or her appellate, post-conviction, and habeas corpus remedies.

There is no particular form required, but a prisoner may use the form provided by the governor's office.

Once the application is completed, the prisoner is required by Oregon law to mail a copy to: the director of the Department of Corrections, the Oregon State Board of Parole, the district attorney for the county where the prisoner was sentenced, and the district attorney of the county where the prisoner is confined.

The clemency process may be started by requesting clemency forms from the address below.

Governor's Office
160 State Capitol
900 Court Street Northeast
Salem, OR 97301
Telephone: (503) 378-3111

PENNSYLVANIA

Applicable Forms of Executive Clemency

The governor of Pennsylvania has the authority to grant pardons, reprieves, and commutations, and to remit fines and forfeitures after conviction for any offense against the State of Pennsylvania, except in cases of impeachment.

Eligibility

All prisoners are eligible to apply for a conditional commutation of sentence. Any other form of clemency is dependent upon the circumstances of each particular case.

Application Process

The prisoner must submit the original clemency application and ten photocopies to the Pennsylvania Board of Pardons. Six photocopies of all supporting documents must also be included. All questions must be answered in the prisoner's own words, and he or she must personally sign and date where indicated. If the Board has questions regarding the prisoner's application, the person he or she names as a representative will be contacted.

The application must also be accompanied with a twenty dollar, non-refundable filing fee, in the form of a cashier's or certified check, money order, or institution check, made payable to the Commonwealth of Pennsylvania. The Board may waive the filing fee upon proof of indigence. The official form to proceed without payment of the filing fee may be obtained from the secretary of the Board and filed in lieu of the fee.

The Board will grant a public hearing on the application if two of the five Board members approve. When all information has been compiled, a hearing will be scheduled. The person representing the prisoner will be notified whether or not a hearing has been granted, and, if so, will be informed of its time and place. Before the hearing, a legal notice will be published in a newspaper of general circulation in the county where the offense occurred. The notice will include the prisoner's name, conviction, and the date and place where the hearing will be held. Publication is required for every application heard by the Board.

The Board consists of the lieutenant governor, attorney general, and three members appointed by the governor with consent of a majority of the members.

The prisoner may not appear at a hearing. Be or she may designate another person to appear on his or her behalf—either privately retained legal counsel or a requested representative from the Department of Corrections.

At a hearing, fifteen minutes will be allotted for argument in support of the application, and an equal amount of time will be allotted for argument in opposition to the application. In death penalty cases, thirty minutes will be allotted for each side.

Following the hearing, the Board will issue a recommendation and submit the case to the governor for review and a final decision. The prisoner will be notified of the Board's decision within fourteen days of the hearing.

If probation or parole is violated following any granting of commutation, or if the prisoner is convicted of a new offense, the commutation will be voided and revoked.

The clemency process may be started by requesting clemency forms from the address below.

Pennsylvania Board of Pardons
333 Market Street, 15th Floor
Harrisburg, PA 17126
Telephone: (717) 787-2596

RHODE ISLAND

Applicable Forms of Executive Clemency

The governor of Rhode Island has the authority to grant conditional pardons after conviction for any offense against the State of Rhode Island.

Eligibility

All prisoners are eligible to apply for a conditional pardon. Any other form of clemency is dependent upon the circumstances of each particular case.

Application Process

There is no formal, prescribed application form or process. To apply, the prisoner is required to submit a written petition to the Office of the Governor. The petition should include: a copy of the prisoner's current BCI (official criminal history) report from the state in which he or she resides or resided; a full description of the underlying offense(s) of the current incarceration; copies of any official court documents regarding the disposition of the case, the duration of sentence, and the amount of time already served; information regarding the prisoner's conduct while incarcerated; and any other information that the prisoner believes would be helpful to the governor in making an informed decision.

The prisoner is encouraged to present his or her most compelling arguments in support of the requested relief. There are no formal deadlines and no time periods within which a petition must be considered or decided by the governor. If granted, the conditional pardon may be revoked if any of the conditions are violated.

The clemency process may be started by sending a petition to the address below.

Office of the Governor
State House, Room 115
Providence, RI 02903
Telephone: {401) 222-2080

SOUTH CAROLINA

Applicable Forms of Executive Clemency

The governor of South Carolina has the authority to grant reprieves, and to commute sentences of death to sentences of life imprisonment only. The South Carolina Department of Probation, Parole, and Pardon Board has sole authority to grant pardons.

Eligibility

All prisoners are eligible to apply for a pardon anytime before becoming eligible for parole. A pardon may only be granted upon proof of extraordinary circumstances. The Board will decide, based on its findings and the information provided by the prisoner, if the evidence demonstrates extraordinary circumstances.

Application Process

The application for a pardon (provided by the Board) must be filled out completely, and signed and dated by the prisoner. He or she must list the name, address, and telephone number of each reference listed so the Board may contact them.

The application must also be accompanied with a one hundred dollar, non-refundable, filing fee in the form of a money order or cashier's check, made payable to the South Carolina Department of Probation, Parole, and Pardon Services. No pardon will be granted unless all restitution and collections fees are paid in full. It is the prisoner's responsibility to attach to the pardon application a certified statement from the appropriate authority showing that all restitution and collections fees have been paid. If the filing fee is not included with the application, it will be returned.

Consideration of an application takes on average seven to nine months before a hearing may be scheduled, in order to verify references and information.

The Board's decision will be the final determination of pardon eligibility. In order for a Pardon Certificate to be granted, a favorable Order of Pardon must be signed by two-thirds of the Board.

The clemency process may be started by requesting pardon application forms from the address below.

Division of Paroles and Pardons
South Carolina Department of Probation, Parole, and Pardon Service
2221 Devine Street, Suite 600
P.O. Box 50666
Columbia, SC 29250
Telephone: (803) 734-9202

SOUTH DAKOTA

Applicable Forms of Executive Clemency

The governor of South Dakota has the authority to grant pardons, reprieves, and commutations, and to remit fines and forfeitures after conviction for any offense against South Dakota.

Eligibility

All prisoners are eligible to apply for a commutation of sentence. Any other form of clemency is dependent upon the circumstances of each particular case.

Application Process

In the application process there are seven steps that must be completed before a hearing can be granted. The prisoner must complete a form that authorizes the South Dakota Board of Pardons and Paroles (BPP) to obtain a current FBI criminal history report; complete an application for clemency; write a personal letter to the BPP explaining why he or she should be granted clemency; publish a notice in the newspaper where the offense occurred; complete a form PA-4 (provided by the BPP) and send it to the prosecuting attorney in the county where the conviction occurred; obtain a certified copy of his or her Judgment and Sentence from the court clerk where the sentence was imposed; and submit letters of support from employers, friends, family, etc.

The clemency process may be stared by requesting application for clemency forms from the address below.

South Dakota Board of Pardons and Paroles
1600 North Drive
Box 5911
Sioux Falls, SD 57117
Telephone: (605) 367-5040

TENNESSEE

Applicable Forms of Executive Clemency

The governor of Tennessee has the authority to grant pardons, reprieves, and commutations after conviction for any offense against the State of Tennessee, except in cases of impeachment.

Eligibility

All prisoners are eligible to apply for a commutation of sentence. Any other form of clemency is dependent upon the circumstances of each particular case.

Application Process

The Board of Probation and Parole Executive Clemency Unit is responsible for processing pardon, commutation, and exoneration applications. In preparing an application, the prisoner should attach a cover letter specifying which type of relief he or she is requesting.

When an application is received, it is forwarded to the Board members for review to determine if a hearing is warranted. The prisoner will be advised in writing whether or not a hearing will be granted. If the hearing is granted, the Board will make a non-binding recommendation to the governor as to whether or not clemency should be granted. The governor considers both favorable and unfavorable recommendations. The prisoner will be notified of the Board's recommendation and the governor's final decision in writing.

The governor will give serious consideration to commutation of sentence requests where the prisoner has demonstrated, by clear and convincing evidence, that he or she has made exceptional strides in self-development and improvement, and would be a law-abiding citizen. The prisoner must provide information indicating that he or she has been rehabilitated; is no longer a threat to society; has demonstrated, to the extent his or her age and health permits, a desire and an ability to maintain gainful employment, and fairness supports the prisoner's application; or is suffering from a terminal illness or has a severe and chronic disability that would be substantially improved by release from incarceration.

The clemency process may be started by requesting clemency forms from the address below.

Board Operation Division
State of Tennessee
404 James Robertson Parkway, Suite 1300
Nashville, TN 27243
Telephone: (615) 741-1150

TEXAS

Applicable Forms of Executive Clemency

The governor of Texas has the authority to grant pardons, reprieves, and commutations, and to remit fines and forfeitures after conviction for any offense against the State of Texas, except treason and cases of impeachment.

Eligibility

All prisoners are eligible to apply for a commutation of sentence. Any other form of clemency is dependent upon the circumstances of each particular case.

Application Process

The Texas Board of Pardons and Paroles (BPP) reviews applications for clemency and issues recommendations to the governor. In order for the Board to consider an application, it must receive a completed application, signed and dated by the prisoner, and written recommendations by a majority of the current trial officials (the present sheriff, prosecuting attorney, and judge) in the county and court where the offense occurred.

A recommendation of a trial official must include: a statement that the penalty imposed now appears to be excessive, a recommendation of a definite term now considered to be just and proper by the official; a statement of the reasons for the recommendation, based upon facts directly related to the case, which were in existence but not available to the court or jury at the time of the trial; or a statutory change in penalty for the crime which would appear to make the original penalty excessive.

If the Board recommends a commutation, the governor will make the final decision. The prisoner will be notified in writing of the final action.

The clemency process may be started by requesting clemency forms form the address below.

Executive Clemency Section
Texas Board of Pardons and Paroles
8610 Shoal Creek Boulevard
Austin, TX 78757
Telephone: (512) 406-5852

UTAH

Applicable Forms of Executive Clemency

The Utah Board of Pardons and Parole has the authority to grant pardons, reprieves, commutations, and to remit fines and forfeitures after conviction for any offense against the State of Utah, except treason and cases of impeachment.

Eligibility

All prisoners are eligible to apply for a commutation of sentence. Any other form of clemency is dependent upon the circumstances of each particular case.

Application Process

The Board has not developed a formal clemency application. It only requires that a prisoner make his or her request for clemency in writing, providing: name and DOC ID number, current address, offense(s) and date of conviction(s), and the reason(s) why clemency should be granted.

The Board consists of five members. A majority vote (at least three of the five members) is required for clemency relief to be granted. Although it is administratively related to the Department of Corrections, the Board's decisions are autonomous.

It takes thirty days for a reply from the Board. If it finds a case meritorious, the full Board will conduct a hearing in which the prisoner and the state may present evidence and arguments. Prisoners are not provided an attorney but are permitted to retain one. Hearings are open to the general public and media. A typical commutation hearing lasts about twenty minutes. The Board's decision is final and not subject to judicial review.

The clemency process may be started by submitting a clemency application to the address below.

State of Utah Board of Pardons and Parole
448 East Winchester Street, Suite 300
Murray, UT 84107
Telephone: (801) 261-6464

VERMONT

Applicable Forms of Executive Clemency

The governor of Vermont has the authority to grant pardons and to remit fines after conviction for any offense against the State of Vermont.

Eligibility

All prisoners are eligible to apply for a conditional pardon or remission of fines. Any other form of clemency is dependent upon the circumstances of each particular case.

Application Process

Applications are available upon request. Once an application is completed, it should be returned to the governor's office with a letter indicating that the application is for a "conditional pardon."

By submitting the application, the prisoner consents to the release of his or her record to the governor, and to the public release of the prisoner's name.

The governor's office will send a letter to the commissioner of corrections to initiate a conditional pardon investigation. Once the application is reviewed, the commissioner of corrections may assign the investigation to the appropriate area manager, who will then instruct the facility superintendent to conduct an investigation to determine if cause exists to require a hearing.

If such cause exists, the facility superintendent will recommend that a hearing be held. The area manager will review the investigation report, measuring the information gathered against pardon policy and procedures and the guidelines for determining compelling reason for the prisoner's request. The area manager will send a memo to the commissioner stating the rationale for a positive or negative recommendation for the conditional pardon.

The commissioner will forward the recommendation of the Department of Corrections (DOC) to the governor. If the recommendation is positive, the commissioner will present written rationale for his or her decision. If it is negative, the commissioner will forward the case, along with a letter expressing his or her position, to the governor and secretary of Civil and Military Affairs. The DOC's investigation should be completed within thirty days of being assigned to the area manager.

The governor will review the DOC's recommendation and the prisoner's file before making a decision. The prisoner will be notified of the decision in writing.

The clemency process may be started by requesting conditional pardon forms from the address below.

Governor's Office
109 State Street Pavilion
Montpelier, VT 05609
Telephone: (802) 828-3333

VIRGINIA

Applicable Forms of Executive Clemency

The governor of Virginia has the authority to grant simple, conditional, or absolute pardons, reprieves, and commutations of sentences of death, and to remit fines after conviction for any offense against the State of Virginia.

Eligibility

All prisoners are eligible to apply for a conditional pardon. Any other form of clemency is dependent upon the circumstances of each particular case.

Application Process

There is no formal form for a conditional pardon. The prisoner is only required to make his or her request in writing, providing: name and DOC ID number, current address, offense(s) and date of conviction(s), and the reason(s) why a conditional pardon should be granted.

Consideration for a conditional pardon takes over one year. Once a petition is received, it is reviewed. If it is determined that the case warrants investigation, the Virginia Board of Parole will conduct an investigation and issue a recommendation to the governor.

The prisoner should provide all relevant information he or she wishes to have considered. The petition process does not include any hearing, meeting, or conference with the prisoner or people acting on his or her behalf.

Conditional pardon requests are processed by the Office of the Secretary of the Commonwealth. If the Office finds a request has merit, it will conduct a thorough investigation. Except for those dealing with medical pardons, these investigations may take as long as a year to complete. Once a decision is rendered, the prisoner will be notified in writing.

The clemency process may be started by submitting a petition to the address below.

Office of the Secretary of the Commonwealth
P.O. Box 2454
Richmond, VA 23218
Telephone: (804) 692-2542 or (804) 786-2441

WASHINGTON

Applicable Forms of Executive Clemency

The governor of Washington has the authority to grant pardons, reprieves, and commutations after conviction for any offense against the State of Washington.

Eligibility

All prisoners are eligible to apply for a commutation of sentence. Any other form of clemency is dependent upon the circumstances of each particular case.

If the Washington Clemency and Pardons Board reviews an application and finds no compelling justification or extraordinary circumstances to recommend clemency, it is the Board's policy to deny any subsequent application unless there is a substantial change in the facts of the case since the past petition filed.

Application Process

The prisoner is required to submit the original and five photocopies of his or her clemency application and accompanying documents to the Office of the Governor.

The application must include a waiver to grant the Board access to information about the prisoner, including work records, medical records, criminal history records, financial records, and psychological records.

The Board's review committee reviews all pending requests for clemency and determines which petitions will be heard by the full Board. It will only review the cases referred by the review committee. If the Board reviews a case, it will issue a recommendation to the governor, who reviews the case for possible executive action.

The clemency process may be started by requesting clemency application forms from the address below.

Chair, Clemency and Pardons Board
Office of the Governor
Legislative Building
P.O. Box 40002
Olympia, WA 98504
Telephone: (360) 753-6780

WEST VIRGINIA

Applicable Forms of Executive Clemency

The governor of west Virginia has the authority to grant pardons and to remit fines after conviction for any offense against the State of West Virginia.

Eligibility

Prisoners are eligible to apply for a pardon to reduce their sentence once they become eligible for parole. In extraordinary circumstances, applications may be accepted prior to a prisoner becoming parole eligible. If serving a life sentence, the prisoner must have served fifteen years before he or she is eligible to apply for a time reduction. Any other form of clemency is dependent upon the circumstances of each particular case.

Any prisoner who has previously been denied executive clemency by the governor is not eligible to reapply until three years have passed from the date of the denial.

Application Process

The application must be completed in full, including responses of "does not apply" where appropriate. All concurrent or consecutive sentences must be noted separately on the application.

The release of information statement on the application must be signed, to give the West Virginia Division of Corrections and the West Virginia Board of Parole access to information regarding the prisoner's medical condition, criminal history, treatment history, and plans.

When the application is received, the Governor's Office will forward it to the Board, which then compiles a written report addressing factors such as: the circumstance of the crime, criminal history, employment and education history, drug and alcohol use, institutional conduct and work history, as well as public and official sentiment. Upon completion of the written report, the Board will make a recommendation to the governor regarding the request for pardon or any other form of clemency.

The prisoner will be notified in writing of the governor's response within eight weeks of the application being submitted by the Board.

The clemency process may be started by requesting clemency application forms from the address below.

Governor's Office
West Virginia State Capitol
1900 Kanawha Boulevard East
Charleston, WV 25305
Telephone: (888) 438-2731

WISCONSIN

Applicable Forms of Executive Clemency

The governor of Wisconsin has the authority to grant pardons, reprieves, and commutations after conviction for any offense against the State of Wisconsin.

Eligibility

Executive clemency rules require the prisoner to obtain an Eligibility Rule Waiver from the Wisconsin Pardon Advisory Board, permitting him or her to apply for clemency while incarcerated. A waiver will be granted if the prisoner can demonstrate that there are extraordinary circumstances showing that he or she should be eligible to apply.

If the prisoner's application is denied, he or she may reapply no sooner than eighteen months after the date of denial.

Application Process

The prisoner must first obtain a waiver, and may request an Eligibility Rule Waiver form from the Board. If the waiver request is accepted, the prisoner will be mailed application to be completed and returned.

Each application is handled on a case by case basis. Some of the factors considered by the Board and the governor include: the seriousness of the offense, whether a significant and documented need for clemency exists, the prisoner's criminal record, the length of time since the offense occurred, the prisoner's personal development and progress since the offense was committed, and community or other civic service performed by the prisoner.

The prisoner is not required to retain an attorney to file for executive clemency. It is suggested that the prisoner obtain and submit letters from friends, family, etc., recommending clemency.

The prisoner must submit a certified copy of his or her judgment of conviction, criminal complaint, and docket (sometimes called the judgment roll or minutes).

The application includes forms that must be sent to the prisoner's sentencing judge, prosecuting attorney, and warden informing them of the clemency application. The prisoner must also inform a local newspaper, in the county where the offense occurred, that he or she is requesting clemency with the forms provided by the Board.

Once the application is returned, the prisoner will be notified, via mail, when and where his or her Board hearing will be held. The Board meets several times a year. Although there is no requirement that the prisoner appear at the hearing, it is highly recommended. The Board will ask the prisoner questions and the prisoner will be afforded an opportunity to present his or her reason for seeking a pardon or commutation of sentence. The hearing will be open to the public and media. When possible, family, friends, and other supporters will be permitted to speak on the prisoner's behalf. The prisoner will appear before the Board for about fifteen minutes.

The Board consists of six members, including representatives from the Department of Justice, the Department of Corrections, three members of the public, and (typically) the governor's legal counsel. Each member is appointed by the governor.

The Board meets after the hearing, votes whether to make a positive or negative recommendation, and forwards its recommendation to the governor. The governor reviews the prisoner's file and makes the final decision to grant or deny clemency. The prisoner will be notified of the final decision in writing.

The clemency process may be started by requesting an Eligibility Rule Waiver form from the address below.

Pardon Advisory Board
Office of the Governor
State Capitol
Room 115 East
P.O. Box 7863
Madison, WI 53707
Telephone: (608) 266-1212

WYOMING

Applicable Forms of Executive Clemency

The governor of Wyoming has the authority to grant pardons, reprieves, and commutations after conviction for any offense against the State of Wyoming.

Eligibility

All prisoners are eligible to apply for a commutation of sentence. Any other form of clemency is dependent upon the circumstances of each particular case.

Application Process

Although the governor has the authority to grant clemency, the governor relies on the Wyoming Board of Parole to refer cases for consideration. The process is usually initiated at the request of the prisoner by his or her caseworker.

Working with the prisoner, the caseworker will prepare a commutation request to be forwarded to the Board. Typical information in the commutation request packet includes, but is not limited to: the prisoner's name, DOC ID number, current address, criminal history, education, involvement in programs, attitude toward rehabilitation, and personal letter. A recommendation by the institution will also accompany.

Commutation of sentence requests are initially addressed before the three-member panel that conducts the prisoner's annual review hearing, but may be brought before the Board prior to such hearing if the warden presents the prisoner's case as a special one. The Board of Parole has a total of seven members. The three-member panel will submit any commutation recommendation to a quorum (four members) of the Board for further review and to decide whether the case will be forwarded to the governor.

Before a decision is made by the Board, comments are requested from the sentencing judge, prosecuting attorney, and the victim or victim's family. Once all the information is reviewed by the Board, its recommendation and the file will be forwarded to the governor for a final decision. The prisoner will be notified of the governor's decision in writing.

The clemency process may be started by requesting clemency forms from the address below.

Wyoming Board of Parole
3120 Old Faithful, Suite 100
Cheyenne, WY 82002
Telephone: (307) 777-5444

UNITED STATES

Applicable Forms of Executive Clemency

The president of the United States has the authority to grant pardons, reprieves, and commutations, and to remit fines for any offense against the United States federal government.

Eligibility

No petition for pardon should be filed until at least five years after the date of release of the prisoner from confinement. Generally, no petition should be submitted by a person who is on probation, parole, or supervised release.

No petition for commutation of sentence, including remission of fines, should be filed if other forms of judicial or administrative relief are available, except upon a showing of exceptional circumstances. Any other form of clemency is dependent upon the circumstances of each particular case.

Application Process

The prisoner seeking executive clemency by pardon, reprieve, commutation of sentence, or remission of fines must execute a formal petition. The petition must be addressed to the president of the United States and submitted to the pardon attorney at the Department of Justice. Petitions relating to military offenses are ineligible for this process. Petitions and other required forms may be obtained from the pardon attorney. Prisoners may also may obtain commutation petition forms from the wardens of federal penal institutions.

A prisoner applying for executive clemency with respect to military offenses should submit his or her petition directly to the secretary of the military department that had original jurisdiction over the court-martial trial and conviction of the prisoner. In such a case, a form furnished by the pardon attorney may be used, but it should be modified to meet the needs of the particular case. Each petition for executive clemency should include the information required in the form prescribed by the attorney general.

Upon receipt of a clemency petition, the attorney general will cause an investigation to be made of the matter as he or she may deem necessary and appropriate, using the services of, or obtaining reports from, appropriate officials and agencies of the government, including the Federal Bureau of Investigation.

When a prisoner requests clemency for a conviction of a felony offense for which there was a victim, and the attorney general concludes from the information developed in the clemency case that the case warrants contacting the victim, the attorney general will make a reasonable effort to notify the victim that a clemency petition has been filed, that the victim may submit comments regarding clemency, and give victim notification if the clemency request is ultimately granted or denied by the President.

In determining whether contacting the victim is warranted, the attorney general may consider the seriousness and recency of the offense, the nature and extent of harm to the victim, the prisoner's overall criminal history and history of violent behavior, and the likelihood that clemency could be recommended in the case.

The attorney general will review each petition and all pertinent information developed by the investigation and will determine whether the request for clemency merits favorable action by the president. The attorney general will report in writing his or her recommendation to the president.

When a petition for pardon is granted, the prisoner or his or her attorney will be notified of such action, and the warrant pardon will be mailed to the prisoner. When a commutation of sentence is granted, the prisoner will be notified of such action, and the warrant of commutation will be sent to the prisoner through the officer in charge of his or her place of confinement, or directly to the prisoner if he or she is on parole, probation, or supervised release.

Whenever the president notifies the attorney general that the prisoner's clemency request has been denied, the attorney general will advise the prisoner and close the case.

Except in cases in which a sentence of death has been imposed, whenever the attorney general recommends that the president deny a request for clemency and the president does not disapprove or take other action with respect to that adverse recommendation within thirty days after the date of its submission to him, it will be presumed that the president concurs with the attorney general's recommendation, at which point the attorney general will advise the prisoner and close the case.

The clemency process may be started by requesting clemency forms from the address below.

Pardon Attorney
500 First Street Northwest, Suite 400
Washington, DC 20530
Telephone: (202) 616-6070

ACKNOWLEDGMENTS

First, I must thank my mother, Barbara Bristor, for all her help with this book: Internet research, printing and mailing information; and for her endless support as my most devoted fan.

I would like to thank Byron Case, for his deft editing, turning many of my clunky, grammatically incorrect sentences into sensible prose, as well for his countless and much-appreciated advice: the man is a machine with a manual of style and complete encyclopedia set in his head.

And last, but not least, I would like to thank my publisher, redbat books' Kristin Summers. Without her, this book would not have been a reality.

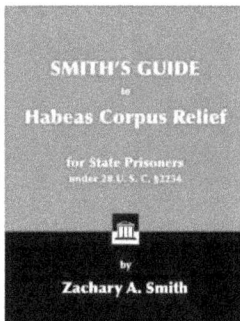

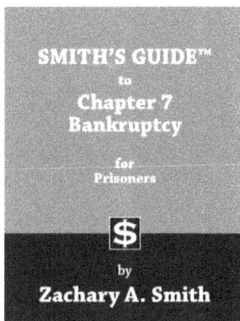

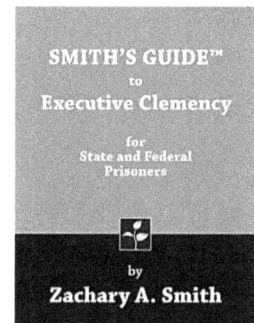

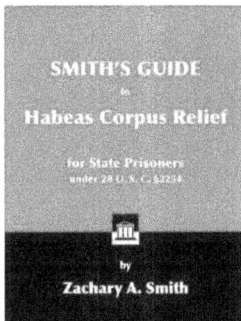

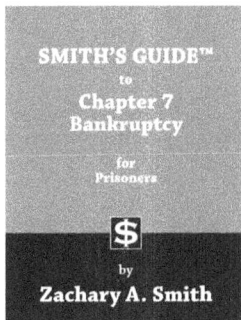

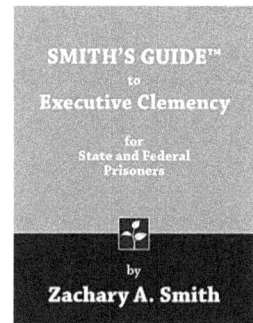

www.ingramcontent.com/pod-product-compliance
Lightning Source LLC
Chambersburg PA
CBHW080520220326
41599CB00032B/6143
* 9 7 8 0 9 8 9 5 9 2 4 1 3 *